M000306804

Of Friends and Foes

Of Friends and Foes

Reputation and Learning in International Politics

MARK J.C. CRESCENZI

OXFORD
UNIVERSITY PRESS

OXFORD
UNIVERSITY PRESS

Oxford University Press is a department of the University of Oxford. It furthers
the University's objective of excellence in research, scholarship, and education
by publishing worldwide. Oxford is a registered trade mark of Oxford University
Press in the UK and in certain other countries.

Published in the United States of America by Oxford University Press
198 Madison Avenue, New York, NY 10016, United States of America.

© Oxford University Press 2018

All rights reserved. No part of this publication may be reproduced, stored in
a retrieval system, or transmitted, in any form or by any means, without the
prior permission in writing of Oxford University Press, or as expressly permitted
by law, by license or under terms agreed with the appropriate reproduction
rights organization. Inquiries concerning reproduction outside the scope of the
above should be sent to the Rights Department, Oxford University Press, at the
address above.

You must not circulate this work in any other form
and you must impose this same condition on any acquirer.

CIP data is on file at the Library of Congress
ISBN 978-0-19-060952-8 (Hbk.)
ISBN 978-0-19-060953-5 (Pbk.)

1 3 5 7 9 8 6 4 2

Paperback printed by WebCom, Inc., Canada
Hardback printed by Bridgeport National Bindery, Inc., United States of America

CONTENTS

FIGURES

TABLES

PREFACE

This book sets out a theory of how reputation affects both conflict and cooperation in world politics. That is, of course, a rather ambitious goal, accomplished only by standing on the scholarly shoulders of so many who have worked on reputation before me. In a way, it is surprising to me that I have written a book on reputation. When I started working on the research that would eventually evolve into this book, I had in mind a methodological innovation that would allow scholars to embrace the complexities of world politics without losing sight of the powerful analysis that we leverage when we focus in on dyads, or pairs of states interacting with one another. I labeled this complexity "Relational Interdependence" and began the process of trying to harness the way states observe the world, and to apply those observations to their dyadic interactions.

Dyads are useful in that they have an actor and a target, a victim and a perpetrator, or a winner and a loser. The simple elegance of the Prisoner's Dilemma game relies on this platform: two actors, strategically interacting with important consquences. Yet scholars and non-specialists alike are quick to point out that the world is more complicated than that. When we think in terms of dyads, we assume away much of this complexity. This assumption has proven to be remarkably productive, and in my opinion worth saving. So, I set out create a mathematical model that would enable scholars to see the processes interactions that take place outside of the dyad, but were clearly still important to the states within it.

One group of these extra-dyadic dimensions can be classified as spatial, like neighborhoods or regions, or friends and enemies nearby. But the organizing principle need not be based on distance. Scholars have long understood the importance of trade networks, colonial ties, and similarities in language and shared culture. As I worked on the modeling process and the moving parts that I thought were most important in this process, I kept circling around the puzzle of information. Reputation is really just one such dimension of this extra-dyadic information, and the need for information is the key to understanding when and why reputations matter.

Parts of the book are informed by three articles I published in the *American Journal of Political Science, Journal of Peace Research,* and *International Studies Quarterly.* For two of these articles my graduate students joined me as research assistants and coauthors. Together, this collection of publications introduced the technical details of the model and provided important quantitative empirical evidence supporting the arguments we set forth about reputation's influence on conflict and cooperation. Given these three publications, the natural question is, why do we need the book?

I wrote the book for three reasons. First, once the articles were complete, there was still much more to say about the concept of reputation and the mechanisms that link reputation and political outcomes. I realized that the nuance of a full discussion of the concept of reputation required space beyond the concise focus of a collection of articles. Second, my own thoughts on the role reputation plays in world politics have evolved over time. As I began to understand how one model of reputation could be useful to understanding both conflict and cooperation, it became useful to produce one document to represent the full evolution of the argument. Third, this book allows me to provide a more complete theoretical and empirical discussion of reputation. The theoretical discussion in the first part of the book is designed to be a careful and accessible introduction to the concept of reputation, while at the same time establishing a new way to think about reputation as a dynamic concept. The qualitative illustrations that I include in the book are an essential component of the overall picture, and they provide valuable complements to the quantitative analyses herein. Together, these components allow me to provide a more coherent argument that will hopefully stand the test of time.

The book is designed to be accessible to a wide audience. Readers without any background in statistical analysis can still glean the key lessons learned in Chapters 4 and 5 by focusing on the discussion and the figures that graphically represent the analyses. The theoretical discussion is designed to be accessible to undergraduate students and non-specialist readers (i.e., everyone), while being careful and specific enough to be useful for scholars conducting their own research in world politics. Finally, the entire project is designed to enable scholars to incorporate reputation as a variable in their existing analyses of political interactions. Data and replication files are freely accessible online.

Lastly, I would like to acknowledge the tremendous help I received along the way. This research would have never been possible without a lot of help from a long list of talented people. I would like to thank the National Science foundation for providing support for this research (SES-0450111 and SES-07294050). Thanks also to David McBride, Claire Sibley, Katie Weaver, Kristen Browning, and the production team at Oxford University Press for guidance and support throughout the publication process. Jacob Kathman, Katja Kleinberg, Stephen Long, and Reed Wood were essential contributors to the project and coauthors of the articles mentioned above. Bailee Donahue, Rachel Myrick, Lindsay Reid, Kai Stern, and Rob Williams helped with research and editing. Navin Bapat, Stephen Gent, Kelly Kadera, and Patricia Sullivan provided advice and support, and Dina Zinnes's mentorship helped me develop a dynamic view of the world and political processes. The work Andrew Enterline and I did years earlier on the behavioral history of dyads and the Interstate Interaction Scores we built are a cornerstone of this research, and his enthusiasm for this project has been invaluable. He was outdone only by Anita Crescenzi, who has unceasingly supported me as I struggled with these pages. Her patience went way above and beyond the call, and I am grateful.

Of Friends and Foes

1

Introduction

We don't see things as they are, we see them as we are.
—Anais Nin

Reputation is in the eyes of the beholder.
—Jonathan Mercer

In this book, I develop a theory of reputation formation and learning that captures complex relational dynamics. I then pair it with a theory of international politics that helps us understand how reputations exacerbate or ameliorate the problems of credible commitment. The resulting analysis yields new insight into how states perceive the actions of one another, and how those perceptions can affect peace and conflict in the future.

Reputations throughout history have had an important influence on world politics. A reputation for honoring one's obligations in a treaty, for example, can make a state a more attractive ally. A reputation for war and conflict can trigger more of the same, leading to a cycle of violence that exacerbates security challenges. For much of the Cold War, the involved states understood reputation to be a shield of sorts, thwarting would-be aggressors from striking first. Yet, reputation has also been an elusive concept. In politics and in political science research we see a lot of words like "trust," "credibility," "resolve," "integrity," "risk," "known commodity," and "brand," to name a few, overlapping with "reputation" like in a Venn diagram. As a result, the concept of reputation often gets stretched or diluted, weakening our ability to ascertain its role in cooperation and conflict.

It was not always this complicated, at least in the way we thought reputation mattered. Not too long ago, the idea that reputation was essential to avoiding war was an integral part of theories of international politics. Deterrence could only be accomplished with a reputation for toughness and a willingness to punish when tread upon. Cooperation in the anarchical international system could only be fashioned out of the combination of repeated interaction and an emerging reputation for being trustworthy. But, disagreement persistently surrounded the question of whether such reputations for being cooperative and trustworthy would hold up in the event of a major political crisis that could trigger international war. The result was a tension among scholars regarding which type of reputation was more important: a reputation for toughness or a reputation for cooperation.[1]

After the end of the Cold War—an event that shook the world and the core foundations of the study of international relations—scholars began to challenge the notion that reputations worked the way we previously thought. Whereas the old debate centered around which type of reputation was more likely to bring peace and harmony, new research emerged to challenge the clarity (and thus utility) of a state's reputation. Rather than characterizing reputation as a simple, one-dimensional characteristic of a government, the focus shifted to thinking of reputations as uniquely linked to the context of the moment and the psychology of perception. Jonathan Mercer (1996) argued that the complexity of these perceptions had been vastly understated, and the simplistic representations of reputation trivialized and misrepresented a complicated phenomenon. At best, we were oversimplifying the picture. At worst, we risked making dangerous policy decisions that wasted resources and lives in pursuit of a tough identity that might not produce the peace dividend it was designed to engender. With the Cold War over for only about a decade, the debate had shifted from what kind of reputation mattered to the question of whether reputation really could matter to policymakers at all.[2]

Not long after the relevance of a state's reputation was challenged, the wheels seemed to come off the reputation bus entirely. In an effort to uncover the role of reputation (or, in this case, "past actions") in the decision to go to war, Daryl Press found just the opposite.[3] Rather than relying on what the enemies of a state have done in the past, Press argued, state leaders become so focused on the crisis at hand that historical or reputational information has no real presence in the decision-making process. Instead, the information at hand that defines the immediate crisis takes precedence, and past actions do not influence policy.

---

[1] See, for example, Schelling, 1966; Axelrod and Keohane, 1985a; Huth, 1988; Huth and Russett, 1993.

[2] See Mercer, 1996; Copeland, 1997; Huth, 1997; Mercer, 1997.

[3] Press, 2005.

As such, the vast efforts devoted to cultivating and maintaining reputations throughout the Cold War not only fail to influence policy decisions in times of crisis, they fail to manifest the very reputations they were meant to produce. It is not just that reputations exist but do not matter—they are not part of the discussion at all.

But the idea that reputations are not relevant to world politics in times of national security crises is difficult to accept. Outside of the study of war and deterrence, reputation has been an important concept in fields such as sociology, anthropology, economics, and biology. Recently, Nowak and Sigmund set forth a compelling argument for indirect reciprocity as a mechanism for cooperation and even altruism.[4] The study of economic cooperation in world politics has also been influenced by reputation.[5] The consequence has been puzzling: why does the concept of reputation play a continuing role in so many areas of scholarly inquiry, and yet it has faced what appeared to be an existential challenge in the study of international security?

Even in the study of international security, advances were made just as the death of reputation was being announced. Danilovic (2002), for example, teaches us that some deterrent threats are more inherently credible than others, suggesting that in the right geopolitical context, reputation still matters. Her work with Clare also suggests that states may overcompensate when they have a reputation for being irresolute, and that reputation is best understood within the context of a state's interests. Sartori (2005) shows us that reputations change over time, suggesting that the evolution of reputation can be an important piece of the puzzle.[6]

We also seek out and use reputational information in our daily economic lives. Years ago I tried to purchase the Pixar movie classic, *Toy Story*, as a Christmas present for my two-year-old son.[7] Like any good academic, I left my purchase until the last minute, only to realize that Disney (which owns Pixar, and distributes the *Toy Story* DVD) only releases its DVDs in discrete windows. As luck would have it, this was not one of those windows. Not one to give up easily, I turned to the online mega-flea mart, eBay, in search of the film. I found three sellers who had the DVD and could ship it to me before Christmas, but

[4] Nowak and Sigmund, 1998; Nowak and Sigmund, 2005; Nowak and Highfield, 2011.

[5] See, for example, Axelrod and Keohane, 1985b; Tomz, 2007.

[6] Danilovic, 2002; Clare and Danilovic, 2010; Clare and Danilovic, 2012; Sartori, 2005.

[7] For anyone thinking this might not qualify as an "important decision," I urge you to find a young sleep-deprived mother or father with a two-year-old son who has asked for one thing for Christmas.

these sellers were all between eight and ten thousand miles away from me. Since it was my first time on eBay, it is safe to say I had no purchasing history with any of them. Pricing was similar, and all three sellers claimed a delivery date that would meet my needs. All of the additional information available to me could be found in the sellers' "feedback" scores, also known as "seller ratings." The feedback scores were aggregate scores based on positive or negative reviews of the sellers provided by past buyers. I knew nothing about these past buyers (which bothered me), but their reactions to their purchasing experiences with the sellers were provided by eBay as a reputation mechanism. With pricing and shipping information relatively equal and thus uninformative, I chose the seller with the best feedback score, entered my credit card information, and hoped for the best.[8]

There is a simple structure undergirding my interaction with the sellers on eBay that is useful for understanding how reputation works and when it matters. I found myself in a situation in which I had to choose whether to cooperate with someone who held a private information advantage, and I had to make a choice. In choosing between my options, I was primarily concerned with maximizing the probability that the seller would follow through with his or her end of the bargain. Put another way, the information I was seeking pertained to the reputation of the seller to as it related to whether he or she fulfilled his or her obligations. Economic exchanges between the sellers and previous buyers who had left feedback were the source of that information, and in this case all of the buyers were equally useful to me, with the exception of timeliness. The older the feedback, the less relevant it was to my decision, because the ability or willingness to fulfill obligations can change over time.

I only turned to this reputational information because I could not adequately ascertain the credibility of the sellers without it. Had I developed my own

[8] You will be pleased to know that the DVD arrived in time, but I am still not certain of its authenticity. More interestingly, it turns out that the introduction of the seller-ratings system was the innovation that enabled eBay's (and in a way, all of e-commerce's) revolutionary success. Early in 1996, eBay's founder, Pierre Omidyar, penned a letter to his customers detailing the new system. While eBay's launch in 1995 was successful, brick-and-mortar stores were fighting back by highlighting the risks of buying products from unknown sellers with nothing but a promise of product quality and returnability. The infusion of fear into the online transaction was working, and customers became wary (often unnecessarily so) of remote sellers whom they could not see nor speak with. Omidyar's rating innovation infused new information into the online transaction, helping buyers overcome their trepidations and solidifying online shopping as a commercial force that appears here to stay.

purchasing history with one of these sellers previously, the seller rating would be less important. Lastly, the ratings were a product of the sellers' relationships with other buyers. As a result, ultimately what mattered was the buyers' perceptions of the quality of those relationships, and the way I used those perceptions as proxies for my own expectations. The feedback mechanism was invented by eBay's founders in an effort to convey reputational information and motivate good behavior. The system was designed such that it promoted cooperation. The system has been adopted with minor differences by other online firms such as Amazon, as well as purveyors of reputations about local businesses such as Yelp.

In the second chapter of this book, I will argue that reputation works in similar ways in the realm of international politics. Reputations form and evolve within a system of actors that can observe behavior over time. Those observations provide opportunities for indirect or vicarious learning. The need for indirect learning is motivated by missing information relevant to the bargaining process. The ability to garner meaningful information about a potential friend or foe depends on the opportunity to observe reputation information, the quality of this information, and the specifics of the information needs. When all of these conditions are present, reputations can affect the decisions world leaders make, and they can influence the determination of friend or foe.

This is just one piece of the puzzle, however. We cannot properly understand the impact of reputation on world politics until we understand its origins and dynamics, but we also cannot stop there. Understanding reputation's role in these strategic puzzles sheds light upon its role in cooperation and conflict. If we focus only on reputations without placing this information in the context of broader political processes, we can easily misunderstand when we should expect reputations to matter.

Thus, while the first goal of this book is to develop a new theory of reputation dynamics, the second goal is to improve our understanding of whether and when reputations influence cooperation and conflict. There is reason to believe that we still have work to do with respect to understanding how and when reputations matter in world politics. Think for a moment about the two fundamental causal mechanisms that have been identified as key ingredients that trigger war: private information, and problems of credible commitment.[9] Reputational information

---

[9] While not universally accepted as necessary components of an explanation for war, these two mechanisms are widely held by rationalists to be essential to understanding political violence. See, for example, Morrow, 1989, Fearon, 1995, Bueno de Mesquita and Lalman, 1992 and Powell, 1999, 2002, 2004a, and 2004b. Scholars outside the rationalist camp do not necessarily disagree with the

matters when the problems of private information and credible commitment exist. The first, private information, stems from the fundamental inability to know the capabilities or intentions of one's enemy. The existence of private information leads to inefficient negotiations and the ability to bluff, both of which can exacerbate the probability of violence. Credible commitment problems can be even more pernicious, as they get to the heart of the challenge states face when negotiating agreements that need to be durable in order to be effective at managing peace between potential belligerents. In both mechanisms, states (and the leaders that govern them) struggle to know the intentions, capabilities, and limitations of one another. Given these struggles, it is easy to conclude that leaders will task their policymaking teams with uncovering every possible source of knowledge that may help them ascertain the secrets and habits of the enemy. While it is certainly possible that there is no room in crisis negotiations for reputational information, it is likely that we have yet to identify the ways decision makers use this knowledge when anticipating the actions of others.

It is also important to recognize that we are not in complete control of our reputations. Think back to the aftermath of the terrorist attack against the United States on September 11, 2001, and the Bush administration's attempts to redefine its national security policy. The United States was not new to being a target of terrorism, but the severity of the attack and the ability to hit such a vital and symbolic homeland target placed the United States in unfamiliar territory. Uncharted waters make us nervous by nature, as we eagerly seek to get our bearings and resolve the uncertainty. In the months that followed the September 11 attacks, political forces both within the United States and beyond looked for signals and clarity in the policy response of the Bush administration.

For most observers, there were two limitations to the ability to resolve this uncertainty. First, foreign governments were forced to observe US actions indirectly. Offers of help could be heard from every corner of the world, but ultimately the United States had to formulate a coherent response on its own. Second, nations viewed the actions of the United States through diverse perspectives shaped by identity and history. While allies viewed American policy changes in search of precedent and sometimes in fear of commitment implications, other states viewed these actions with an eye on how they would be treated by the United States in the future. One such state was North Korea.

importance of incomplete information and/or credible commitment problems, but they rarely see these issues as sufficient for explaining war.

Shortly after George W. Bush issued his ultimatum against Saddam Hussein's Iraqi regime to disarm and step down or face war with the United States, North Korea's Kim Jong-il slipped into a rare level of seclusion. Daily reports of his activities disappeared from North Korea's official media. In a culture where the primary focus of the society is on the Dear Leader, such an absence of information is highly unusual.[10] It is easy to imagine that leaders in Iran and Syria were paying close attention as well. The United States started its campaign to remove Saddam Hussein with a "surgical strike" prior to the stated expiration of President Bush's ultimatum calling for Hussein to step down. Given the explicit association between Iraq, Iran, and North Korea, the other leaders had reason to believe that President Bush might ask the US military to take advantage of such opportunities to remove them from power as well. Indeed, in the immediate "postwar" period, the Bush Administration seemed to be counting on the assumption that US actions in Iraq would serve as a signal of resolve. In a speech to his troops on May 1, 2003, President Bush tied the events in Iraq to other governments:[11]

> Our war against terror is proceeding according to principles that I have made clear to all: Any person involved in committing or planning terrorist attacks against the American people becomes an enemy of this country, and a target of American justice. . . . Any person, organization, or government that supports, protects, or harbors terrorists is complicit in the murder of the innocent, and equally guilty of terrorist crimes. Any outlaw regime that has ties to terrorist groups and seeks or possesses weapons of mass destruction is a grave danger to the civilized world – and will be confronted.

It is likely that President Bush intended this speech to serve as a signal of resolve, both to his domestic audience and to potential foes. But what if these statements were perceived by these foes as a signal of aggression rather than resolve? Should Iran and North Korea have understood President Bush to be expressing a warning to cooperate, or a warning that war was coming? As conditions in Iraq unraveled, leaders in North Korea and Iran regained their voices and presence in the news, but what are the enduring lessons that they will take away from the US foreign policy toward Iraq?

[10] Shanker, 2002.
[11] Bush, 2003.

If we evaluate the sequence of events, there are two lessons that emerge. First, there is always a difference between the image we wish to portray and the image that is perceived by others. In other words, the reputation we have and the reputation we want are not always the same. One key to solving the puzzle of reputation is to shed our tendency to associate a single reputation with any given country in the system. This one state–one reputation approach fits with the assumption that a state chooses it reputation, and that this reputation is manipulable and consistently observed by everyone else.

Second, context matters, and in this case the context of proxy similarity is important. Most of the state leaders in the world did not disappear from public view in reaction to the surgical strike against Hussein. I believe North Korea's Kim Jong-il took his precautions because he considered Iraq to be a particularly good proxy for North Korea in terms of forming a reputational perception of the United States. The leaders of states like Mexico, France, and Russia did not respond in the same way because Iraq was dissimilar either in its political (dis)affiliation with the United States or its capability. Because North Korea was making a determination about the United States' intent to target them specifically, these proxy qualities were more important.

This illustration differs from my eBay story, of course. Besides being more salient to the topic at hand, it differs particularly in one key dimension: the need for relational proxy information. In the eBay story, I only needed to know if one of the sellers was trustworthy. All of the buyers providing the information that generated a seller's feedback rating were equally useful to me. North Korea, on the other hand, needed to know if the United States was showing aggression toward states like itself. The United States does not treat all other states equally. Instead, it shapes its foreign policy based on interests and capabilities. The distinction here is one of objective versus relational proxy information. Understanding when the quality of proxies matters is an important step toward solving the reputation puzzle.

Reconsidering Reputation: Actors and Proxy Information

In our efforts to understand international politics, we frequently focus on the interactions of two sides (e.g., the United States and the Soviet Union, Russia and Georgia, or Iran and Iraq). All of these pairings, or *dyads*, occur within a political environment. Any scholar in the field knows this, so it is worth pondering why we are so reluctant to walk away from the notion of two actors or two sides in our analyses.[12] One option would be to focus only on the environment, and return to the study of international systems. We spent more than two decades exploring the role of the international system as a determinant of interstate relations, to mixed reviews. Focusing only on the environment or system sacrifices too much at the state and dyadic levels of analysis. Somewhere in between the grand theories of global system structure and the isolating of the strategic dynamics of two governments, however, there is a wealth of information that can help us understand war and peace. One such wellspring of information can be found by focusing on how governments react to the actions their partners and enemies carry out toward others.

This does not mean we need to abandon the dyadic level of analysis. In fact, we lose sight of the ultimate goal if we do: namely, understanding how reputation impacts these dyadic interactions. In my view, this is a mistake that is often made when scholars turn to network analysis. Nobody can argue that these complex networks do not exist, or that they do not influence the decisions leaders make in crafting domestic and foreign policy. Yet if we are unable to connect these complex or environmental phenomena back to state behavior, the implications of our work can be difficult to process. When I turn to the study of extra-dyadic information here to craft a theory of reputation, my goal is not to abandon the fundamentals of state and dyadic analyses. Rather, I simply wish to emphasize that dyads are always informed by their political and historical environments, and reputation is one such conduit to this context. Reputation can be thought of as one way states process vicarious behavioral history to inform their interactions with one another. This is where things can get a bit confusing, because even though we ultimately seek to understand the impact of one state's reputation on the behavior of another, we cannot appreciate the complexities of this reputation without bringing in more information.

To tell this story we need three sets of actors. First, we need a *protagonist*. In the eBay story above this role is played by me. In world politics this role is played by the state that is trying to predict the behavior of its partner, or enemy. For example, if Latvia were to run into trouble with Russia, and trying to gauge whether Russia might use military force against it, Latvia is the protagonist. Second, we need an *antagonist*, or second actor.[13] These are the two key actors

[12] Many scholars have done just that, examining the world through the complex lens of network analysis or computational modeling.

[13] I am using the term "antagonist" more broadly than is commonly done in literary studies. Technically, I should label this second actor the *deuteragonist*, which is a more general term (but I

within a dyad in international relations, and the mechanism bringing reputation to the foreground is the fact that the protagonist needs information about the antagonist. In the eBay story the antagonist is the sellers, and in the Latvia example the antagonist is Russia. More generally, the antagonist is a potential partner or enemy, and the subject of our protagonist's focus. Lastly, in order for the protagonist to observe the antagonist's reputation, we need at least one *proxy*, or third actor, who has already interacted with the antagonist.[14] In the eBay story the other buyers that came before me are proxies for me. They have direct experience with the seller, and have passed on some of that information to me through eBay's feedback mechanism. In the Latvia example the proxies for Latvia include Georgia, Ukraine, Turkmenistan, and Belarus, all of whom have had salient interactions with Russia.

In world politics generally, this is the set of states that have interacted with the antagonist in the past. Often there are many proxy states, sometimes dozens. The model I develop in the next chapter can handle that, will address this in more detail and even embraces it, because sometimes not all proxies are equally valuable for the protagonist. The astute reader will notice that the two examples in the previous paragraph are different in many ways, but particularly in the proxies available to the two protagonists. In the eBay story, I have no need to evaluate the quality of the buyers, or the extent to which they are like me. All of the other buyers are equally useful to me. This is not true for Latvia and its pursuit of information about Russia's intentions to use force. Russia's intentions are likely to be conditioned by the qualities of its targets, and Latvia's regime has a lot more in common with Georgia and Ukraine than it does with Belarus. When the protagonist needs to know whether the antagonist will cooperate or conflict with proxies that are similar, we need to find a way to represent that extra layer of information in the theory.

The protagonist is trying to evaluate the intentions of the antagonist in an effort to anticipate its behavior. If I concede this territory, will they still attack me? If I sign this treaty, will they abide by its terms? If I join this country in an alliance, will they be there when I need them? These questions hint at the

had to look that up, so common sense suggests it is a poor fit if I am trying to actually communicate with the reader). If the situation concerns the possibility of conflict then the term "antagonist" fits well. But reputation is just as important in cooperation puzzles, and the second actor is not always at odds with the protagonist.

[14] The literary-studies equivalent for the proxy is a tritagonist. But this particular actor (or set of actors) serves a special purpose for the protagonist: namely, by serving as an example, and providing expectations for how the protagonist expects to be treated by the antagonist.

need for information that can never fully exist, and reputation is simply one of the tools we use to address this void. The type of reputational information we seek is inextricably tied to these questions. Thus, reputations exist within the context of types of interactions. The protagonist is essentially looking for precedent; past behavior by the antagonist that fits the current situation well. The protagonist is trying to learn what it can about the antagonist, and we can think of the other states as potential learning opportunities. This means that in order for reputations to emerge, the antagonist must have a history of interaction with other states in the system.[15] Like any historical relationship, these interaction histories will vary in quality and quantity.

If you put all three of these pieces together—the protagonist, antagonist, and proxies—we have a recipe for reputation. Once we understand how these histories translate into reputations, we can then turn to the issue of impact. The second goal of this book is to present a new theory of the link between reputation, cooperation, and conflict. In essence, evaluating this impact becomes a question of how states act upon the reputations of others with respect to the context of the political issue at stake. Traditionally, states have operated under the assumption that governments need to cultivate reputations for toughness. The idea was to use history as precedent, and to show one's enemies that the costs of war outweighed the benefits (think of it as "Don't Mess with Texas" on an international level).[16] But the mechanics of this strategy have always been obscure to me, and one of the tasks of this second goal is to empirically re-evaluate the notion that a reputation for violence leads to peace.

In fact, an important takeaway message of this book is that a reputation for using militarized violence does not generate a peace dividend as has traditionally been assumed. The key to the problem lies in the reputations we have versus the reputations we seek. The goal may be to cultivate a reputation for being tough, but what often emerges instead is a reputation for aggression or incompetence.

---

[15] In Chapter 2, I explore the assumptions we make about initial conditions and reputations. As a default, I propose that we consider the initial condition to be no reputation at all, which means no meaningful information. A risk-averse protagonist may set the initial reputation of its antagonist as hostile, while the eternal optimist may assume its partners are honest until proven otherwise. The theory of reputation developed in the next chapter gives the reader the freedom to customize the model to fit his or her research needs.

[16] Oddly, "Don't Mess with Texas" was a phrase developed in the mid-1980s by the Texas Department of Transportation as an anti-littering slogan. It quickly came to symbolize the identity of Texans, however, and very few of us outside of Texas imagine the words have anything to do with litter.

Whereas toughness can send the signal that deters an enemy, aggression can signal an inability to commit to peace. I systematically examine the impact of a reputation for violence in Chapter 5, and in doing so I find compelling evidence that suggests violence begets violence. As the early phase of the twenty-first century has thus far been characterized by renewed tension between great powers such as the United States and Russia, the policy implications of this finding are non-trivial, to say the least.

History, Perception, and World Politics

All of this is putting the cart before the horse, however, so perhaps it is best to introduce some history that illustrates the role of reputation in times of crisis. In the early part of 1812, Tsar Alexander I was trying to decide whether Napoleon and his army planned to invade Russia. The two leaders had already accumulated quite a bit of history, including years of war and a secret treaty in 1807 wherein they pledged fealty to one another. But Napoleon was also busy taming the rest of the continent, and Alexander watched these interactions with great interest.

I can think of few better leaders to illustrate the concepts of reputation and identity than Napoleon Bonaparte. Napoleon will always be known as one of the most brilliant, audacious, and ambitious leaders in history, and few others so singularly combined political and military roles to become one of the most powerful men in history. I first learned about him in primary school, and I can still recall my first image of him on his horse, sitting as tall as possible with his hand in his coat. When we study him now, he is almost larger than life; a unique and dangerous mix of arrogance and genius. Despite this reputation for near-invincibility and military brilliance, however, Russia did not back down when France attacked in 1812. If his reputation had worked as he intended, Napoleon should have been able to extract whatever he wanted from Alexander without the need to invade.

But what happens if we think more carefully about Napoleon's reputation, particularly from Alexander's perspective? In this example, consider Alexander (and Russia) as the protagonist, and Napoleon (and France) as the antagonist. The proxy states are all the other actors in Europe, including Spain, the Grand Duchy of Warsaw, Great Britain, and Prussia. Viewing this slice of history in this way sheds interesting light on Alexander's decisions surrounding the early days of the Russo-French war of 1812. Remember that the puzzle Alexander faced was whether or not Napoleon would start a new war with Russia. As such, it was Napoleon's reputation for aggression and using force to resolve disputes that mattered to Alexander. If reputation works the way we have classically thought of it, then Napoleon's reputation for military mastery should have triggered acquiescence from Russia. If reputation works the way I think it does, however, then Napoleon's reputation for aggression undermined his ability to credibly commit to peace with Russia, thereby removing the option to acquiesce.

It is easy to forget how important the first two decades of the nineteenth century were to the formation of international politics as we understand them today. If Napoleon had succeeded in implementing and enforcing his vision of the Continental System, British influence would have been greatly diminished. From there it is easy to envision a remarkably different future for Europe. If I can demonstrate that reputation mattered in this formative moment in world history, then perhaps it will be worth suffering through a little political science in the following chapters.

It is also easy to forget just how much changed in European politics between 1805 and 1815. At the beginning of this ten-year span, Napoleon elevated himself to emperor and conquered most of Continental Europe. Imperial France was at war with the Third Coalition, formed by Austria, Russia, and the United Kingdom, and despite the British control of the sea, Napoleon prevailed. In 1806, the Fourth Coalition (Russia, Prussia, Saxony, Sweden, and the United Kingdom) tried once again to stem the tide of French imperialism, but by 1807, Tsar Alexander I of Russia had had enough. In July of that year, Alexander signed the Treaty of Tilsit, granting major concessions to Napoleon and France in an attempt to stem the tide of war. With Russia subdued but not defeated, Napoleon turned his attention westward, toward the British.

Just five years after the treaty was signed, however, Russia and France found themselves at war again. In a series of events that are often used to demonstrate the folly of Napoleon's hubris as well as the seemingly unique ability of the Russian people to bend without breaking, Napoleon's invasion into Russia failed in large part because Alexander anticipated it and implemented an extraordinary strategy of retreat and scorched-earth tactics. The French army suffered enormous losses in Napoleon's attempt to defeat the Russian army, and the image of Napoleon's invincibility was tarnished. More than any other moment in this chaotic time, this defeat initiated the unraveling of the Napoleonic Empire and any hope of a Continental System.

The questions at hand are, what caused Russia to be so skeptical of France's promise of cooperation in the months and years after Tilsit, and why did Alexander anticipate Napoleon's invasion in 1812? Had Russia simply complied with the treaty and believed Napoleon when he pledged brotherhood with Alexander, the war in 1812 would have likely solidified Napoleon's hold on the continent. Part of the answer to these questions can be found in Napoleon's reputation as it was perceived by Alexander. Returning briefly to the language I introduced earlier, Alexander in this situation is the protagonist, and Napoleon is the antagonist. Alexander is in dire need of information, and this case it is information about Napoleon's intention to either abide by his treaty with Alexander or to invade Russia.

Looking back, this reputation information began to emerge not long after the Treaty of Tilsit was signed in 1807. After Tilsit, a chilly peace emerged between France and Russia. Napoleon focused on enforcing the Continental System. His plan was to deny Great Britain any access to the rest of Europe, and the resulting blockade would in theory break the British economy. This "Continental Blockade," as it was also called, relied on a complete denial of access to trade, which proved to be exceedingly difficult. Napoleon sought an embargo that would prevent the British any safe harbor and effectively strangle their economy.

Wanting and getting a blockade are two different things, of course, and while most of Continental Europe was forced to comply with the emperor's wishes, Portugal was autonomous enough to continue its economic relationship with Great Britain. The Treaty of Tilsit included Russia's formal acquiescence with the Blockade, but international politics is replete with agreements that are difficult to implement. Despite Alexander's pledge to be faithful to France and a secret agreement to help one another, Russian compliance was persistently difficult to procure. For one thing, ordinary Russian citizens had come to know Napoleon as the embodiment of the Great Satan, and they struggled to change their perception of him when their own emperor announced the new alliance. More importantly, Russian military and political elites were reluctant to give up hard-won gains in the Russo-Turkish war, England bought a lot of Russian grain, and not everyone was pleased about joining the French in a new war against the British.[17]

Not long after Tilsit, Napoleon's behavior elsewhere in Europe provided important clues to Alexander regarding the French emperor's intentions. In the fall of 1807, Napoleon signed the Treaty of Fountainebleau with Spain. The treaty allowed Napoleon to transport his forces through Spain with the stated intent of invading Portugal. Spain's alliance with France granted this permission in exchange for assurances that King Charles IV would remain in charge of his

[17] Cate, 1985.

continental possessions south of the Pyrenees.[18] On the face of it, the purpose of the alliance was to join Spanish with French forces to oppose the common threat of Great Britain. In fact, the treaty served as a Trojan Horse of sorts, allowing hundreds of thousands of French forces into Spain; subsequently, Napoleon deposed King Charles IV and inserted his own puppet regime.[19] If we consider Spain as a proxy for Russia, the lesson that Alexander learns is that a treaty with Napoleon can quickly lead to French occupation. In Chapter 3, I will return to this example to demonstrate that this was indeed the historical dynamic that motivated the French invasion of Russia, and the dramatic and painful strategies the Russians endured to defeat the imposing French army.

Defining Reputation, Cooperation, and Conflict

Similar examples permeate world politics. Of course, this claim that governments observe the behavior of their peers is easy enough to make, and it would seem ridiculous to assume otherwise. The more important and difficult questions to answer, however, are whether and when governments *systematically* alter their foreign policy behavior based on such knowledge. In other words, when do these observations of reputation influence behavior?

Like any big question in the study of world politics, there are many competing answers. In this book I argue that actions in world politics generate information that is valuable not only for those who are directly involved in the situation, but also for members of the global community who have a relationship with the actor(s). I focus my thoughts on the states in the global system, but the arguments set forth here are applicable to other levels of analysis as well. One way to think about this indirect, vicarious information that emerges from state action is through the concept of a state's reputation.

At this point, it is necessary to define some of the key terms I will be using in this book. "Reputation" is a loaded term in the field of political science, and later in the book I will discuss how that baggage has affected the conclusions we tend to draw about reputation's role in politics. For the purposes of this

[18] Burnham, 2000.

[19] The Spanish resistance that resulted would prove to be far more difficult to suppress than Napoleon imagined, and over the next half-decade he squandered tremendous resources and men in an effort to control Spain and Portugal. He ultimately failed, and his betrayal of the 1807 treaty caused the Spanish resistance to ally with the British, a relationship that would sow the seeds of Napoleon's eventual defeat at Waterloo in 1815. See Dwyer, 2001.

project, I focus on the behavioral contributions to a state's reputation. That is, reputation is a product of past behavior and perception. The behavior is that of the antagonist, perceived by the protagonist. This form of reputation is informed by the interaction between behavior and perception, where behavior is at least in part controlled by the antagonist, but perceptions are not.

For those who may object to labeling this kind of information as reputation, there are other options. Nowak uses the term "indirect reciprocity," but this encompasses strategies as well as information, and serves as the basis for his explanation of cooperation within and among groups. "Reciprocity" is also a richly studied concept in world politics in its own right.[20] Instead of reciprocity, one could replace the word "reputation" with "vicarious experiential learning," which gets to the mechanism that drives the formation and maintenance of reputations. This alternative wording has "learning" in it, however, which is also loaded. For readers troubled by both "reputation" and "learning," try "vicarious experiential observation processes." That rolls off the tongue, right? When I first began writing on this subject, I used the term "relational interdependence," but I have since come to see reputation as a particular instantiation of that broader set of international ties and linkages. Reputation, or reputational learning, are good terms for this information, but only if we can shake the habit of thinking of them only in the context of deterrence.

There are, of course, a multitude of stories about reputations that tend to lead us in different directions. Reputation can be nearly synonymous with the concept of a brand in the business world, a concept that should remind scholars of politics of the notions of identity and roles. Commercial brands are cultivated with the hopes of conveying quality, consistency, innovation, and value. These positive associations can easily be replaced by negative images of shoddy workmanship, inconsistency, outdated technology, and overpriced products. Such changes conjure up the enduring issues of how reputations change and how reputations can be manipulated strategically. To make matters even more complicated, these images can be perceived differently by other businesses or consumers. Businesses, of course, have figured this out, and tailor their images to different types of consumers. Some firms may focus on a single image that will resonate with one market but not others, while other firms may try to develop multiple brands to appeal to a wide band of consumers. Why then, do we typically think of a state as only having one fixed reputation that is consistently observed by the other states in the international system?

[20] Crescenzi, Best, and Kwon, 2010.

Back in the global political arena, positive and negative reputations are abundant. Countries have reputations for being trustworthy or deceitful, friendly to international investment or hostile to foreign business, conciliatory or belligerent, and of course, resolute or irresolute. Understanding the origins and dynamics of this diverse collection of reputations is one of the goals of this book. But somewhere along the way we crossed the wires of reputation with the notions of cooperation and deterrence in the study of world politics. Reputation has been touted as a cornerstone of cooperation,[21] a solution to the the security dilemma, and a source of credibility in deterrence.[22]

Reputation's role in these deterrence theories was often simple and unidimensional. Governments either had a reputation for being tough or weak, for example, and a tough reputation was critical to deterring potential challenges. This logic underpinned the "Peace Through Strength" approach to foreign policy employed by President Ronald Reagan at the tail end of the Cold War.[23] The notion of using a reputation for toughness to deter potential challengers is an intuitive and appealing idea, and it could be said that it served as a foundation for American foreign policy during the Cold War, but the entire argument rests on particular assumptions about the formation and projection of a state or government's reputation. Typically, the conventional wisdom assumed that a state cultivated one reputation that had to be preserved with repeated demonstrations of a willingness to use force. This reputation was considered to be essentially under the control of the state itself. More importantly, reputations were considered to be singular, and commonly perceived throughout the international system.

In order to restore reputation's place in the causal story of peace and conflict, I recast the concept to embrace its complexities.[24] States may have multiple reputations in the eyes of partners and enemies. A state can have a reputation for being reliable and honest in the eyes of one partner, but at the same time harbor a reputation for being aggressive and untrustworthy in the eyes of another state.

[21] Axelrod and Keohane (1985a) say it plainly: "Such reputations may become important assets, precisely because others will be more willing to make agreements with governments that can be expected to respond to cooperation with cooperation" (p. 250). More recently, Michael Tomz (2007) established the role of reputation in international cooperation by examining the emergence of cooperation between governments and foreign investors.

[22] Huth, 1997.

[23] Beschloss and Sidey, 2009.

[24] Much of this complexity was identified by Mercer (1996). His conclusion, however, was that these complexities and idiosyncrasies rendered the study of reputation implausible.

Great Britain perceived a positive reputation for the United States during the Cold War, but the Soviets did not. Even on one dimension of political activity, such as a state's proclivity for initiating violence, we may have reason to expect a diverse set of perceived reputations. This is not always the case, however; and this is a topic I return to in Chapters 2 and 3. Reputations can be durable, but they do degrade over time unless they are nurtured. And while reputation plays an important role in world politics, it is not the only cause of peace or conflict. My goal is to embed reputation within the framework of what we already know to be the major causes of war.

Reputation is thus contextual and in the eyes of the beholder. Because of this, reputational information can influence one actor's behavior while being completely dismissed by another. Ignoring this context is the easiest path toward misunderstanding the impact of reputation. But just because reputational information is contextual does not mean it cannot be influential or evaluated by scholars. The key is to find a way to incorporate this context into a theory of reputation without losing sight of the underlying processes at work. If we focus too heavily on context, we are forced to abandon the notion of understanding reputation's influence in a broad sense. If we fail to focus on context enough, however, we may mistake the contextual dimension of reputation as noise or complexity. In this book, I attempt to strike the right balance between generalizability and contextual richness, producing a theory of reputation and politics that is both portable and useful in helping scholars evaluate the whens, whys, and hows of reputation.

Connecting Reputation to Cooperation and Conflict: Elusive in Observation or Influence?

Reputation's influence is one of the last concepts in the study of politics that remains poorly understood. We often give it too much credit, claiming that reputation can entirely explain or account for instances of cooperation or successful deterrence. Or, we give it no credit at all, arguing that reputations either don't exist, or are not useful or relevant when it comes to leaders making their foreign-policy decisions. In this book I will make the case that reputations are important phenomena that influence international politics, but reputation need not be the only influence to be influential. Reputation conditions the environment within which decisions are made. For a government with a reputation for violating agreements, such as North Korea, the challenge of crafting agreements that will trigger cooperation from any state interacting with North Korea becomes far more difficult. On the other hand, a government with a reputation for abiding by its agreements in similar situations may be able to leverage this identity to signal credibility in potential commitments. This perceived credibility may be an important piece of the cooperation puzzle. One challenge scholars face is to not lose sight of the need to understand the way the same historical information might be interpreted as different signals to different actors.

In the pages that follow I develop an explanation of reputation that states generate through their behavior over time, and then pose the following questions. If this information exists, what do governments do with it? How do state leaders interpret the actions of their friends and foes? For example, does the war between the United States and Iraq influence the North Korean government's belief that war between the United States and North Korea is coming? More generally, do nations alter their behavior with others based on what these other nations are doing elsewhere? To answer these questions, I develop a theory of how reputational information is perceived by other states, drawing from cognitive balance theory and social learning models as well as theories of rivalry and interaction history. A critical component of this theory, however, is understanding when and how reputational information influences foreign policy choices.

There are two specific pieces of this puzzle to sort out. First, how does a state (or more specifically, its policymakers) process the information contained in international relations where that state is not directly involved? Second, once this information is processed, what do policymakers do with it? Does this information affect the choices made in international politics?[25] I argue that reputation matters when there is an opportunity for it to inform problems of private information with respect to credible commitment. States who develop reputations for upholding their agreements are more likely to convince others that they will keep their word. In this case, the reputation helps ameliorate the concerns that come with anarchy and uncertainty in world politics. On the other hand, states who have a history of resolving disputes with violence will develop

---

[25] Three related perspectives contribute to my solution to the second piece of the puzzle. Russell Leng's research on repeated interaction and rivalry (1983, 1988, 2000) provides a platform by delineating an experiential model of direct learning within dyads. The rivalry literature provides a rich conceptual context of viewing dyads as dyanamic, evolutionary political arenas (Diehl and Goertz, 2001). Finally, Andrew Enterline and I develop a flexible model of direct historical learning within dyads that can be expanded to address extra-dyadic learning (Crescenzi and Enterline, 2001). I will build off of this platform to incorporate reputational learning into this dynamic relationship framework.

a reputation for being unable to commit to peace. Such a reputation exacerbates fears of commitment problems, making negotiations in times of crisis more difficult and thus increasing the chance of conflict. In effect, reputation contributes to policymakers' beliefs that they are dealing with a trustworthy state.[26] Whether this contribution is sufficient to make the difference between cooperation and conflict depends on the setting, but in Part Two of the book I show that this contribution is both significant and systematic in world politics.

This broader puzzle is also one of substance and research design. The dyadic level of analysis (studying the interaction between pairs of states) has dominated the study of international conflict for the last two decades.[27] It is a natural fit with the parallel emphasis on strategic interaction, but it is not ideally suited to incorporate information that lies beyond the dyad itself.[28] While we have recently made theoretical and empirical progress regarding the dependence of dyadic observations across time,[29] we still have very little understanding of how the political choices made by the two states (and their governments) within a dyad are influenced by other states and other dyads. Scholars have recently renewed their focus on this spatial interdependence and these networks,[30] but we are only beginning to understand how these phenomena relate back to the dyadic level of analysis. My goal here is to be able to assess the impact of this particular form of reputation on crises between states; therefore, preserving the ability to consider reputation at the dyadic level of analysis is important.

Plan of the Book

This book has two parts. The first, composed of the next two chapters, pursues the goal of establishing a theory of reputation dynamics and a theory of reputation's impact in world politics. The second, composed of chapters 4 and 5, is an empirical evaluation of the influence of reputation. I then conclude with

---

[26] See also important work done by Sartori (2002) and Kydd (2005) on the topic of trust and trustworthiness in world politics.

[27] Bremer, 1992.

[28] Strategic interaction, or a rationalist approach to the study of world politics, has made great strides toward understanding the inefficient choice to use violence rather than reach an agreement. A list of references would be too long to include here, but see Bueno de Mesquita (1981a) and Fearon (1994) for two foundational examples.

[29] Raknerud and Hegre, 1997; Beck, Katz, and Tucker, 1998; and Crescenzi and Enterline, 2001.

[30] Signorino and Ritter, 1999; Heagerty, Ward, and Gleditsch, 2002; Ward and Gleditsch, 2002; and Hoff and Ward, 2004.

a discussion of the policy implications of this new understanding of reputation and politics.

Part One: A Theory of Reputation and Its Place in World Politics

The concept of reputation has long puzzled scholars and policymakers. Chapter 2 examines how reputation is both pervasive and evasive in world politics. The notion of reputation has been discussed as far back as Thucydides and by many of the world's current political leaders. In this chapter I present a dynamic and transparent model of reputation. The model emerges from a simple "the friend of my friend is my friend" logic,[31] and it allows me to show how reputations form within the eyes of the beholder. By anchoring a state's reputation in its historical behavior beyond the dyad, I am able to demonstrate how one state, such as France, can have a very different reputation from the perspective of Poland than it does from the perspective of North Korea. I also draw from my previous work on the evolution of interstate relationships to show how this reputational information waxes and wanes across time.[32]

In the next chapter, I carve out a new focus on reputation that leads to observable traces of its influence. By stepping back from highly specific types of reputation (often associated with deterrence), and thinking theoretically about the way in which states process reputational information, I am able to recast the debate on reputation and move the literature forward. Building on the extant literature,[33] I show how we have failed to properly theorize or observe the implications of reputation in politics. Chapter 3 establishes a theory of reputation and politics that is connected with what we currently know about problems of credible commitment and bargaining. I then distill this theory down into key hypotheses linking a state's reputation for *competence* during crises and cooperation to expectations of future behavior and effects on phenomena relating to conflict and cooperation.

Throughout these two theoretical chapters, I make extensive use of empirical illustrations with the goal of helping the reader understand the process and importance of reputation dynamics. I highlight the role of reputation in the crafting of British foreign policy toward the Soviet Union in the aftermath of World War II. I specifically focus on early 1946 and the relationship between George Kennan (at the time, the US Chargé d'Affaires in Moscow) and Frank

---

[31] Heider, 1946; and Harary, 1959.
[32] Crescenzi and Enterline, 2001.
[33] Schelling, 1966; Mercer, 1996; and Press, 2005.

Roberts (British Chargé d'Affaires in Moscow). Kennan's famous "Long Cable" to Washington is widely credited as one of the key influences in the hard line America took with the Soviets in the early years of the Cold War. Roberts, however, issued three telegrams of his own to the British Foreign Ministry shortly after Kennan's memo went to DC. The parallels between the two sets of documents are clear,[34] and in this chapter I show that Roberts's trust and reliance on Kennan's expertise allowed him to evaluate the government in Moscow based on reputational information. His decision to parallel Kennan's assessment enabled the British Foreign Ministry to do the same, shaping British foreign policy such that it was highly compatible with American foreign policy. This illustration demonstrates both the causal process that links reputation to foreign policy decisions, and how reputation can have a dramatic impact on international politics. Illustrations are not empirical tests, however, so the second part of the book is devoted to rigorously testing the predictions that emerge from reputational learning theory.

Part Two: The Influence of Reputation on Cooperation and Conflict

With a theory of reputation dynamics in place, the second half of the book turns to historical evaluations of the implications of the reputational learning model. While the model is designed to be applicable to a wide variety of political interactions, I focus my attention on alliance formation, the onset of militarized violence (disputes), and war. An alliance between two or more states is one of the most difficult forms of cooperation to obtain (compared, for example, to trade or diplomatic offices). The formation of alliances always involves elite political actors, and often has to face a number of political and bureaucratic obstacles. Alliances also tend to be rare events, and state performance is always uncertain. They provide an excellent test of the reputational learning model.

Chapter 4 examines the impact of reputation on the occurrence of conflict between states. While the role of historical violence between nations in the incidence of militarized conflict is well established, the role of indirect, reputational information is not. The entire rivalry literature, for example, is built upon the premise that politics among nations should be studied as long temporal relationships, wherein multiple conflicts cannot be considered independent from one another.[35] More generally, Andrew Enterline and I demonstrate that a history of violence between nations is a powerful predictor of future militarized

---

[34] Greenwood, 1990.

[35] See Diehl and Goertz, 2001.

disputes.[36] The argument is fairly intuitive: interstate conflict leaves an indelible mark on the nations involved, and these memories influence foreign policy decision-making in times of crisis. Together, these two streams of information place crises and crisis behavior in macro-relational and historical contexts. As I discussed earlier, however, this perspective does not yet translate to reputational histories.

In Chapter 4, I draw from the implications of reputational learning theory to examine the question of whether a reputation for crisis incompetence influences the onset of militarized violence. Care is taken to implement empirical illustrations of how reputational information is processed by states when dealing with peace and conflict. I then operationalize this learning model using data on conflict history, foreign policy similarity, and power similarity to empirically test the argument that a state is more likely to fight an opponent that has engaged in conflict with that state's peers. The empirical analysis in this chapter supports the notion that states are indeed paying close attention to the way their potential enemies treat their friends. When states face opponents that are historically hostile towards other, similar countries, militarized conflict is more likely to occur. This result undermines the previous position in the literature that advocates a deterrent effect to violence, and it also counters the argument that reputations do not matter in times of crisis. Instead, this chapter demonstrates that understanding how reputations indirectly influence decision-making can generate more valid analyses of the impact of reputation on conflict.

Chapter 4 then completes this empirical analysis with a focus on the question of whether these contextual sources of reputation remain important when states escalate from militarized conflict to full-blown war.[37] It is one thing to argue that historical and reputational contexts are relevant when political crises turn violent; it is quite another to conclude that these contexts are also relevant when these crises escalate to war. Do these factors permanently inhibit the ability of states to negotiate their way out of crises, or does the specter of war cause states to shed this historical knowledge?[38] Or, does a reputation for toughness lend credibility in brinksmanship?[39] The reputational learning model developed in Chapter 3 suggests otherwise. Indeed, a reputation for violence and escalation makes a crisis *more* dangerous, not less.

[36] Crescenzi and Enterline, 2001.
[37] Senese and Vasquez, 2008.
[38] Press, 2005.
[39] Schelling, 1966.

I test this hypothesis using semi-parametric hazard analysis on data for war onset covering all international dyads from 1817 to 2000, as well as a sample containing only politically relevant dyads.[40] I find that historical and reputational contexts have an important inflammatory impact on the decision to go to war. When states engage in crisis-driven behavior in a context rich with direct and indirect historical conflict, the onset of war is more likely, because such reputations undermine the credibility of settlement options. The results indicate that a direct history of conflict between a dyad increases the odds of war onset. Additionally, the odds of war onset increase when either state within the dyad has a reputation for using force in times of crisis.

With this analysis of the link between reputation and conflict in place, Chapter 5 draws from the implications of the reputational learning model developed in Chapter 3 to evaluate the question of how reputations for credibility and reliability influence international political cooperation. I investigate the extent to which states value reputations for upholding agreements when making their alliance formation decisions. While states hope to satisfy a number of interests by carefully considering the characteristics of potential allies, the expected reliability of future partners is an important component of an alliance seeker's decision calculus. Thus, my specific focus in this chapter is on the question of whether a state's historical reputation for alliance reliability influences its likelihood of being sought by other states as an ally.

States form alliances for multiple reasons, behind which lie an assumption of reliability. That is, states choose to ally with partners when they have some positive expectation that the alliance will hold in the event of conflict. Otherwise, the basis for the alliance is undermined. Any alliance in which a partner fails (or is expected to fail) to live up to its commitments is largely devoid of merit. Moreover, the failure of an alliance likely renders the abandoned partner *more* vulnerable than it was prior to its formation. Indeed, the level of security that a state hopes to achieve by forming an alliance is only relevant to the extent that the alliance seeker believes its partner will live up to its obligations. Consequently, states choose their partners carefully, preferring those likely to honor their agreements.

Based on this argument, I establish that reputations for reliability can affect alliance formation choices. While a reputation for reliability is not the only influence on alliance partner choices, I demonstrate that it is an especially important one. Clearly, an ally is not particularly useful unless it brings security

---

[40] Maoz and Russett, 1993.

goods to the table (or trade, or some other policy dimension). But the benefits that another state can bring to an alliance relationship may be mitigated by how trustworthy that ally is when its resources and efforts are actually needed. In this chapter, I develop the notion of a reputation for reliability and apply it to the phenomenon of alliance formation. To examine the argument, I operationalize the reputational learning model from Chapter 3 and present an alliance reputation measure that reflects the historical reliability of a state. I use this variable to test the notion that a reputation for being a reliable ally makes a state a more attractive partner for future alliances. The empirical research at the end of this chapter provides support for this reliability reputation hypothesis, suggesting that when states develop reputational identities (in this case for being reliable allies), those identities can provide useful and actionable information for other actors in the international arena. The chapter also makes use of qualitative empirical illustrations drawn from European history, centering around Britain's use of reputational information when gauging whether to pursue an alliance with Germany as opposed to with Japan at the end of the nineteenth century.

In Chapter 6, I address the policy implications of the reputational learning model, and discuss possible extensions of the model and its applicability to puzzles in world politics. The key policy result is that the classic Cold War logic of peace through strength is flawed. States who develop a propensity to use violence do not deter opponents; rather, they entrench them. A reputation for violence generates priors that undermine bargaining environments. In short, states can no longer trust that their opponent will stick to a deal, so they prepare to fight instead. In this way, a violent reputation can trigger the conflict spiral, rather than produce peace through deterrence. I conclude with a reflection on the policy implications of this logic for the United States in a post-nuclear, post-Cold War world.

The journey to this policy implication starts with a better theory of how reputations form. In the next chapter, I endeavor to change the way we think about state reputations. By shifting our focus from the reputations states want to the reputations they get in the eyes of others, I lay the foundation for the concept that enables us to better understand the link between reputation and politics.

0190609532-043

PART ONE

A THEORY OF REPUTATION AND ITS PLACE IN WORLD POLITICS

2

The Dynamics of Reputation

Great-power virtue makes for good words, but truly effective prosely-
tizing, as missionaries know, requires the fear of God.
—Josef Joffe and James Davis

But memory plays tricks. Memory is another word for story, and
nothing is more unreliable.
—Ann-Marie MacDonald

By now you have hopefully come to the realization that reputation is both
pervasive and evasive in world politics. This is the heart of the problem. We
live with the ideas of reputation, status, brand, and identity, but these terms can
seem both ubiquitous and vague. Some of us care about this conundrum more
than others, which in and of itself is important information. If you stop ordinary
people on the street and ask them if their reputation matters to them, most, if
not all, of them will say that it does. If you ask them if their own reputation
matters to others, again they are likely to agree. Now ask them if their country's
reputation matters in the world, and I suspect they will agree, but with far less
confidence in their answer. Ask them to characterize their country's reputation,
and you may get many answers. Not only is the concept of reputation difficult to
circumnavigate, but also, the role of reputation in politics can be just as vexing.

Part of the problem is that there are two pieces to the puzzle: formative and
causative. The first is the question of how reputations form and evolve. Who
is involved? Who controls reputations? How do reputations emerge, change,
and fade away? If we ignore these questions, we inevitably make the mistake of
oversimplifying reputation dynamics. The second puzzle piece is the question of
whether reputations affect political outcomes, like conflict and cooperation, in
world politics. These are the questions of causation, not formation. Can a state's
reputation increase or decrease its chances for war? If states form reputations for

being trustworthy, do these reputations lead to more cooperation? We cannot improve our understanding of reputation's role in world politics unless we sort out both pieces.

In this chapter, I tackle the first challenge of building a model of reputation formation and evolution. I identify a functional, dynamic model of reputation, with particular emphasis on states in the context of world politics. I will argue here that states and their leaders indeed have reputations, but these reputations are complex and multidimensional. This complexity is due in part to the realization that these reputations are tied to those that perceive them. In other words, a state's reputation depends in part on the other states observing its behavior. Complex does not mean intractable—however, we can better understand a state's reputation by thinking theoretically about these perceptions and observations. I will present a model of reputation dynamics in this chapter that helps us focus on a state's reputational information as it is viewed by other states. The result is a reputation learning model that captures some of the complex dynamics of reputation without sacrificing the ability to think about this phenomenon systematically and analytically.

Before I present the reputation learning model, it is worth taking a brief look at the history of scholarship on the subject of reputation in world politics. Like many important topics of our (or any) field, the study of reputation has developed its own baggage over the years. That baggage has both shaped recent research and constrained the debate on reputation's role and relevance in world politics, and one cannot properly move forward with a renewed treatment of the concept without understanding its past usage. Ironically, the concept of reputation has a bit of a reputation problem. The story of whether and how reputations matter in world politics is a troubled one. It is therefore also useful to place research in the field of international relations within the broader context of how reputation is evaluated throughout the social and natural sciences. Doing so will help the reader appreciate the ubiquitous and pervasive presence of reputation, which may help lighten the load of the baggage that has constrained the study of reputation for so long.

The Origins of Reputation in the Study of International Relations

The notion of political reputation has been discussed as far back as Ancient Greece, and remains pertinent to many of the world's current political leaders. It has been called upon to rescue politics from the threat of an anarchical international system, accused of motivating governments to sacrifice their own soldiers on the battlefield, and debunked as a mythical political concept. On a smaller scale, scientists use it to explain learning among individuals, even among fish. At the same time, its existence and its importance are challenged. How can we find a way forward, toward a better understanding of reputation in politics?

If we step back and look at the arguments in a new way, it becomes clear that we are closer than it seems to a new path forward. Mercer rightly criticizes any characterization that treats reputation as singular and manipulable, but he gives up too much when he concludes that reputations are so unique and short-lived that they have an indeterminate impact on politics. Reputations are more complex and dynamic than we have traditionally given them credit for, but we can model these complexities and reveal the systematic influence reputations have on cooperation and conflict among states in world politics.

The origins of reputation's central role in politics can be traced at least as far back as Ancient Greece and the writings of Thucydides. In his iconic *History of the Peloponnesian War*, written in 431 BCE, Thucydides observes Pericles referring to Athens' reputation as something to be cherished and tended, but also as a clear and useful tool of foreign policy:

> For Athens alone of her contemporaries is found when tested to be greater than her reputation, and alone gives no occasion to her assailants to blush at the antagonist by whom they have been worsted, or to her subjects to question her title by merit to rule. Rather, the admiration of the present and succeeding ages will be ours, since we have not left our power without witness, but have shown it by mighty proofs; and far from needing a Homer for our panegyrist, or other of his craft whose verses might charm for the moment only for the impression which they gave to melt at the touch of fact, we have forced every sea and land to be the highway of our daring, and everywhere, whether for evil or for good, have left imperishable monuments behind us. Such is the Athens for which these men, in the assertion of their resolve not to lose her, nobly fought and died; and well may every one of their survivors be ready to suffer in her cause.

I am neither the first, nor, I suspect, the last scholar to call upon this classic text when introducing the concept of reputation. For Thucydides, reputation was a key component of political motivation, irrevocably influenced by and intertwined with the importance of honor and admiration, as well as responsibility and duty. When you read the above selection, however, notice how important reputation is as a signaling mechanism for Pericles. The "mighty proofs" are designed to signal Athens' power, will, and above all commitment to its resolve. This would become a theme that resonated with the foreign policy choices made by the United States during the Cold War. Nobody embodied the logic of reputation as *the* key to successfully deterring the Soviets more than Thomas Schelling.[1] Whereas Pericles could be accused of caring about Athen's honor and duty and the need to maintain one's reputation for such things, Schelling was much more concerned with communicating one's reputation for political *action*.

> [T]here is also a more serious kind of "face," the kind that in modern jargon is known as a country's "image," consisting of other countries' beliefs (their leaders' beliefs, that is) about how the country can be expected to behave. It relates not to a country's "worth" or "status" or even "honor," but to its reputation for action. If the question is raised whether this kind of "face" is worth fighting for, the answer is that this kind of face is one of the few things worth fighting over. ... We lost thirty thousand dead in Korea to save face for the United States and the United Nations, not to save South Korea for the South Koreans, and it was undoubtedly worth it. Soviet expectations about the behavior of the United States are one of the most valuable assets we possess in world affairs.[2]

Note the language in that last sentence. Schelling assumes that one can "possess" this information, and even more importantly, manage it. Such management can be costly (in his example, costly in lives), but the underlying logic is that if one is willing to invest the proper resources, then one can obtain the reputation needed to signal credibility to one's adversaries. This logic became conventional wisdom during the Cold War, and remains a dominant paradigm for thinking about reputation in world politics.

Two decades later, a compatible discussion of reputation was used to emphasize the role of reciprocity in international cooperation. Axelrod and Keohane argued persuasively that a reputation for practicing reciprocity could foster cooperation between governments when it would otherwise be scarce:

---

[1] Schelling, 1966.
[2] Schelling, 1966, p. 124–25.

Such reputations may become important assets, precisely because others will become more willing to make agreements with governments that can be expected to respond to cooperation with cooperation.[3]

Propelling reputation's role in both the security/conflict puzzle and the political economy/cooperation arena was the the idea that simple games of interaction that predicted myopic non-cooperative behavior by states would yield very different results when we analyzed these games as repeated interactions over time. Both approaches considered reputation to be a state characteristic that was manipulable and independently valuable. Whether the issue at hand was fighting over the spread of communism or coordinating the norms of non-discrimination and the GATT (General Agreement on Tariffs and Trade), reputation mattered. Particularly for Schelling and the Cold War, reputation mattered enough to fight over it, with the expectation that it would save future lives through deterrence.

Reputation's Fall From Grace

Not so long ago, however, the notion that a state could possess a reputation at all was contested. Jonathan Mercer challenged the idea that the reputation one strives for can be the reputation one gets. Instead, the images of states' actions, intentions, characters, and futures are socially constructed over time and unique to the complex array of timing, relationships, and frames of reference.[4] For Mercer, these complexities made it impossible to arrive at generalizable conclusions regarding reputation and deterrence. It was not that reputations were irrelevant, just that our ability as scholars to systematically predict the effects of reputation on political behavior is so constrained as to be a fruitless endeavor.

Building off of this first salvo against the conventional wisdom of reputation's import, Press (2005) examined the role of reputation in the specific context of crisis decision-making. He found that even when he focused his historical analysis to control for all the problems raised by Mercer, governments were simply too concerned with the present crisis to pay any attention to the signals

---

[3] Axelrod and Keohane, 1985b, p. 250. The true mission of this research was to promote the importance of international institutions in achieving cooperation. Axelrod and Keohane go on to argue that "since governments with good reputations can more easily make agreements than governments with bad ones, international regimes can help to facilitate cooperation by making it both easier and more desirable to acquire a good reputation."

[4] Mercer, 1996.

of the past.[5] Not only is reputation an impossible concept for study, Press's conclusion was that when it really matters the most, political leaders relegate such information to the background and focus on the pressing issues of the current moment.

Recent work pushes against this Mercer/Press notion that reputation is irrelevant. Clare and Danilovic (2012) demonstrate that context indeed matters, but its complexity need not overwhelm the scholar's ability to find evidence of reputation. Sechser (2010) finds that states form reputations for alliance behavior that meaningfully affects future alliances and security crises. Studies by Kertzer (2016) and Weisiger and Yarhi-Milo (2015) show that resolve and the reputation for resolve can be uncovered at the micro-level through innovative research designs.

Sartori (2005) provides an important piece of the puzzle by demonstrating that states can develop reputations for bluffing. Moreover, "reputations for bluffing hurt a state's credibility and lessen the effectiveness of its diplomacy."[6] States that develop reputations for honesty were found to be more effective in their diplomatic efforts. Sartori's contribution can be easily overlooked if we simply decide that Sartori and Press are at odds. What Sartori shows us is that a state's reputation can have important effects on a crisis *before* it emerges. The logical result produces a selection effect problem for studies like Press's because he only examines political interactions that have already escalated to international crises. More broadly, Sartori shows us that a reputation for honesty can be an important component of a state's identity in world politics, and that reputation does not only have to refer to the credibility of signaling in crisis politics. Similarly, Kydd (2005) broadens our understanding of the puzzle by focusing on trust. Trust and reputation are not identical, but for Kydd trust is defined as "a belief that the other side is trustworthy, that is, willing to reciprocate cooperation."[7]

Kydd is focused primarily on the emergence of trust or mistrust within a dyadic relationship, and is thus more in line with the concept of direct reciprocity, but it is easy to make the mistake of confusing direct reciprocity (and the historical relationship that emerges as a result) with the indirect information that creates a reputation. Reputations are important to states only when they

---

[5] Press (2005) uses the term "Past Action Theory" instead of reputation, but the terms are analogous for the purposes of this study.

[6] Sartori, 2005, p. 14.

[7] Kydd, 2005, p. 3.

are looking for information about the intentions, capabilities, or some other characteristic of a friend or foe. Moreover, any theory that only evaluates two actors and their interactions must treat reputational information as exogenous. Perhaps if we can identify the mechanics of reputation as dynamic, indirect reciprocity, we will find ways to understand reputations impact on politics.

The juxtaposition of Mercer's and Press's conclusions against the conventional wisdom that reputation somehow matters and the desire for political leaders to establish reputations for the sake of policy gains is striking, and it presents a puzzle for scholars and policymakers. If reputations do not matter or are indecipherable (or both), then leaders should be unconstrained by the past or their fear of conditioning the future. Before we walk away from the possibility that reputation might matter in world politics (and the idea that we as observers of history can translate a systematic understanding of reputation and politics into explanation and prediction), however, it may be that the key is to step back and place the role of reputation's influence within the broader context of the dynamics of learning and observation. In the scientific study of international politics, researchers frequently assume that dyadic interactions are independent across space. In this case, space can be defined in terms of geographic or relational qualities. Two states are usually treated as independent from other states, dyads, and institutions. Clearly, we are aware of the problems associated with this assumption. Scholars have long been aware of the importance of studying world politics beyond the basic dyad-year unit of analysis.[8] The assumption is not made out of ignorance; rather, it stems from challenges associated with theoretical clarity and research design.

Within the dyadic level of analysis (which has dominated the scientific study of international processes for the last two decades), researchers have primarily been preoccupied with the equally important problem of temporal dependence (that is, the problem of treating an observation of a dyad in one year as independent from observations in prior or subsequent years). While great progress has been made toward solving the problems associated with temporal interdependence, issues of research design have forced the assumption of spatial independence to remain in much of the extant empirical research. Over the last thirty years, explicit research dealing with spatial interdependence has typically been at the systemic level of analysis.

Relaxing the assumption that the dyads in the international system are independent from each other has been an infrequent but useful exercise. Richardson

---

[8] Deutsch, 1954.

(1960), for example, developed a model of arms races capable of capturing N-nations. Deutsch (1954) understood the spatial interdependence of the international community well. Schrodt and Mintz (1988) conceptualized spatial interdependence as a conditional probability problem. Others have used Richardson's N-nation model to study the qualities of balance and stability in the structure of the international system.[9] The problem of structure (polarity) and stability in the international system has driven most of the research that considers extra-dyadic information and international conflict.[10] Ultimately, these works are focused on the overall stability and peace of the international system, and they remain focused, accordingly, at the systemic level of analysis.

The study of contagion is a second example.[11] War contagion, or diffusion, is the notion that as war breaks out, it tends to draw other countries into its grasp. Conflict begets conflict, and the effect is spatial rather than temporal. But the logic of war contagion or diffusion is that the spread of war is rather immediate and directly associated with an original conflict. Of primary importance to this literature is the understanding of how war can spread to a systemic war like both of the World Wars.

Recently, the focus has been on the problem of temporal dependence in the dyad-year research design.[12] Intuitively we know that historical behavior between two nations is likely to influence present and future behavior between these same actors. Solutions to this problem have either focused on treating this temporal dependence as noise in the data to be corrected for,[13] or as a theoretical explanation for conflict.[14] All of these studies, save Raknerud and Hegre, preserve the assumption that each unique dyad in the international system is independent from the others.[15] Since the initial round of research by Raknerud and Hegre (1997) and Beck, Katz, and Tucker (1998), dealing with temporal dependence in the dyad-year research design has become a standard issue.

---

[9] Schrodt, 1978.

[10] S. C. Lee, Muncaster, and Zinnes, 1994; Zinnes and Muncaster, 1997.

[11] Levy, 1982; Houweling and Siccama, 1985; Most and Starr, 1989; R. Siverson and Starr, 1991; Kadera, 1998.

[12] Beck, Katz, and Tucker, 1998; Raknerud and Hegre, 1997; Crescenzi and Enterline, 2001; Russett and Oneal, 2001.

[13] Beck, Katz, and Tucker, 1998.

[14] Crescenzi and Enterline, 2001; Diehl and Goertz, 2001.

[15] Raknerud and Hegre (1997) also consider the problem of contemporaneous spatial diffusion, such as war with a third country.

More recently, the problem of spatial interdependence has been embraced by political methodologists who clearly identify the problem (from an econometric perspective) of treating dyads independently.[16] Their approach differs from mine in that they characterize space as geographic distance, while I treat the spatial dimension as one of relational distance. The two dimensions likely overlap, and both provide meaningful information to the study of dyads. In a renewed focus on the spatial diffusion of war, Ward and Gleditsch (2002) attempt to fix the problem of spatial interdependence by incorporating information about the involvement of proximate states in war. Heagerty, Ward, and Gleditsch (2002) warn that ignoring the problem of spatial interdependence can lead to erroneous empirical findings, and thus jeopardize the predictive capabilities of current empirical models. The approach taken here differs from these works in that I emphasize the need to explicitly model the phenomena that may be causing the spatial interdependence. Problems of estimation are important, but theoretical models concerning the role of this interdependence in interstate conflict can also go a long way toward improving empirical research.

Reputations Abound

The study of world politics is not alone in its investigation of reputation. Schiller (2000), for example, emphasizes the importance of reputation to senators in American politics. She argues "securing an independent reputation is the most powerful incentive for senators from the same state to contrast their representational portfolios" (2000, p. 88). In the field of social psychology, Craik (2009) focuses on the social network as the key structure that separates reputations from direct sources of information. In his book summing up over two decades of research on reputation, Craik begins by explaining that reputation is socially generated and fundamentally tied to social life:

> Reputation is not located on or in a person, like a left elbow or a knack for languages. Reputation is a dispersed phenomenon that is to be found in the beliefs and assertions of an extensive number of other individuals. Having a reputation has to do with an external, extended, and distributed entity ... Reputation is part of the social environment but uniquely referenced to a specific person. (2009, p. xvii)

[16] Beck and Katz, 1995; Heagerty, Ward, and Gleditsch, 2002; Ward and Gleditsch, 2002.

This suggests that reputations are not wholly controlled by the their subjects; rather, reputations are shaped in systematic ways by social environments. It is this overlay between the roles and contexts of the global political environment combined with the unique behavioral patterns of the individual state that makes the concept of reputation so complex. Not only is the notion of a reputation dependent on a community environment; Craik argues its genesis is rooted in the interpersonal relationships that form social communities:

> Seldom do any two or more persons regularly spend 24 hours per day within each other's gaze. Indeed, much more typical are the instances in which direct observation of an acquaintance is episodic, quite fleeting, highly selective, and often separated by considerable periods of time across the life span. Nevertheless, through the ongoing flows of chat, the eyes and minds of other community members are mobilized to complement our own direct observations of and interactions with others, as well as our recollections of them. Thus, reputational information is a team effort on the surveillance side. (2009, p. 29)

Here we see evidence that reputational information emerges as a result of the need or desire for knowledge that is created by the inability to maintain direct observation over time. This gap in information is both critical and variable. It is critical in the sense that without it, there is no need for reputation. That is not to say that reputations only exist when needed, but it does suggest that reputational information is more likely to be utilized by others when the need arises from scarcity in direct observation. The gap is also variable, both across space and time. We interact with some more than others as a function of location, environment and circumstance. Understanding when the gap exists and is salient to political decision making can help us understand when reputations matter in world politics.

With these discussions in mind, in the next section I lay out how I think reputations emerge and evolve in world politics. The emphasis in this theory building exercise will be to juxtapose the sociopolitical context of interstate behavior with the unique collection of events associated with each state in the international system. The goal is to embrace the challenge of representing reputations as unique constructs that are still recognizable, useful, and in some ways predictable. If successful, we will have a new model of this complex concept that we can use to make predictions about how reputations influence political behavior in the global arena.

How Reputation Works in the International Arena

This discussion of the literature, both within international relations and beyond, suggests reputation is an important but complex and elusive phenomenon. Frequently, the concept is not well defined, and scholars leave the mechanics of reputation essentially blocked from sight. This approach is what made the classic reputation literature vulnerable to Mercer's critique. Therefore, it makes sense to be clear about the way reputations form and change over time. As such before I present an argument that links reputation to cooperation and conflict in world politics, the rest of this chapter is devoted to modeling the concept of reputation in world politics.

Reputations are perceived, and ultimately these perceptions are critical to understanding changes in political behavior. A theory of reputation needs to incorporate the mechanism of perception. Herein lies one of the key problems with past theories of reputation. It should be clear by now that many scholars (and policymakers) think of reputation as something that can be easily controlled. Self-control over one's reputation is an essential assumption of deterrence in foreign policy. One has to treat it this way if one wants to consider reputation as a signal that a threat to punish is a credible threat. The whole idea behind "peace through strength" is that a state signals that it is strong and should not be dismissed by demonstrating such strength and resolve in prior behavior. As such, much of the research on reputation centers around the ability to communicate signals that allow a state to convey the reputation it wants, and then we evaluate critically the question of whether or not this signaling process works in the sense of altering the policy choices of one's friends and enemies.

A reputation isn't strictly or easily controlled by the one who holds it. That is not to say, however, that one's reputation is completely controlled by others. It simply means that actions are perceived through filters, and ignoring that fact can lead to erroneous predictions about the impact of one's behavior on future interactions. What looks like toughness to one actor may look like belligerence, incompetence, or willful disregard to another. The challenge we face when thinking about reputation is to incorporate the "in the eyes of the beholder" dimension without losing our focus on patterns of behavior.

Moreover, reputations are collections of information and perceptions, aggregated across time and space. This is where dynamics become important. Reputations not only vary based on differences in perceptions; they evolve over time in reaction to shifting opinions and data. Past actions play an important role, but information degrades as it ages. Reputation can't be signaled anew in the process of negotiating a treaty, or in talks over a land dispute. We do not choose our reputation at specific or discrete times. Reputations are a function of repeated and contextual behavior. We earn them and lose them over time.

By focusing on these two dimensions—that is, perception and temporal dynamics—we can get a better understanding of the complexities of reputation without losing our ability to grasp its effects. Moreover, there are good guides for thinking theoretically about how states perceive the reputations of their partners and enemies. All that is required is a brief journey outside the comfort zone of political science. I build upon the basics of cognitive balance theory to create one possible model of reputation perception. I then incorporate a dynamic component to model the way reputation information changes over time. The result is a reputational learning model that grounds reputation and its perception within the dyad while incorporating key information from proxies.[17] In the pages of this chapter I will explain these two components (perception and dynamics) separately, then combine them into a full model of reputational learning.

Perceptions: How do Nations Observe Extra-dyadic Information?

Politics is the result not only of man's varying aspirations, but also of man's varying evaluation of the situation which confronts him.[18]

Let me return to the trio of actors I briefly introduced in the first chapter: the protagonist, antagonist, and proxy states. Typically, we focus our attention on the interactions that take place between two states. This leaves out the proxy states, and focuses only on the protagonist and antagonist. We call this the dyadic level of analysis. It is a powerful and flexible way to study international relations because it is intuitive, it highlights the interaction between governments,[19] and it lends itself easily to the notion of strategic interaction. The best and perhaps

[17] There are many options when building a model of reputational learning, some of which I will discuss in this book. One of the more important decisions I had to make concerned whether to frame this theory within a dyadic level of analysis (meaning, pairs of actors), or abandon the dyad in favor of networks or neighborhoods of states. So much of what we know about international peace and conflict is rooted in the dyadic level of analysis, however, so I placed a premium on developing a theory that fits within general models of conflict processes. The benefit of this decision will be evident in the next chapter.

[18] Haas and Whiting, 1956, p. 1.

[19] This interaction is what separates the study of international relations from comparative politics. The line between the two fields is blurry and artificial in many ways, but at the center of each field

State I observes J's behavior toward I over time

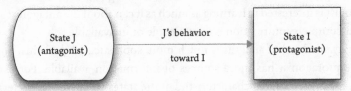

Figure 2.1 The Directed Interstate Interaction: The Antagonist's Behavior Toward the Protagonist.

most important example of a dyad in recent history is the interaction between the United States and the Soviet Union during the Cold War.[20] Throughout the Cold War, it seemed that the interplay between the two superpowers was *the* focus of the world. The rivalry dominated the global political arena, and I grew up thinking about the chess match between the two governments.[21] During my own childhood and youth in the United States, it seemed like we were always trying to figure out the plans and intentions of the Soviets. This perspective falls within the purview of the dyadic level of analysis, with a simple but effective focus on the two major players. When we focus on how one side of the dyad treats the other, we often call this a directed dyad analysis. I label these states as State I and State J, just to remind us this is a general model of interstate interaction. In this directed dyad analysis, State I is observing and anticipating State J's behavior toward State I. Figure 2.1 visually represents these interactions.

As you can see, State I is the protagonist; it is the state that is observing the actions being made toward it by the antagonist, which is State J. For the time being, think of these actions broadly. The protagonist may be experiencing conflict or cooperation from the antagonist, and there is no reason at the moment to assign blame or initiation to these actions. Like all political or social

is a core difference. International politics is concerned with this interaction between states, and comparative politics is concerned with interaction within the state.

[20] It is no accident that the dyadic level of analysis was born out of the Cold War. If you compare Bruce Bueno de Mesquita's *The War Trap* (1981) with his subsequent *War and Reason* (1992), for example, the shift in focus is clear. In addition, Stuart Bremer's (1992) data and research design innovations not only launched a new generation of data analysis in the study of peace and conflict; it also provided a much-needed empirical framework to match the theoretical progress in the field.

[21] We all did. I can remember nuclear attack drills in elementary school, and in the sixth grade my teacher had a poster of the nuclear arms race on the wall of my classroom. The US–Soviet rivalry was ubiquitous, if exaggerated, in our lives.

relationships, however, uncertainty exists to varying degrees. I assume that the protagonist is interested in learning as much as it can about the antagonist's plans, but that complete information is unattainable or unavailable.

The dyadic level of analysis is much more sophisticated than this, however, and the protagonist has more sources of information available. For example, we can specify individual characteristics of the states (monadic characteristics), including institutional structures (e.g., parliamentary democracy). The dyad also exists within an international system, whose structure may be relevant (e.g., bipolar versus multipolar). Moreover, we can introduce extra-dyadic information into the analysis. In particular, the protagonist is able to observe the antagonist's interactions with other states. I call these proxy states (labeled as K states in Figure 2.2 below), because I wish to focus on how the protagonist evaluates these interactions with respect to what it expects the antagonist to do to the protagonist. Reputation comes from this extra-dyadic information.

In short, the protagonist attempts to learn from the antagonist's behavior with others. In and of itself, this is not a controversial assertion. Game theoretic models focusing on the problems of private information are often built upon the idea that the protagonist learns from the actions of the antagonist. The only difference here is that I wish to explore the extent to which the protagonist learns from the actions of the antagonist with others.

This raises the important question of how the protagonist processes these events. To illustrate one way states may systematically process extra-dyadic interactions, Lee, Muncaster, and Zinnes (1994, p. 336) introduce an important

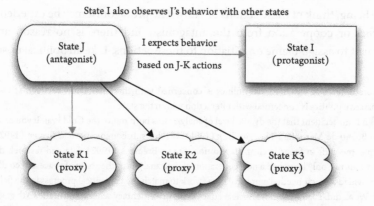

Figure 2.2 Observing Extra-Dyadic Interstate Interaction: The Protagonist observes the Antagonist's behavior with other (Proxy) states.

insight regarding how states may learn from the behavior of other states. Using Heider's rule, they establish a simple basis for interpreting state behavior (which is illustrated in Figures 2.3, 2.4, 2.5, and 2.6):[22]

> *The friend of my friend is my friend,*
> *the friend of my enemy is my enemy,*
> *the enemy of my enemy is my friend,*
> *the enemy of my friend is my enemy.*

Even though this often is referred to as Heider's rule, the origins of these phrases are both ancient and disputed. The most popular line in these phrases is "the enemy of my enemy is my friend," and it has been used to suggest a strictly strategic motivation for an often unusual alliance. While the original text is often described as an Arabic proverb,[23] it appears to trace back to an ancient Hindu

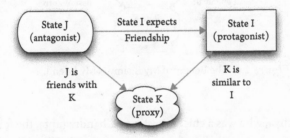

Figure 2.3 The Friend of My Friend is My Friend.

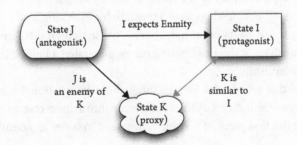

Figure 2.4 The Enemy of My Friend is My Enemy.

---

[22] Heider, 1946; Harary, 1959.

[23] A recent such example takes place in the 2013 movie, *Star Trek Into Darkness*, where Captain James T. Kirk uses the rule to rationalize his temporary alliance with Khan. Incidentally, Spock's retort

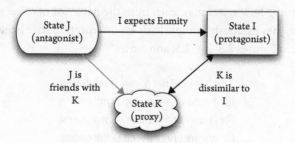

Figure 2.5 The Friend of My Enemy is My Enemy.

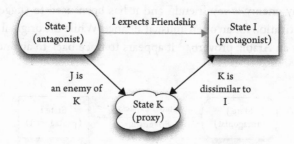

Figure 2.6 The Enemy of My Enemy is My Friend.

scholar, Kautilya, who was a chief minister to Chandragupta, the founder of the Maurya Empire at the tail end of the fourth century BCE.[24] Kautilya spoke of circles of states, and was interested in a set of rules that would allow him to advise Chandragupta with respect to the rulers of nearby kingdoms. He assumed that immediately neighboring kings were a threat to his own king, and a neighboring king is also a threat to its other neighbors. This shared enmity, created by the spatial relationships of the neighboring rulers, generated a linkage that held the potential of friendship.[25]

How does this set of rules help us think about international relations? The axioms transpose an indirect dyadic relationship into a direct one, and in so doing they provide the first piece of the puzzle we need in order to assemble a better

that the creator of this rule was subsequently beheaded by one such strategic ally is, as far as I can decipher, untrue. See Wickman, 2013.

[24] See Modelski, 1964. Modelski also evaluates Kautilya's contributions to foreign policy in an international relations context.

[25] See Modelski, 1964, p. 554.

theory of reputational learning. There are two components to the transposition that are important. The first component involves mirroring, or proxying. The protagonist is determining its relationship with the antagonist based on how the antagonist treats others. The second component is the focus, or subject of the proxy dimension for the protagonist. In Heider's rule, this focus is on friendship and enmity. In particular, the proxy lens is the protagonist's friends and enemies. If you treat my friend as your friend, that is good enough for me to decide that you are my friend as well. Similarly, if you treat my enemy as your enemy, our common opposition can be a platform for our friendship.

I have split the rule into these two components because I want to use the mechanics of the first component while adapting the second. Others have similarly adapted the rule to develop a more general model of behavior. Harary, Norman, and Cartwright (1965), Newcomb (1953), and Newcomb (1961) form the basic logic of cognitive balance theory. In fact, Heider's rule represents a folk interpretation of the logic behind balance theory. Balance theorists were concerned with the ability of the self (Heider) or the ability of groups (Harary, Norman, and Cartwright) to reconcile relationships that were unbalanced. Using the classic logic of the P-O-X triad, the theory focuses on the calculations of person P concerning his/her relationship with some other person O. Both P and O have a relationship or level of attraction to object X.[26] The first person, P, evaluates O's relationship with X in light of P's own relationship with X. If the two individuals share an equal attraction with the object X, the P–O dyadic relationship is said to be balanced. Similarly, if the two individuals both find X to be unattractive, the P–O dyad is balanced. If their feelings toward X are inconsistent, however, the relationship is unbalanced. For example, if P is attracted to X but O is not, the dyad is unbalanced and a fundamental tension results.

For Heider, this tension was internal to P, as P grapples with how the inconsistency should manifest itself in the overall dyadic relationship. For example, is O's dislike of baseball enough to cause P and O to not be friends? The focus is on the dyadic P–O relationship, from the perspective of one person in particular. Heider and Newcomb assumed a basic desire for harmony over tension. Critics of cognitive balance theory cite its myopic focus on triads as too simple to account for the complexities of group dynamics, as well as its basic qualitative

[26] The object, X, may also be a third individual. But more frequently the theory was applied to study how a relationship between two individuals became unbalanced when it was discovered that they held different feelings toward a separate concept or item, like politics or baseball.

assessment of relationships (+ or -) as too vague to produce accurate forecasts of social behavior.[27]

While Heider's focus was on the impact of imbalance internal to P, my focus is slightly different in that I want to know how balance and imbalance enhance or denigrate interstate relations between the protagonist and the antagonist. Balance theory is willing to entertain a wide variety of others, but here I want to focus in on proxy states that are similar to the protagonist because they provide the protagonist with good learning opportunities. As such, allow me to restate Heider's rule in the following manner.

> *The friend of someone like me is my friend,*
> *the friend of someone not like me is my enemy,*
> *the enemy of someone not like me is my friend,*
> *the enemy of someone like me is my enemy.*

Friendship and enmity may not be so easily discarded, however. One option would be to treat similarity and friendship as two distinct dimensions.[28] Friend-ship/enmity and similarity/dissimilarity could be thought of as forces that work together when they align, but cancel one another out when they are at odds.[29] It is easier to simply consider the role of friendship (and its absence) in the observation of similarity. The point here is to introduce a broader concept of similarity, or proxy, than friendship, but not to confuse the learning dynamic in the process. Most importantly, we need to think of this similarity condition beyond the simple categories of friend and enemy. A more accurate theory would allow the protagonist to evaluate a proxy state in a more complex fashion, with proxies ranging from very similar (e.g., Britain and the United States in the 1980s) to completely dissimilar (e.g., Sierra Leone and the United States in the 1990s).

This new set of rules assumes that the protagonist treats similar proxy states like friends under the old rules, and dissimilar proxy states like enemies.

---

[27] Cognitive balance theory has taken its lumps, but primarily as a theoretical explanation for group structure within social network theory. In the early twenty-first century, it appears to be enjoying a bit of a renaissance (see Hummon and Doreian, 2003) with a renewed focus on the internal tension variant.

[28] This is a topic I will return to in the quantitative empirical chapters later in the book.

[29] For example, the friend of a friend who is like me is my friend, but a friend of a friend who is not like me is perhaps less so. Even more confusing is the notion of a friend of an enemy who is like me.

But it could also be that dissimilar proxy states are simply uninformative for the protagonist. That is, the protagonist only learns from proxy states that demonstrate some meaningful degree of similarity. In this case, the rules look more like the following:

The friend of someone like me is my friend,
the friend of someone not like me is neither my friend nor my enemy,
the enemy of someone not like me is neither my enemy nor my friend,
the enemy of someone like me is my enemy.

With both sets of rules, there is an opportunity to add a layer of complexity to the basic model by incorporating the degree to which relationships are friendly, hostile, similar, or dissimilar. Whereas the original rules essentially present these qualities as on or off, present or absent, we know that some streams of information are going to be stronger than others. I could do this categorically ("best" friends versus acquaintances, "arch" enemies versus mild annoyances), but any lines drawn here are arbitrary and I prefer to think of these as variables along a continuum.

A Dynamic Model of Reputational Learning

Having established a broad, indirect, learning-focused conceptualization of reputation above, the next step is to clearly specify a model of these reputational dynamics. The process of formalizing the theoretical discussion forces sorely needed clarity. The risk of any formalization is losing the nuances gained from language, but the upside is a powerful, transparent model of reputational dynamics that improves our ability to evaluate reputation's impact on international relations.

To begin with, recall that the key to reputation is indirect, vicariously obtained information. We need a model that helps us identify how a state learns about another state by looking at that state's interactions with others. Given three countries, $I, J,$ and $K,$ I can learn about J by looking at how J has historically interacted with K. States focus on this extra-dyadic behavior of other states, but they weight this information based on the specific characteristics of the states involved. More specifically, I weights this information based on how similar it is to K. The more similar I and K are, the more I is able to treat K as a proxy. These weights determine the relevance of the JK relationship to I. If there is anything tricky about this setup, it is the argument that I weights the historical interaction within the JK dyad with a relevance comparison between I and K to learn about potential future interaction within the IJ dyad.

Foreign policy similarity is one comparison characteristic used by I to determine how useful K is as a proxy.[30] The more similar the foreign policy portfolios of I and K, the more highly I values the information coming from the JK dyad. Dissimilarity between I and K is important too. Heider's rules stipulate that "the enemy of my enemy is my friend," so if J demonstrates hostility toward K but K's foreign policy portfolio is dissimilar from I's, I may treat this as positive information about J.

Relative power is another important relevance characteristic (Kadera, 2001; Waltz, 1979). For instance, small states learn more from the way their opponents treat other small states than they do from the way their opponents treat major powers. More generally, when I assesses the way its opponent J treats K, it weights J's behavior based on the power similarity between I and K. Similar power characteristics between I and K inform I that what J does to K, it thus might also do to I. Conversely, as the disparity of power between I and K increases, the JK dyad becomes a less useful source of information for I.

For simplicity, I will call this the Reputation Learning Model. The use of the term "reputation" refers simply to the vicarious experiential dimension of the information being processed (i.e., there is no direct interactive history between I and J used to form this information). Clearly, this is not the only form of reputation in world politics, but it is a form of reputation. Equation 2.1 formalizes this discussion with the following Reputation (R) model:

$$R_{ijN} = \frac{\sum_{c \neq i,j}^{N} \rho_{jk}\phi_{ik}\psi_{ik}}{N-2} \tag{2.1}$$

where N is the size of the system

ρ_{jk} is the relationship over time between J and K, $\rho_{jk} \in (-1,1)$,

ϕ_{ik} is the policy similarity between I and K, $\phi_{ik} \in (-1,1)$,

ψ_{ik} is the power similarity between I and K, $\psi_{ik} \in (0,1)$.

[30] For example, Bueno de Mesquita (1981b) uses foreign policy similarity to help determine the expected utility of conflict.

The three variables in the model, ρ_{jk}, ϕ_{ik}, and ψ_{ik}, capture the extra-dyadic relationship and the qualities of policy and power similarity, respectively. Together, their product is the weighted information that I seeks regarding J's extra-dyadic behavior. This product is calculated for every state K in the international system besides I and J. The products are then aggregated and normalized for system size, $R_{ijN} \in (-1,1)$, where one indicates J's extra-dyadic behavior is perfectly compatible with I, and negative one indicates perfect incompatibility. Normalizing in this fashion not only brings the aggregated products within the intuitive -1 to 1 range, it allows us to compare scores across different system sizes.

The R model captures the essence of learning from J's ties with other states, and it reflects the core logic of Heider's rule. For example, when $\rho_{jk} < 0$ and $\phi_{ik} > 0$, then I gets information about J that is akin to "the enemy of my friend is my enemy." If $\rho_{jk} < 0$ and $\phi_{ik} < 0$, however, then the information provided reflects "the enemy of my enemy is my friend." Similarly, $\rho_{jk} > 0$ combined with $\phi_{ik} < 0$ suggests "the friend of my enemy is my enemy." Finally, $\rho_{jk} > 0$ and $\phi_{ik} > 0$ corresponds to "the friend of my friend is my friend."

The model is also more subtle and informative than Heider's rule and cognitive balance theory. It captures the degree of relevance for each proxy state, as well as the degree of hostility or cooperation between the proxy state and the dyadic counterpart. This ability to compare relative cooperation and conflict addresses one of the long-standing criticisms of balance theory: namely, that its qualitative formulation is too simple. The power similarity dimension adds further nuance to the learning model, allowing states to filter this information based on the capability similarity of a proxy state, regardless of its foreign policy similarity. Note also that this model is directional: R_{ijN} and R_{jiN} need not be equal.

The functional form of the model is designed to emphasize the interaction among the individual components. The extreme regions of the calculation for each combination of I, J, and K states (-1,1) can only be reached when all three components (ρ_{jk}, ϕ_{ik}, and ψ_{ik}) are at their extremes. Zero values for any component reduce the value of the calculation to zero. Thus, zero is designed to reflect the notion of neutrality, or a lack of behavioral or relevance information.

Time as a Dimension of Proxy Quality

One remaining piece of the puzzle is how to deal with the passing of time when thinking about proxy states. At the outset, this requires a logistical choice on the part of the researcher. As discussed earlier in this chapter,

quantitative methodologists appropriately identify past observations as a potentially confounding issue for empirical studies. In this theory stage of the book
econometric concerns are minimal, but the theoretical question of how to
think about time matters a lot for a working model of reputation dynamics. By thinking theoretically about temporal dynamics here in the theory
section of the book, the final model will be better suited for empirical analysis
later on.

For nearly two decades, Andrew Enterline and I have modeled the impact of
dyadic interstate relationships over time, using an emphasis on new information
in the present along with the fading impact of past actions.[31] Applying a
straightforward exponential decay model, we argued that historical interstate
relationships form and evolve over time, recent events matter more than events
farther away in time, as time passes without any events this decay process speeds
up, and as a history accumulates between two countries, this fading or decay
slows down.

With these processes in mind, the next step is to specify the ρ_{jk} parameter of
the reputation model as a dynamic process of growth and decay:

$$\rho_{jkt} = (e^{-\left(\frac{\tau}{\sigma}\right)})\rho_{jk(t-1)} + \left(\frac{\upsilon}{\tau}\right) - \left(\frac{\omega}{\tau}\right). \tag{2.2}$$

where τ is the amount of time that has past since the last behavior was observed,
σ captures the amount of observed conflict or cooperation that accumulates
over time, υ identifies the occurrence of J cooperating with K at time t, and
ω identifies the occurrence of J experiencing conflict with K at time t. The
exponential decay model is accelerated by τ, which means the behavioral history
becomes less informative as time passes without cooperation or conflict. At
the same time, information decay slows down as σ increases. This reflects the
assumption that a state's historical policy choices have a cumulative impact.
Finally, τ diminishes the impact of the shocks of new cooperation or conflict.
This reflects my assumption that events that occur regularly are more informative
than events that are infrequent (and thus potentially interpreted as random or
mistakes). For simplicity, I bound this function between 1 (J always cooperates
with K) and -1 (J always fights with K), with 0 representing no information
(or a perfect mix of information that cancels itself out) regarding the $\overrightarrow{JK}$ dyadic

---

[31] Crescenzi and Enterline, 1999; Crescenzi, Enterline, and Long, 2008.

relationship.[32] The result is a simple but dynamic representation of the evolution of *J*'s history directed toward proxy states (*K* states).[33]

Stepping back to view the overall model, the reputation learning model satisfies the need to capture both the behavioral and the relational components of extra-dyadic learning. It reflects an explicit set of assumptions about how states learn, assumptions that are derived from previous research on learning and cognitive balance theory. Yet the model goes beyond these roots to provide a novel perspective on how we understand the process of learning from extra-dyadic activity. While it serves as a lucid platform for research, it is not intended to represent the *only* form of learning for states. Certainly there are others; some are complementary, and some might overlap with this representation. Ultimately, the question of how useful this model is as a representation of state learning must be answered through empirical application. In this vein, the next chapter provides a discussion of the causal linkage between learning and conflict, setting the stage for Part II of the book, an empirical examination that puts the reputation learning model to the test.

Models of political behavior, however, can seem very abstract, and theories that deal with the dynamics of space and time can be absolutely perplexing. The next chapter builds a theory of how reputations affect political outcomes, and the latter half of the book will use quantitative historical data to evaluate the argument that reputation systematically influences cooperation and conflict between states. Before moving on to those discussions, however, it may be useful for the reader to explore an illustration of how reputation forms and can make a difference in world politics. In the next section of this chapter I attempt to do just that, by examining the role of reputational information in one aspect of the origins of the Cold War.[34]

[32] See Crescenzi, Enterline, and Long (2008) for a detailed discussion of the structure of this model as well as the bounding function.

[33] Modeling the proxies' historical relationships in this manner allows the researcher considerable flexibility. For instance, one could weight the relevance of cooperation versus conflict by altering the parameters, perhaps to test an argument about the psychological impacts of the two qualitatively different types of events. The speed at which information from old events diminish can be customized by altering the time parameters, perhaps matching unique constants to types of governments (e.g., parliamentary democracies versus autocratic dictatorships) or leadership tenure.

[34] This illustration relies on the archival research and analysis conducted by others, such as Greenwood (1990, 2000), Jensen (1993), and Zametica (1990a, 1990b). The application of this research to the idea of reputation formation is my contribution, but I could not have made this argument without Greenwood's (1990) astute observations about the similarities between Kennan's

Specifically, I focus on the importance of Britain's observations of American behavior as the United States forged its policy stance with respect to the Soviet Union. In this illustration, my purpose is to focus on why some political actors lean on reputational information, and how proxies matter. In the immediate aftermath of World War Two, the British faced distressing uncertainty about the permanence of the American presence, as well as Stalin's intentions for co-managing Europe. The need for information was great, and the future was far from certain. The dialogue over how to move forward was intense in the Foreign Office, but it was also taking place between two senior diplomats in Moscow. Frank Roberts, then the senior diplomatic officer in Moscow, sent several key memos detailing the intentions and motivations of the Soviet Union in early 1946. The memos played an important role in setting British–Soviet policy, confirming the home office's intuition that the wartime alliance with the Soviets would have to be abandoned. Interestingly, Roberts's memos were based in large part on reputational information, garnered from discussions with George Kennan, who was at the time running the American Embassy in Moscow. Kennan's "Long Memo" is famously regarded as the most important foreign policy memo ever written. Roberts's memos were composed around the same time, and he and Kennan had many long discussions about the intentions and trustworthiness of the Soviets. Roberts's reliance on Kennan's Soviet expertise, combined with their friendship and shared circumstances, resulted in a parallel set of memos that dovetailed Britain's response to Stalin's ambitions with the Americans. Roberts's "enemy of my friend is my enemy" approach was an important piece of the puzzle as Britain cobbled together its post-war strategy. The Kennan–Roberts interaction was a microcosm of a larger discourse, and it illustrates how reputational information can play a role in foreign policy choices. More broadly, this case demonstrates how reputation mattered in one of the most important historical crossroads of world politics.

The Long Memos, Containment, and the Origins of the Cold War: An Empirical Illustration of Reputational Learning

In the early months of 1946, the major powers of the world were still reeling from the end of the Second World War. Less than a year after Germany's surrender

Long Memo and Roberts's Cables. I cross-checked their analysis with the archives when possible, and am grateful for their research.

and just a few short months after the war came to its bracing end in the Pacific, the Western powers struggled to decode the intentions and trustworthiness of the Soviets. Wariness of the Soviets emerged from disagreements over whether and when to withdraw from Iran after Germany's surrender. President Truman had observed troubling signals from the Soviets, Prime Minister Attlee was gravitating toward Churchill's views on the problem, and concerns about Soviet expansion were on the rise.[35] All too quickly, the British and Americans were forced to grapple with the complicated process of deciphering Stalin's intentions and commitments.

Just a few months prior, the autumn of 1945 had presented a very different outlook. This was particularly true in the case of Great Britain. With the fall of Nazi Germany, attention had turned to the future of Europe. The British faced the daunting task of determining a way forward that did not lead to the same bitter collapse of post-World War I politics. Reparations, consequences, economies, and alliances were all like balls in the air to be juggled. At Potsdam, the Big Three met to navigate the waters of post-war territory and the future of Europe. As late as October 1945, the British government entertained the idea that its cooperation with the Soviets during the war would provide the seed for a continued alliance that would allow the two states to co-govern a new Europe. Indeed, there were many in Britain who questioned the Americans' willingness to be a part of the solution. Memories of America's isolationism were still fresh in everyone's minds, and the heroics of the US military could not completely erase that political image. Nobody expected enmity from the Americans, but leaders were cautious about putting their faith in the US as a key partner moving forward. If the Americans couldn't be counted on to help Britain manage Germany, the Soviets were the only logical alternative.

By March of 1946 Truman had received Kennan's Long Memo, and former Prime Minister Winston Churchill had just delivered his now famous "Iron Curtain" speech. Churchill's speech at Westminster College took an aggressive hard line against the Soviets, prompting much discussion back in London. Prime Minister Attlee was just a few months into his position, and despite his close relationship with Churchill, he and his Labour Party coalition had to determine whether or not to embrace Churchill's call to resist Soviet aggression. Churchill had overplayed his hand in his failed bid to retain his position as prime minister, and his speech could be interpreted in the same vein. In essence, the British

[35] Lenczowski, 1990; McCullough, 1992.

government faced the daunting post-war task of deciding whether the Soviet Union was friend or foe.

The Americans, of course, faced a similar crossroads. Truman was able to rely on Kennan's alarming evaluation of Soviet expansionism—an assessment that fit Truman's concerns from his interactions with Stalin at Potsdam. Prime Minister Attlee, however, had mostly indirect information (Churchill, Truman, Kennan) at his disposal. It is in this context that Foreign Secretary Bevin and the British Foreign Office asked Frank Roberts to provide a direct evaluation of the Soviet Union's intentions. Like Kennan, Roberts was the Chargé de Affairs in the British office in Moscow, and the senior diplomat in residence at the time. Indeed, the two career diplomats displayed "striking parallels" at the time.[36] Both were awaiting their respective ambassadors, and both were called upon to report their analysis of the Soviet's intentions during a remarkably tense time. But unlike Kennan, Roberts was not an expert in all things Russian.[37] By his own admission, Roberts's own expertise was Germany:

> Another difference between us is that, whilst the Soviet Union has remained an absorbing interest for me, . . ., Germany has been my first concern both before and after retirement from the Foreign Service, and I have not been so directly and constantly involved with Soviet affairs as George Kennan still is.[38]

This is not to say, of course, that Roberts was uninformed about Soviet policy. His experiences with the Soviet regime began at least as far back as the Yalta Conference. By 1946, however, Kennan had accumulated almost two decades of expertise concerning the Russian people, and the stakes were at their highest to accurately assess the intentions of the Soviet regime. He was considered by Roberts to be an excellent authority on Russian affairs. Moreover, the two became good friends during their time together in Moscow, and had long discussions about the Soviets. As such, it makes sense that Roberts must have known that Kennan had more and better information about the Soviets than did he, and that their similarities made Kennan an excellent proxy for his own direct observations of the Soviets' intentions. Roberts himself recognized

---

[36] Greenwood, 1990, p. 105.

[37] Zametica writes plainly that Roberts considered himself a skilled diplomat, but "he was in no sense a Russian expert" (1990, p. 46).

[38] From Roberts's foreword in Greenwood's (1990, p. 103) evaluation of the two sets of memos.

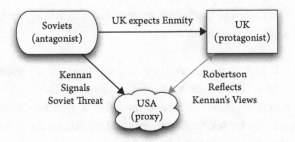

Figure 2.7 The UK Perceives Soviet Threat: Learning from Kennan's Warning in the Long Memo.

Kennan's expertise, as well as his willingness to rely upon it to assess what I argue to have been the Soviets' reputation for aggression:

> So it is particularly interesting to be reminded by Dr Greenwood of such an important early chapter in my diplomatic career and of such a happy relationship with George Kennan, whose far deeper knowledge of the Soviet Union was perhaps at that time balanced to some extent by my wider experience in the wartime Foreign Office. Such "collusion" as there was between us amounted to making a similar assessment of Stalin's policies, shared by many others then in Moscow, against the background of Russian and Soviet traditions and of the wartime Anglo-American partnership.[39]

Using the conceptual map of the reputation-building process from Figure 2.6, we can see that Roberts used Kennan as a proxy for his own analysis of the Soviet Union, as is illustrated in Figure 2.7.[40] The quality of Kennan as a proxy for Roberts enables him to transpose Kennan's views to his own.

Roberts, in his interactions with Kennan during the drafting of both memos, made several observations about the Soviets. Perhaps none are more important than his ultimate assessment that the Soviet regime is incompetent with respect to reason and diplomacy. In other words, they cannot be reasoned with, and thus

---

[39] Greenwood, 1990, p. 104.

[40] This is an adaptation, of course, in that both Roberts and Kennan are not unitary actors in their respective governments. Every unitary actor assumption is an oversimplification, and the aggregation function that shapes the social construction of state reputations from elites to the state level is discussed in the next chapter.

accommodation cannot be the British strategy. Kennan brutally makes this point in the final section of his memo:

> Finally, it is seemingly inaccessible to considerations of reality in its basic reactions. For it, the vast fund of objective fact about human society is not, as tested and re-formed, but a grab bag from which individual items are selected arbitrarily and tendenciously to bolster an outlook already preconceived.[41]

Roberts arrives at a similar conclusion in his cable to London just a few weeks later, albeit in more detail:

> But however well – or ill – informed the Kremlin may be on the situation in the outside world it is certainly incapable, in conducting international relations, of the give-and-take which is normal and, indeed, essential between other States. When British delegates negotiate an agreement with delegates from any country other than the Soviet Union, there is usually an honest endeavor on both sides to understand the point of view of the other and to arrive at an agreement which must to some extent represent a compromise between the interests of both. ... The Soviet Union, however, does not conceive international relations in this sense at all. She approaches a partner, whom she regards as potentially hostile, endeavors to exact the maximum advantage for the Soviet Union, if possible without any return, and, having obtained what she wants, reopens this issue or raises another at the earliest possible moment in order to achieve the next item on her programme.[42]

At the time of this writing, Roberts had barely a year's experience in Moscow, and much of his direct experience with the Soviets took place in the context of the Yalta Conference. Yet he writes about the Soviets with certainty, as if he has deciphered their true character. As such, it seems like Roberts's assessment is a combination of his direct observations and his reliance on Kennan's. This is a useful illustration of the mechanism by which reputations manifest in world politics through indirect observation, not only because it highlights the role of reputation in one of the most salient moments in world history, but also because

---

[41] From Kennan's 1946 "Long Memo," reprinted in Jensen (1993, p. 29).
[42] From Roberts' 1946 Cables, reprinted in Jensen (1993, p. 50).

it hints at one of the elements of reputation that I consider to be consistent across cooperation and conflict: competence. With this conceptualization of reputation dynamics in place, the next chapter tackles the question of how reputations matter once they are formed. The notion of using reputation to evaluate a state's competence proves to be a useful way to think about reputation's influence, and provides the basis for the empirical prediction that fuels the analysis in the latter half of the book.

3

How Reputation Matters in
International Relations

> How can one commit himself in advance to an act that he would in
> fact prefer not to carry out in the event, in order that his commitment
> may deter the other party? ... One may try to stake his reputation on
> fulfillment, in a matter that impresses the threatened person.
>
> —Thomas Schelling

> ... the credibility of US threats and promises does not hinge on
> establishing a history of resolute actions.
>
> —Daryl G. Press

Reputation has been called upon to rescue politics from anarchy, accused of
motivating governments to sacrifice their own soldiers, and debunked as a
mythical political force. Mired in debate, scholars shifted their attention away
from reputation to focus on other determinants of political behavior in world
politics. But since the late twentieth century, we have seen an increased emphasis
on the role of private information and commitment problems in the occurrence
of conflict. Scholars have also investigated the role of domestic political structures and behavior, and particular issues such as territorial disputes or ethnic
differences, setting concepts like reputation aside in favor of more tangible
topics. But reputation is too important to stay off the scholarly radar for long.

How do reputations influence political cooperation and conflict among governments? The classic logic in the security realm often subsumes this question
within the focused debate over whether deterrence works. Indeed, when the
issue at hand is one of resolve, reputation can play a very specific and significant
role.[1] In cooperation studies, however, reputation plays a much more basic role as

---

[1] See Clare and Danilovic, 2010; Clare and Danilovic, 2012; and Kertzer, 2016, for analyses of
resolve in world politics.

a source of information and precedent. The challenge at hand, then, is to reconcile this specific deterrence mechanism with the broader concept of reputation. My starting point for this reconciliation is the context surrounding the need for a reputation on a global level in the first place. Past scholars have often argued that this context is so important and unique that it renders reputational information meaningless,[2] but I will make the case in this chapter that no matter the context, states and their leaders use reputational information to ascertain the competence of their potential partner or opponent. Viewed through the lens of competence or incompetence, reputation helps states evaluate the strategies of others within the contexts of cooperation and conflict.

In this chapter, I revisit the strategic interaction between France and Russia in the early nineteenth century to illustrate the role that reputation can play in informing states and leaders about the competence of others. This case is also useful in demonstrating how reputation informs us about aggression as a form of incompetence. Most important, the case provides a clear example of how states can project a reputation for aggression and incompetence when their intent was to project a reputation that would compel others to cooperate without using force. With this illustration in place, I then contrast this new focus on competence and aggression with the way we traditionally conceptualize reputation in deterrence contexts, and establish the need to think theoretically about reputation outside of deterrence and resolve. Finally, I develop my own theoretical argument linking reputation with cooperation and with conflict.

Napoleon's Reputation and the Patriotic War of 1812

Returning to the example from the first chapter, a closer look into Alexander's perceptions of Napoleon shows that he evaluated Napoleon's actions within the context of roles France and Russia had taken on during the previous decade. Russia and France had fought one another repeatedly in their recent past, but they also went to great lengths to establish a new peace. The treaty of Tilsit was ambitious, and in some ways audacious. The agreement was a difficult strategic shift for Alexander, both domestically and internationally. The agreement also included a secret clause that excluded Prussia. More than anything else, the treaty represented an about-face for Alexander with respect to Napoleon's machinations.

[2] Mercer, 1996; Press, 2005.

Alexander faced domestic challenges to this treaty, as one can imagine the past conflict with Napoleon had generated considerable hostility toward France. The Russian government had fomented this hostility, going so far as to encourage the rumor among the peasantry that Napoleon was in league with the devil, as noted earlier. This proved to be quite a hurdle for the Russian elites after the treaty was signed, as the message reportedly morphed into the conclusion that Napoleon *was* the devil. Not surprisingly, signing a treaty with Napoleon was met with considerable consternation within Russia, particularly in the rural west.

Yet the treaty signaled a trial of peace between the two states, and Russia cautiously hoped for a lasting break from war. That the digestion of a treaty with Napoleon was so difficult for Russia and yet Alexander pressed forward was an indication of Alexander's desire for peace. Above all else, he wished to avoid protracted conflict with the French. He feared that his military would not survive against the legendary French army and Napoleon's battlefield genius, and he worried that Russia itself would not survive more war. Fyffe summarizes the impact and importance of the treaty almost as a seismic shock to the politics of Europe:

> Such was this vast and threatening scheme, conceived by the man whose whole career had been one consistent struggle for personal domination, accepted by the man who among the rulers of the Continent had hitherto shown the greatest power of acting for a European end, and of interesting himself in a cause not directly his own.[3]

Indeed, both leaders had high hopes for the agreement. For Alexander, the hope was to avoid more war with the French juggernaut. France's army seemed nearly invincible, and Alexander sought time to deal with internal stability challenges. Napoleon's hopes were tied to the enforcement of the Continental Blockade, which would starve his chief rival, the British. He also sought to improve his position to the east efficiently, without war if possible. The two leaders engaged in long and intimate negotiations on the barge at Tilsit, forging what appeared to be a new bond of understanding:

> Alexander surrendered himself to the addresses of a conqueror who seemed to ask for nothing and promise everything. The negotiations were prolonged; the relations of the two monarchs became more and

[3] Fyffe, 1896, p. 340–41.

more intimate; and the issue of the struggle for life or death was that Russia accepted the whole scheme of Napoleonic conquest, and took its place by the side of the despoiler for its share of the prey.[4]

Napoleon's goal of enforcing the blockade to keep the British out of the Continent meant his forces and influence were distributed throughout Europe. Russia was second only to England on the list of dangerous opponents, but as 1806 drew to a close, the Fourth Coalition had failed to gain any traction against the French Empire. Prussia fell to Napoleon's forces in less than three weeks, failing to sustain any resistance or garner military victories. The easy victories against the Prussians seemed to catapult Napoleon's army into Poland, setting up the Duchy of Warsaw and preparing to meet the Russians in battle once again. France's decisive victory against the Russians at the Battle of Friedland in June 1807 ended the War of the Fourth Coalition and set the stage for the Treaty at Tilsit. The treaty enabled Napoleon to refocus his efforts on England and Sweden, at least providing a pause against the stubborn resistance of the Russians. For Alexander's part, the agreement appeared to promise substantial rewards as a major partner in Napoleon's ambitions, including the territorial gains of Sweden and the Ottoman Empire once the fighting was over. The two powers also signed a secret treaty at Tilsit, one day after penning the main agreement with Prussia, that joined the two powers in an alliance against England and Sweden.

Given the domestic costs Alexander faced in signing the Treaty of Tilsit, and the grand concessions offered by Napoleon for what seemed to be a great bargain, this new agreement had the appearance of remaking the map of Europe in dramatic fashion. Moving forward, however, both sides faced incomplete information about the credibility of the commitments promised at Tilsit. Those uncertainties motivated the need for additional information, including reputational information.

Napoleon was chiefly concerned with whether Russia would abide by the Continental Blockade and cease trading with England. The question was, could he count on Russia to maintain what were essentially sanctions against the British? The blockade was painful for everyone, with the goal of starving the British into submission. Napoleon knew that Alexander would have difficulty enforcing the blockade throughout the Russian economy.

[4] Fyffe, 1896, p. 338.

Alexander's fears were considerably more dire. The question for Russia was, would France honor its allegiance to Russia and the promises made at Tilsit when and if England and Sweden were defeated? Would France be content to let Russia stand as a partner, or would it use its new focus and power to finish its sweeping conquest of Europe?

If we look closely at this slice of history, we can see the difference between uncertainty and reputation. Napoleon was uncertain about whether he could trust Russia to maintain the blockade. Alexander was uncertain about whether Napoleon would honor the treaty. Both leaders sought to eliminate these uncertainties, and in the process they turned to one another's reputations for help. But, reputations are simply information, and this information can be imperfectly applied to try to solve uncertainty problems.

Focusing on Alexander's uncertainty problems, he looked at all possible sources of information to answer his questions about Napoleon's credibility. In constant pursuit of answers to these questions, Alexander paid close attention to Napoleon's behavior throughout the continent. Reputational streams of information were important precisely because of the lingering uncertainty in the relationship.

One of the most incongruous streams of information for Alexander resulted from Napoleon's close ties to the Duchy of Warsaw, led by the French Emperor's close ally, King Frederick Augustus I of Saxony. Two days after Tsar Alexander and Napoleon signed their agreement in Tilsit, a second treaty united France and Prussia in an alliance that parsed lands and carved out new leadership. The territory given up by Prussia became the Grand Duchy of Warsaw. The new Duchy of Warsaw quickly emerged as a quasi-independent state, firmly in line with Napoleon's France. Frederick Augustus's devotion to Napoleon and the Grand Duchy of Warsaw's territorial expansion was a constant signal to Alexander of Napoleon's aggression. This was particularly the case after the Duchy's war with Austria in 1809, where French troops directly assisted and fought to help the Duchy defeat Austria and seize even more territory. The large and continuous presence of French troops in the Grand Duchy symbolized the decline of Prussia and a threat to Russian territory. If we consider Prussia as a proxy for Russia, Alexander must have concluded that Napoleon had no intention of leaving Russia alone.

Figure 3.1 illustrates how this vicarious learning process affected Alexander's perception of Napoleon's and France's intentions for future expansion. Given its satellite status, nothing the Duchy did was carried out without Napoleon's permission. The steady decline of Prussian territory combined with the defeat of

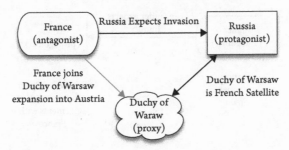

Figure 3.1 The Duchy of Warsaw: Russia observes
France's Relentless Expansionism.

the Austrians in 1809 strongly indicated to Alexander that Napoleon's eastward
expansionism would never stop.

But what about the treaty itself, binding Alexander and Napoleon as brothers,
and the two nations in an alliance? Returning to the brief discussion in Chapter
1, there is ample evidence that Alexander learned quickly that Napoleon's
willingness to abide by his signed agreements was suspect. As discussed in
Chapter 1, shortly after signing the treaty at Tilsit, Napoleon signed an agreement
with the Spanish government, the Treaty of Fountainebleau. This treaty was
designed to allow Napoleon to transport his forces through Spain with safe
passage. Napoleon's goal at the time was to use his expert land forces to bring
the Portuguese in line with the blockade. King Charles IV of Spain agreed to
grant French troops safe passage, and in return Napoleon provided assurances
that King Charles IV would remain in charge of his continental possessions
south of the Pyrenees.[5] On paper, the agreement brought together the Spanish
and French troops into a single unified force, and enabled Napoleon to reach
Portugal without encountering his nemesis, the British Navy. Once the French
troops were physically in Spain, however, it became apparent that the Treaty of
Fountainbleau was a Trojan horse. Napoleon used his troops to depose King
Charles IV and install his own puppet regime.[6] Figure 3.2 visualizes the way
Spain and its invasion at the hands of the French served as a proxy for Russia.
Spain and Russia are not perfect proxies, of course, in that Russia at the time
was far more capable and larger geographically, but they shared key regime

[5] Burman, 2000.
[6] Dwyer, 2001.

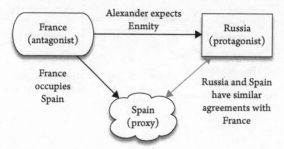

Figure 3.2 Learning from Spain: Russia observes
France's Occupation of Spain.

characteristics and both had signed treaties with Napoleon which included
similar language.

All of this must have contributed to Alexander's skepticism regarding
Napoleon's promises of allegiance. According to one account, by 1811 the
situation seemed inexorably moving toward war. Gibbon writes, "Alexander had
already used all possible endeavors to avert the evils of war. His relation, the duke
of Oldenburgh, had been plundered of his dominions by Bonaparte, in a time
of peace."[7] From the perspective of the Russians, France's aggression seemed to
overwhelm the partnership established a few years before on the barge at Tilsit.

By the spring of 1812, Alexander could no longer ignore all the signs that
pointed to a French invasion. A conversation between Tsar Alexander and John
Quincy Adams in March of 1812 reveals the lack of trust the Russian leader held
for Napoleon. Adams was the first foreign minister sent to Russia by the United
States. From his arrival in 1809, he established a friendship with Alexander that
lasted many years. Both men also had a habit of long morning walks, and would
occasionally walk together. Walking together in the morning in Saint Petersberg,
the two discussed in frank terms the likelihood of a French invasion. Adams
recorded the conversation in his diary, and he seemed struck by Alexander's
certainty.

> And so it is, after all, that war is coming which I have done so much to
> avoid, everthing. I have done everything to prevent this struggle (cette
> lutte), but thus it ends. "But," said I, "are all hopes vanished of still
> preserving the peace?" "At all events," said he, "we shall not begin the

[7] Gibbon, 1819.

war. My will is yet to prevent it, but we expect to be attacked." ... "And then, HE keeps on advancing. He began by taking Swedish Pomerania, and now he has just occupied Prussia – he can't advance much farther without attacking us."[8]

Between his direct interaction and history with Napoleon, Russia's reluctance to stop trading with England, and his observation of Napoleon's interactions with the rest of Europe, Alexander came to the conclusion that war with France was coming. Even after the war began, Napoleon continued to convey a sense of brotherhood and allegiance with Alexander, but by then it was too late. While it is improper to conclude that Napoleon's reputation caused war with Russia in 1812, it clearly exacerbated the fundamental commitment problem that broke the alliance. In short, Napoleon's behavior throughout Europe (and Alexander's perception of that behavior) undermined his ability to credibly commit to the Treaty of Tilsit.

Interestingly, it was Napoleon's reputation for aggression that mattered, not his reputation for military genius. In other words, the reputation Napoleon wanted to have was not the reputation he had in Alexander's eyes. Surely, Napoleon's successes in on the battlefield (particularly the Battle of Wagram in 1809) must have given Alexander pause when he considered defying the Continental Blockade. But along with that image of genius came images of aggression and deception. The occupation of Spain under false pretenses, the occupation of Poland and almost taunting treatment of Prussia, and the mounting French army presence in the Duchy of Warsaw all contributed to Alexander's conclusion that war was coming.

Alexander was not the only one in Russia to perceive Napoleon in this way. As the French went into Spain and then Portugal, and then began to refocus their attention toward the east, the topic of Napoleon's character was often the subject of John Quincy Adams's diary entries. For example, in February of 1812 (shortly before his conversation with Alexander), Adams writes about a meeting with Russia's Foreign Minister, Count Rumyantsev (Romanzof), and the conversation turning quickly to Napoleon.

I heard there were prospects of war between France and Russia, which I lamented. [The Count] had mentioned the Emperor Napoleon ... and

---

[8] See Adams (1914, p. 352). The last sentence is written in French in Adams's diary entry. I use a translation as quoted in Cate (1985).

how much was it to be wished that it were possible the *will* of peace and tranquility could be inspired into his heart. The world might then be allowed to enjoy a little peace. The Count shook his head, and said, "No; it is impossible. Tranquility is not in his nature. I can tell you, in confidence, that he once told me so himself. I was speaking to him about Spain and Portugal, and he said to me, 'I must always be *going*. After the Peace of Tilsit, where could I go but to Spain? I went to Spain because I could not go anywhere else.' "[9]

As for Rumyantsev, his reaction was not what resolve-centered reputation theories would predict. Napoleon had clearly left an impression with the Count that the Emperor was driven to invade, and thus would eventually be driven to invade Russia. Napoleon was resolved, almost certainly. The Count did not, however, conclude that such reputational clarity should motivate capitulation or cooperation. Instead, he concluded, "the circumstances have rendered it proper for us to place ourselves in a state of preparation, as we have accordingly done."[10] Napoleon's reputation for aggression dictated a response counter to his wishes. This is a point worth emphasizing. A typical interpretation of Schelling's concept of reputation would suggest that Napoleon's reputation demonstrated resolve. Such resolve should have motivated conciliation, or even capitulation on the part of Russia. It did not, and instead the Russians prepared for what they perceived as an inevitable first strike.

It is possible to conclude that Emperor Napoleon's mistake was in not understanding how his own reputation was being perceived by the Russians. Napoleon would often send letters expressing strong terms of friendship and kindness to Alexander, and sought to communicate to Alexander that he was different from the rest of Europe's leaders. His actions, however, sent a very different message. In the empirical analysis later in this book, I focus on behavioral sources of information rather than letters, speeches, and text. The reason can be seen here in this illustration. Napoleon often made proclamations of cooperation and trust, followed up by actions that suggested a different path. Ultimately, Alexander's anticipation of invasion was based on indirect observations of Napoleon's behavior in Spain, Portugal, and Prussia. It proved to be correct, and the preparations made by the Russians led to the downfall of Napoleon and his empire.

---

[9] Adams, 1914, p. 336. In his diaries, Adams refers to the Count as either "The Count" or "Romanzoff."

[10] Adams, 1914, p. 336.

Lessons from the History of Napoleon and Alexander

What can we learn from this historical, political event? Specifically, what can we learn from about reputation and how it influenced the events that would lead to the end of the Napoleonic Empire? Scholars focusing on international security tend to make the same mistake Napoleon did, focusing only on the reputation for resolve and its implications for deterrence and compellence. Credibility is important, as I will show below, but the traditional focus is to examine a state's reputation for credibly threatening violence. Russia's conundrum, however, was not in deciphering whether or not France's threats of violence were credible. Rather, the challenge was in determining whether France's promises of peace were credible.

The classic role of reputation in deterrence is a poor fit for understanding cases like the French invasion of Russia in 1812. In a deterrence scenario, reputation matters, but it is the reputation backing up the threat of punishment if defection occurs. Threats of punishing defections are meaningless if the target of those threats finds them incredible. But this scenario is the opposite of what Alexander faced. In the deterrence scenario, we would be focusing on Alexander's ability to use his reputation to credibly threaten Napoleon with a suitable punishment should Napoleon break the treaty. In evaluating the role of reputation in shaping Alexander's decisions, it is better to focus on models of trust and credibility outside of the constraints of deterrence theory.

Studies of cooperation, on the other hand, tend to focus on the characteristics of trustworthiness and credibility. Rather than signaling one's resolve, reputation serves as a measure of commitment, and provides an incomplete but informative signal of the willingness to abide by an agreement or contract. It is useful to step back from this historical example to take a look at some of the prominent theories that link reputation with political cooperation and conflict in world politics. The goal in the next section is to highlight the diversity of theories linking these phenomena, and to emphasize the role of learning when leaders utilize reputational information. I will then offer up my own argument about when and how reputation influences cooperation and conflict in world politics.

Studies of Reputation in World Politics:
What We Already Know

Reputation as a motivator of state behavior is receiving growing attention in international relations research.[11] Similar to arguments in economics about

---

[11] Clare and Danilovic, 2010, 2012; Kertzer, 2016; Weisiger and Yarhi-Milo, 2015.

the behavior of firms in the marketplace, scholars have invoked processes of reputation formation and learning to explain phenomena as diverse as military deterrence,[12] recurring conflict,[13] multilateral cooperation,[14] and international lending.[15] In this section I examine the particular role of reputation in the mechanisms of deterrence and resolve, and contrast this conceptualization with the work linking reputation with cooperation.

Reputation as Precedent: Beyond the Deterrence Frame

In the field of security studies, reputation is a concept that is classically associated with the notion of deterrence, which is the process of preventing another state from doing what it would otherwise do. In its broadest form, general deterrence, this process can refer to a great many things, but it most often refers to preventing another state from initiating war. In its narrowest form, nuclear deterrence, the process refers to preventing one's enemy from launching a first strike of nuclear weapons. Extended deterrence is also important as a process of preventing a state from attacking a third party or third state (e.g., the United States has successfully deterred China from attempting to reacquire Taiwan). One thing these processes all have in common is a credibility mechanism that enables states to succeed in their deterrence attempts.

Deterrence theories assert that deterrence is effective when one state can credibly threaten the other with consequences resulting from initiating violence, and that these consequences outweigh the benefits the attacking state would enjoy from initiating violence.[16] The credibility of the promise to deliver such consequences is derived from a state's capability to deliver and its resolve for doing so. Successful deterrence requires power and resolve. Both are difficult to quantify in their own ways, but power in terms of military capability is at least demonstrable in an objective sense. Resolve, in this case the will to carry out a retaliatory punishment if a state is undeterred, is nearly impossible to fully observe in the field.

[12] Alt, Calvert, and Humes, 1988; Huth, 1988; Nalebuff, 1991; Schelling, 1966.

[13] Diehl and Goertz, 2001; Leng, 1983, 1988; Crescenzi, 2007; Crescenzi, Kathman, and Long, 2007.

[14] Downs and M. J. Jones, 2002; Milgrom, North, and Weingast, 1990.

[15] Simmons, 2000; Simmons and Elkins, 2004; Tomz, 2007.

[16] See Schelling, 1966; Huth, 1997; Huth and Russett, 1984; and Nalebuff, 1991 for classic arguments, and Lebow and Stein (1989) for a classic critique. Achen and Snidal (1989) provide perhaps the best overall evaluation of the logic of deterrence.

And therein lies the inherent need to focus on reputation. Resolve is often promised but costly to demonstrate. In the deterrence frame, having a reputation for being resolute is more efficient than needing to demonstrate resolve constantly. Much of the debate that historically emerged around the notion of reputation in world politics was centered around the question of whether or not this efficiency could actually be obtained in real world politics. Mercer argued that the specific context of each real-world situation would overpower any state's overall efforts to create a generic, across-the-board reputation for resolve. Huth and others pushed back, showing empirically that reputation could have a systematic impact on deterrence outcomes in world politics.[17] More recently, scholars have demonstrated the impact of reputation and resolve in this deterrence crisis environment. Clare and Danilovic (2012) provide a leap forward by demonstrating empirically that reputation can convey information about resolve, but that the impact of this information depends on the interests of the state observing another's reputation. This finding is key to moving to a more interactive concept of reputation. Traditionally, reputations for resolve were identities or roles that were thought to be controlled by the state holding the reputation. Mercer famously demonstrated that what matters is the perception of another state's reputation, but Clare and Danilovic provide the first meaningful clue to show us how this relational perception does not have to lead to overwhelming complexity such that systematic research is precluded. Similarly, Sechser (2010) finds that reputations can matter in some circumstances but not in others. Put simply, if a state's reputation for honesty or honoring its agreements may not matter if the crisis is already past the stage of agreements. Reputation provides information, and if that information is not relevant for the situation at hand, then we are mistaken if we expect reputation to matter. Together, this new research points to the importance of matching the context of the political need for information with the existence of reputational information to fit that need.

Lastly, new work in the early twenty-first century on resolve, status, and honor teaches us that these concepts matter in world politics far beyond the narrow scope of deterrence. Kertzer (2016) teaches us that resolve is nearly ubiquitous in world politics, and sought after as a predictor of success in responding to crises both natural and political. As such, he defines resolve as a matter of "steadfastness of purpose"[18] that cannot be represented properly without integrating the actor's

[17] Huth, 1997.
[18] Kertzer, 2016, p. 3.

ability and willingness to persevere. Viewing resolve this way assists in breaking away from the confining frame of the need to demonstrate threat credibility in deterrence. Furthermore, resolve and reputation do not perfectly match up conceptually or empirically. To the extent to which states seek information from third-party sources about their potential enemy or partner's resolve, the two phenomena can overlap, but resolve is only one form of competence in world politics.

With this new perspective in place, I now turn to a discussion of the role of reputation in cooperative contexts. There are some key differences, particularly the absence of a highly specific crisis-deterrence frame, and some similarities. One particular similarity of note is that reputations in cooperative contexts serve as proxies for competence or trustworthiness. With this common role in information provision in mind, we can begin to see a unified vision of how reputation plays a role in both conflict and cooperation in world politics.

Reputation in Cooperation: Firms, Markets, and Trustworthiness

Given their similarities, scholars have analogized the behavior of states in the international system to the behavior of firms in a free-market economy.[19] While some key differences between the marketplace and the international system obviously exist, with respect to alliance formation the two systems are quite similar. In both, the decisions of the central actors are made in relatively anarchic, competitive environments characterized by limited information. In both systems actors desire resource aggregation and seek partners with complementary or supplementary strengths as a means to expand their prestige in and control over their strategic environment. Because partnerships are important (and common) features of both systems, firms and states alike are acutely aware of the costs imposed by the defection of an ally. For states, defection can leave them vulnerable to aggression from adversaries or can result in declining political influence. For firms, contractual breeches or the dissolution of partnerships can exert strong negative influences on market share, stock values, or net revenues. Consequently, states and firms both seek information that can shed light on the potential partner's loyalty.

Firms often attempt to limit the likelihood of future losses by forming alliances with partners that boast a reputation for credibility in upholding their

[19] Waltz, 1979.

obligations.[20] A reputation for honoring commitments functions as a strategic asset in the process of alliance formation.[21] Past empirical research has shown that a firm's reputation is a powerful signal of its likelihood to cooperate or defect on its future agreements.[22] Accordingly, a firm with a reputation for past reliability is increasingly likely to be selected as an ally in future business dealings.[23] The effect of reputation is present in both dyadic as well as extra-dyadic relationships. That is, the firm's history of trustworthiness may be created through its direct history with its potential partner, but also through its dealings with other past partners, as well as its "general image in the marketplace."[24] Interestingly, research in the fields of business, economics, and marketing has demonstrated that the historical reputation of a firm in the open market is an important predictor of its ability to attract other firms for profitable mergers,[25] set higher prices,[26] and attract quality employees.[27] On the other hand, firms with poor reputations lose market share and earning potential by selecting themselves out of future transactions. In a parallel to states in the international system, these studies often note that in a marketplace of incomplete information, where firms have an inability to portray their true intentions, a firm's reputation acts as a primary information source on which actors make transaction decisions. As firms develop a direct history of transactions, this reputation dimension should diminish in importance. That is, the role of reputation is at its peak in the absence of information provided by direct interactions.

As such, research in business, economics, and marketing has demonstrated that the historical reputation of a firm in the market is an important predictor of its future economic performance. Reputation is particularly relevant to the setting of product prices, assessments of product quality, the negotiation and enforcement of contracts, and the extension of credit.[28] As Allen (1984) argues, a positive reputation for providing quality products is unambiguously beneficial. Obtaining and promoting such a reputation allows firms to sell their goods at

---

[20] Das and Teng, 1998, p. 504.

[21] Barney and Hansen, 1994.

[22] Weigelt and Camerer, 1988.

[23] Dollinger, Golden, and Saxton, 1997.

[24] Das and Teng, 2002, p. 734.

[25] Dollinger, Golden, and Saxton, 1997.

[26] Shapiro, 1983.

[27] Chauvin and Guthrie, 1994.

[28] Allen, 1984; Boot, Greenbaum, and Thakor, 1993; Chauvin and Guthrie, 1994; Wujin Chu and Woosik Chu, 1994; Diamond, 1989; Kim, 1996.

comparably higher prices than their competitors.[29] While firms may pay costs to obtain a positive reputation, this public perception pays dividends in the form of higher asking prices and profit margins. Additionally, in the free market, a reputation for treating employees fairly will allow firms to attract and retain high-quality employees. While a firm is likely to incur costs associated with an investment in employee relations, firms should expect a payoff. A strong workforce with little turnover should yield greater efficiency, generate higher profits, and increase stock prices.[30]

More generally, a firm's reputation is relevant to other companies when considering a potential merger or joint venture. It is this process that is most closely associated with the cooperation competence hypothesis presented below. As with states entering into an agreement or an alliance, the decision of a firm to enter into a business partnership with another entails the possibility of both benefits and risks. Pooling resources to accomplish a common goal may allow firms to dominate markets, produce better products, or thwart the encroachment of rivals. On the other hand, collaboration in a joint venture exposes firms to risks they would not otherwise encounter as independents. By merging, firms tie their future fortunes not only to the future performance of their partner, but also to its business practices, the treatment of its employees, and the quality of their products. Firms therefore have an incentive to scrutinize the past behavior of potential joint-venture partners. To limit the possibility of allying with an ineffective or economically injurious partner, firms rely on the reputations that potential partners have established.[31] The key here is that there exists some risk in engaging in a cooperative arrangement, and the perception of this risk is imperfect. In short, there is a need for more information, and firms use the past actions of their potential partners in an attempt to resolve this need.

The role of reputation in predicting cooperation at the firm level is not just theoretical. Evidence from studies of joint ventures and firm reputations suggests that, on balance, a positive reputation produces more favorable rewards than a negative reputation. Provided that one's reputation is public knowledge, actors should be interested in maintaining a positive reputation so as to enjoy the future benefits that a good reputation bestows. Empirical and theoretical work has formalized the notion that a positive reputation is an asset that generates

[29] Klein and Leffler, 1981; Shapiro, 1983.

[30] Chauvin and Guthrie, 1994.

[31] Weigelt and Camerer, 1988.

future rents.[32] As Weigelt and Camerer note, a firm's reputation is a powerful signal of its likelihood to cooperate or defect on its future agreements. By defecting on agreed transactions, firms lose market share and earning potential by effectively selecting themselves out of future transactions. In fact, the true intentions of a firm are of less consequence to potential business partners. In a world of incomplete information, where firms have an inability to portray their true intentions, a firm's reputation acts as the primary information source on which potential partners make their transaction decisions. Firms therefore have distinct incentives to build and maintain a positive reputation in the market so as to derive future rents. It should come as no surprise that previous research suggests that the better the reputation of the firm, the more likely it is to be selected as a business ally by other companies in the future.[33]

One key difference between corporate and state systems is the presence within domestic markets of legal structures that can punish firms that renege on their contractual obligations. While the government's power to enforce a contract between two independent firms is often limited, domestic legal structures in most developed capitalist states allow the aggrieved party to reclaim at least some portion of the losses accrued from its partner's defection. Unexpected departures, however, can still exert unrecoverable costs. In the international system, states enjoy even less recourse to damages wrought by defection. While limited international legal structures exist, the real potential for one state to extract compensation from another is comparatively small. With the exception of the compensatory mechanisms available through the World Trade Organization or various regional trade organizations for trade-related offenses, states are seldom able to appeal to higher bodies to enforce treaties or to seek compensation for losses resulting from a partner's defection. In this sense, the importance of selecting a reliable alliance partner is even greater for states.

While a level of consensus has been reached in the business literature on the importance of corporate reputation, work on interstate conflict processes has not arrived at similar agreement. Select quantitative studies report a significant effect of reputation on deterrence outcomes.[34] While some research using case analyses casts doubt on the logic of reputations in deterrence and interstate

---

[32] Weigelt and Camerer, 1988; Wilson, 1985.
[33] Dollinger, Golden, and Saxton, 1997.
[34] Huth, 1988, 1997; Huth and Russett, 1984.

bargaining,[35] recent work suggests that reputation affects alliance dynamics. In examining the First Morocco, Bosnia–Herzegovina, and Agadir Crises,[36] G. D. Miller (2003) specifically addresses the effect of state reputation on alliance formation. He notes that reputations were an important factor in Britain's choice of alliance partners in the early twentieth century. Specifically, he finds that "the more reliable a state appears to be, the more autonomy it will have in its alliance choices."[37] Gibler (2008) finds support for his expectation that heads of state form reputations that affect their prospects of forming future alliances. These findings hint at the role of historical interactions and reputation in alliance formation.

The Role of Learning in Reputation Dynamics

The concept of learning and adaptation has a long-standing presence in the study of international relations.[38] Learning is a key component of the way I believe reputations form and evolve, for three reasons. First, learning is *experiential*, and thus well-suited to a behavioral theory of reputation. States learn from the experiences and behavior of other states. This is not to say that states don't learn from other characteristics of states, or the text and rhetoric of leaders. That said, I think it is worthwhile to separate the two streams of information (behavioral from rhetorical). Rhetorical sources of reputation tend to be less grounded in context, and it is important to connect political context with reputation needs.

Second, learning is *diagnostic* in that states use the experiences of others to update their beliefs about the intentions of others. In order for learning to satisfy the diagnostic condition, there must exist a need for diagnosis. Rationalists

[35] Mercer, 1996; Press, 2005.

[36] These three crises occurred between 1905 and 1911, and can be considered precursors to World War I. The First Morocco Crisis took place in 1905 as Germany's Kaiser Wilhelm arrived in Tangiers and declared support for the sultan of Morocco. The secondary intent of the visit was to apply tension to the entente between France and Britain.

In 1911, the Agadir Crisis, also known as the Second Morroco Crisis, flared as France intervened with troops on behalf of the Sultan to put down a rebellion. Germany used the event to leverage territorial gains in what was then known as Middle Congo.

The Bosnia-Herzegovina Crisis occurs in 1908 when Austria-Hungary annexed these territories, which were formerly considered sovereign territory of the Ottoman Empire.

[37] G. D. Miller, 2003, p. 77.

[38] See, for example Jervis, 1976; Dixon, 1983; Leng, 1983, 1988, 1993, 2000; Huth, 1988; Maoz, 1990, 1996; Snyder, 1991; Levy, 1994; Reiter, 1996; Farkas, 1998; Press, 2005.

often simplify this process when building signaling models designed to reveal information about an actor's type. This is a highly stylized form of diagnostic learning, often presented in static and final terms once information about type is conveyed. My own view is that diagnostic learning is rarely so final or permanent. Within the context of an immediate decision motivated by a crisis or a contract, it is often sufficient to approximate a more dynamic learning process with the static updating found in signaling models. A more general approach, taken here, is that the value of the diagnosis is only valuable as long as it applies to the contextual information needs motivating the search for reputation in the first place.

Lastly, learning with respect to reputation is *vicarious*, or diffuse, in that states learn from experiences in which they are not directly involved.[39] Research on learning in foreign policy is most frequently concerned with direct experiential learning at the state and dyadic levels of analysis. For example, Dixon (1983) examines the dynamic, historical sources of affect and their impact on Cold War ties between the United States and the Soviet Union.[40] Reiter (1996) looks at how formative events help states learn about alliances. Snyder (1991) considers how great powers learn and adjust to their early mistakes of overexpansion. Leng (1983) and Crescenzi and Enterline (2001) demonstrate that dyads learn from earlier crises within the dyad and become more bellicose with each other in subsequent crisis situations. Leng (1993, 2000) delves deeply into the dynamic interplay within dyads during crises to understand when states choose dangerous bargaining strategies. All of these studies identify patterns of learning. None of these studies address the ability of states to learn from the indirect behavioral history of their dyadic partners.

Three lines of research are useful in explicating an argument for how the information gleaned from relational interdependence affects the onset of interstate conflict. Leng (1983) provides an important theory of experiential learning in the context of direct dyadic interaction. His Experiential Learning–Realpolitik (ELR) model of crisis-driven bargaining assumes that states learn from their experiences in prior crises. A coercive historical experience leads to an increased probability of employing more coercive bargaining tactics in the future. After careful empirical work, Leng concludes that "coercion begets coercion" (1983,

---

[39] Jervis, 1976; Leng, 1983; Levy, 1994.

[40] Dixon uses the term "affect" to refer to the feelings of one state toward another. In this case, the United States toward the Soviet Union.

p. 412).[41] Leng's ELR model is echoed in the study of rivalry and conflict.[42] Rivalry scholars do an excellent job of conceiving of a dyad as a dynamic, historically dependent entity. While the learning mechanism is not explicit, states within a rivalry dyad are constrained by the experiences of past violence when dealing with current crises. The accumulation of hostility becomes a key component to the rivalry's fundamental relationship. In rivalries, again conflict begets conflict. Here the argument can be a combination of underlying causes and social construction, but the notion of rivalry operating as a cause of violence has a clear evolutionary path. Finally, in my work with Andrew Enterline (2001) we develop a model of the direct dyadic historical relationship that is experiential and cumulative. The model is in line with Leng's crisis learning patterns and rivalry theories in its assumption that conflict in the past leads to higher probabilities of conflict in the future, but it also broadens this argument to a more general treatment of the historical relationship.

Learning in foreign policy can also be attributed to the emergence of roles among states in the international system also plays a key role in the development of global reputation and relationships.[43] Thies (2001) identifies two mechanisms by which roles emerge among states: competition and socialization. Competition gets most of the attention in the general literature, particularly when discussing territorial disputes or interstate rivalries,[44] yet socialization provides the dynamic interaction that also shapes interstate relationships. For Thies, rivalry is best explained using the two dimensions in tandem: "Competition is an environment or situation within which actors find themselves. Socialization, on the other hand, is an ongoing process. Rivalries are ongoing dyadic processes that occur within a competitive environment."[45] Socialization is a social and behavioral form of learning, requiring interaction between units for new information to form. The roles that emerge from this learning process, combined with the competitive nature of the political environment, do not have to be limited to the direct dyadic relationship.

[41] In Leng (1988) the model is referred to as REL, but the argument is consistent and even more logically robust. Leng (1993, 2000) also deals explicitly with experiential learning within the dyad, particularly for enduring rivals. He finds that while this learning can be constrained by realpolitik beliefs, it occurs regularly in enduring rivalries.

[42] Diehl and Goertz, 2001.

[43] Holsti, 1970; Thies, 2001; Thies and Breuning, 2012.

[44] Diehl and Goertz, 2001.

[45] Thies, 2001, p. 700.

In the next section, I provide an argument about how context and behavioral learning combine to generate reputations that influence political outcomes. Using the discussion of reputation dynamics from Chapter 2, I adapt these direct-learning mechanisms to the more indirect process of reputation formation and influence. The triadic mechanics of balance theory represent the basic calculations, with the added complexity of proxy quality and directionality. I assume a different motivation than balance theorists, however, with respect to the actors involved. I argue that states are less concerned with the problems associated with balance, per se, and more concerned with the problems associated with the lack of information and problems of perception. Extra-dyadic information is a valuable source of information about the intentions and competence of one's dyadic counterpart. States use other states as proxies to get a sense of what their dyadic partner would do in situations such as a crisis or a contract.

A Theory of Reputation's Impact on World Politics

The key to unlocking the mystery of reputation and its role in political interaction is to free it from the bonds of the deterrence frame, simply because this frame refers to a highly specific and limited competitive context. If we focus only on the question of whether a state's leaders are *resolved* with respect to an agreement or a crisis, then the entire discussion of how reputation matters revolves around reputation as a signal of resolve. This focus, however, is not fully representative of the role of reputation in world politics. In fact, look closer at the strategic dynamics that cause interstate cooperation to flourish or flounder, and you will see that reputations need to be evaluated within that context. Sticking with the notion that conflict requires a breakdown in information or commitment, for example, we should not automatically conclude that a state's past actions are interpreted within the frame of resolve. If a state's past actions are replete with examples demonstrating an inability to commit to peace, the lesson learned is not that the state is resolved to fight but rather that it may be incompetent in its crisis negotiations.

Even worse, the lesson here could be that the state is reckless and aggressive. Schelling famously argued that such perceived recklessness and aggression could have deterrent capabilities (often referred to as the "madman theory"), but it is just as easy to arrive at the opposite conclusion. Aggression can signal an unwillingness or inability to peacefully navigate a crisis. This inability can stem from incompetence that translates into commitment problems that prevent the state from avoiding conflict. Moreover, the opponent need not know the exact source of the problem to conclude that it exists. The source of the problem could be domestic constraints, for example, or miscalculations about opponents' willingness to pay the costs of fighting. These two sources have very different origins, but they may manifest the same behavior.

In fact, past evidence of conflict primarily signals a history of credibility problems which lead to an increased propensity for violence. Mercer was correct to argue that signals of resolve with respect to war are extremely difficult to communicate due to context and the complexities of relationships, but we should not conclude that the result is a lack of meaningful information. The conclusion is far more pernicious. Actions that can only result from the existence of information and commitment problems signal the presence of these problems. Without countervailing evidence, it is reasonable to assume that past failures in a bargaining environment simply signal incompetence or intransigence, both of which exacerbate the problems of crisis management.

Like most research on learning and conflict (see Reiter, 1996), such an argument is incompatible with purely neorealist theories of world politics. Given that I explicitly argue that states rely upon information other than relative power levels to assess their strategies in crisis situations, this theory of reputation is a combination of rationalist and constructivist thought, with a focus on behavioral signals. I also adopt the structure of the well established two-stage learning→foreign policy process. The first stage involves learning from observation, and interpretation of these observations leads to updating. (That process was the focus of the last chapter.) In stage two, this updating may influence foreign policy behavior.[46] The Reputation Learning model is a model of this first stage, and it is a conceptual model of the learning process. My hope is to generate a model that uniquely captures the first stage, while allowing researchers to apply it to multiple causal analyses that fit in the second. The causal link between learning and foreign policy decision-making must be grounded in the type of political behavior that is being explained.

The basic components outlined in the discussion of learning and reputation do not just apply to the direct historical interactions between states. Indeed, I expect that they hold for vicarious experiential learning as well. Building off of the findings by Leng and supported by my work with Enterline, I argue that states that engage in repeated conflict develop a reputation for aggression

[46] Jervis, 1976; Levy, 1994.

and incompetence during crises. As potential enemies observe this reputation, they develop an expectation for aggression and incompetence from the states in question. Such an expectation creates a commitment problem, which decreases the likelihood of a nonviolent settlement to a crisis. In short, conflict begets conflict, because previous violence signals aggression and incompetence.

This argument has a straightforward cooperation complement. Just as conflict begets conflict, cooperation begets cooperation when a reputation for cooperation provides information about competence in cooperative contexts.[47] States that observe their dyadic partners as historically conflictual with similar proxy states will be more likely to resort to the use of force in times of crisis, but at the same time, states that observe their dyadic partners as historically cooperative with proxy states will be more likely to be cooperative themselves. Both arguments are fueled by the pursuit of information about competence within a particular context. In the absence of complete information, states are forced to generate expectations about the behavior of other states. One possible learning schema for generating these expectations is to observe how other states behave in similar situations, and to then use this observation as a precedent, or "prior," for the current situation. In times of crisis, a nation will observe how its opponent has behaved in similar crises throughout history both within and outside of the dyad. This past behavior sets the stage for bargaining tactics, expectations, and ultimately the decision whether or not to use force.

Overall, the basic logic of this theory is built upon components discussed in the previous chapter: cognitive balance theory combined with triadic interaction models.[48] This theory of reputational learning captures the dynamics of triadic interactions but then reduces this information to the state and dyad levels of analysis. In essence, reputation serves as the mechanism for this information to be translated from triadic to dyadic dimensions. In this book, I focus on one type of political context at a time, and set aside the questions of whether and how a reputation in one arena (e.g., international crises) may influence political behavior in another arena (e.g., trade agreements). While there is some reason to expect that cross-pollination can occur with reputations across contexts, it makes sense to first get a clear grasp on the influence of reputations within context.

[47] Crescenzi and Enterline, 2001; Crescenzi, Enterline, and Long, 2008.

[48] Triadic interaction models similar to those found in Schrodt and Mintz (1988) and Goldstein and Freeman (1990).

Testable Implications of the Reputation Learning Theory

Emerging from this discussion are common elements that provide clues to a shift in the way we can think about the role of reputation. The first is that a state's reputation exacerbates or ameliorates the private information and commitment problems that lie at the heart of cooperation and conflict. Reputation only matters when it is needed, and the source of that need lies in the problems of private information and commitment. States rely on reputation when they are unable to ascertain enough information without it.

Second, It is just as important to pay attention to the context of reputation. We cannot know the impact of a state's reputation on cooperation or conflict until we know the subject of that reputation. A reputation for resolve may be the relevant subject for deterrence contexts, while a reputation for aggression may be relevant for broader investigations of international crises. A reputation for keeping one's promises and agreements can be the relevant subject of cooperation contexts.

Across all of these contexts, however, the function served by reputation is to signal a state's competence. If we can agree that the occurrence of violence is potentially observed as incompetence in handling an international crisis, then a state's violent past may be processed by others as past incompetence. Similarly, a state that signs agreements only when it intends to fulfill them, and then demonstrates that commitment through its upholding of agreements, is likely to convey a reputation for competence in cooperative contexts. In both cases, the context is significantly different but the essential information contained in the state's reputation is consistent. The core argument in this book is that a state's reputation for competence improves that state's chances for cooperation, efficiency, and peace, while a state's reputation for incompetence can make conflict, inefficiency, and war more likely to occur.

Thus, if a state has a reputation for using violence against its enemies in a crisis context, other states will view this behavior as a signal of crisis incompetence. Such an identity makes it that much harder to trust any agreement that allows its enemies to avoid preparations for war. I identify this argument here as the *Crisis Incompetence Hypothesis*:

> A state that has a reputation for incompetence in crises, such as violating agreements or engaging in conflict, is more likely to experience conflict with other states in the international system.

Turning now to cooperation contexts, if a state has a reputation for uphold-ing its agreements, other states will view this behavior as a sign of cooperation competence. This reputation helps alleviate the fears of other states as they ponder the possibilities of new agreements with that state. If a state has a reputation for violating its agreements, however, this reputation amplifies the credibility concerns states must navigate as the try to achieve cooperation. This argument is represented here as the *Cooperation Competence Hypothesis*:

A state that has a reputation for competence in cooperation, such as upholding its agreements and promises, or peacefully navigating crises, is more likely to experience cooperation with other states in the international system.

Lastly, throughout this book there is an important focus on the quality and durability of reputation information. Like all forms of information, it is assumed that the quality of this reputation degrades over time. The essential dynamic of reputation is its tendency to be self-perpetuating but this information fades into the past. This argument is three-fold. The first and more general argument, emerging from the discussion of reputation dynamics in Chapter 2, is actually a specific form of context where the assumption is that temporal distance is a form of contextual distance. This argument is represented in the *Temporal Dynamics Hypothesis*:

Reputational information is dynamic. Past actions matter, but the relevance (and thus impact) of this information degrades over time.

The second argument emerging from Chapter 2 is that not all streams of reputational information are equally useful. When a state is able to observe another's behavior with high-quality proxies, the first state is able to extract better reputational information. In the absence of good proxies, reputational information is harder to find. This can be simply stated as the *Spatial Proxy Hypothesis*:

Reputational information improves with proxy quality.

The third component of temporal dynamics corresponds to the dynamic need for reputation information. As two states develop their own direct history, the reliance on reputation lessens. The argument is simply that direct information is more useful because the proxy is perfect (in that the proxy is the state itself). This argument is represented in the *Direct History Hypothesis*:

> Reputation matters most when a state has little or no direct observations
> of the behavior of the other state. As dyads develop their own direct
> histories, the role of reputation will diminish.

Together, these five hypotheses lay out a new and unique interpretation of the role of reputation in world politics. Reputation affects both conflict and cooperation, it matters most when the source of information is temporally and spatially proximate, and it is most useful in the absence of direct streams of historical information.

Evaluating the Implications of the Reputational Learning Model

With these hypotheses in place, the next part of the book evaluates this approach to reputation in world politics. Testing theories is never as straightforward as it seems, and scholars are rarely able to test entire arguments. In this book, I restrict the hypothesis-testing in the next two chapters to focus on the onset and escalation of conflict and the onset of alliances. For both, there are alternatives that could have been the focus of the empirical analysis. Yet these dependent variables—militarized violence and alliance formation—are at the heart of the study of peace and conflict in world politics. While it may also be fruitful to study the impact of reputation on trade, investments, treaties, and legal disputes, for this author the clear place to start is with the onset of violence and the cooperative alliance commitments that enable states to overcome the security dilemma.

There are alternative explanations, of course, that suggest a different relationship between reputation and politics. The classic view of reputation and resolve, for example, would take issue with the idea that conflict begets conflict. Instead, the alternative argument that comes from this view would be that the use of force can contribute to a reputation for resolve, which can actually reduce the risk of future conflict. As discussed above and by others, this was the logic that drove US policy during the Vietnam War, and to a certain extent the Cold War, writ large. If this view is correct, then a state's ability to demonstrate that it is willing to fight should signal its resolve and deter future challenges, thereby making subsequent conflict less likely.[49] If the deterrence frame is the common context surrounding a state's reputation for conflict, then I should fail to find support for the Crisis Incompetence Hypothesis.

Similarly, a second set of alternatives to the reputational learning theory advanced here comes from the original critique of reputation by Mercer and the more recent discussion of past actions by Press. For very different reasons, these alternatives both point to a fundamental disconnect between reputation and politics. For Mercer, the problem is not that reputations do not exist but rather that they are situational, unique, and so socially complex that their impact on political behavior cannot be broadly or systematically predicted or explained. It is not that reputation does not matter, but rather that its impact on politics is too contextual to provide meaningful information in the future. Press, on the other hand, sees no evidence of reputation's influence even with the focused lens of history. The two alternatives point to the same prediction that reputations do not systematically influence political behavior. If they are correct, I should fail to find support for any of my hypotheses.

Lastly, it is necessary to think about whether it is states or state leaders who possess reputations.[50] The parallel in the business world is the question of whether the firm or its CEO possesses the reputation. In states as well as in firms, the answer is both. Leaders of states embody the identity and competence of their governments, and depending on the type of regime can become synonymous with the state itself. In dictatorships like North Korea, for example, the competence of the leader is central to predicting the competence of the state. But even in these extreme cases, the leader cannot possibly encompass the entirety of a state's competence, and other states know this. In democracies, the overlap between state and leader reputations is smaller but still exists. When President Barack Obama began his term in 2008 and President George W. Bush ended his term, the world perceived a shift in the United States' competence. That said, the entire history of American foreign policy remained intact, and it would be appropriate to assume that America's reputation did not fully reset with this presidential transition.

In an attempt to accommodate this tension, I have incorporated illustrations of leader reputations throughout the book to show how reputations for individual leaders impact political outcomes in international relations. In the next two chapters, however, I collapse this information and treat states as unitary

---

[49] This is a general deterrence argument, not an immediate deterrence one.
[50] Gibler, 2008.

actors. To be clear, nobody who studies world politics thinks that any state
in the history of the international system operates as a unitary actor. Yet this
reduction in information facilitates empirical tests at a very general, systematic
level, complementing the historical illustrations throughout the book, and it
allows me to evaluate the role of reputation with respect to the phenomena of
war and alliance formation in broadest terms. If I am wrong, and reputations
only follow leaders, then I am less likely to find support for either the Crisis
Incompetence Hypothesis or the Cooperation Competence Hypothesis in the
tests that follow.

PART TWO

EVIDENCE: THE INFLUENCE OF REPUTATION ON COOPERATION AND CONFLICT

4

Reputation, Conflict, and War

"I believe that [China's] aggressiveness recently displayed not only in Korea ... reflects predominantly the same lust for the expansion of power which has animated every would-be conqueror since the beginning of time.
...
It has been said in effect that I was a warmonger. Nothing could be further from the truth."

—General Douglas MacArthur

How do states' reputations for using force and going to war influence interstate conflict? In this chapter, I focus on two particular questions relating to the role of reputation and violence. The first is whether reputations for violence influence the onset of new violence. This is the first stage of militarized conflict, the initiation of disputes. The second is whether reputations for escalating violence to war lead to or affect the likelihood that future disputes with other states will be more likely to escalate to war as well. It is one thing to argue that historical and reputational contexts are relevant when political crises turn violent; it is quite another to conclude that these contexts are also relevant when these crises escalate to war. Do these factors permanently inhibit the ability of states to negotiate their way out of crises, or does the specter of war cause states to shed this historical knowledge?

When evaluating the role of reputation in world politics, the place to begin is where the stakes are highest—that is, with the question of how reputations affect military conflict between states in the international system. For much of the Cold War, the conventional wisdom was that having a reputation for being willing to use violence was what kept the West safe from the ever-expanding Soviet threat. Yet, if we remember the statements made by General MacArthur quoted at the beginning of this chapter, we can see that he perceived Chinese military action not as a sign of a tough or resolute reputation, but rather as a sign of an aggressive state. Indeed, his use of words like "expansion" and "conqueror" emphasize an impending threat of invasion. At the same time, only moments later in his speech, MacArthur defends himself against similar charges. His self-perception was that his strength and willingness to use any and all resources to succeed were essential signals to the communists that he was an insurmountable foe not to be challenged. At the same time, however, even his allies in the West perceived him to be aggressive to the point of extreme danger. In an accounting of MacArthur's showdown with Truman during the Korean War, for example, H.W. Brands writes that, "Attlee and many others in Britain could think of no one more frightening than MacArthur to have control of the bomb."[1] It was not just the British who were worried; nearly everyone who looked at MacArthur's past actions expressed concerns about the frightening possibility of World War III.[2]

One interpretation of all this is the reputations that states and their leaders wish to project are not the reputations perceived by others. More specifically, attempts to project a tough or resolute reputation can easily be conflated with threat, and the result can be a projection of aggression. Aggression may look a lot like toughness from the sender's perspective, but the target state comes to very different policy conclusions as a result. Rather than being dissuaded from violence by the show of strength of one's opponent, states may instead be convinced that the opponent is a dangerous threat to be resisted. Thus, the Crisis Incompetence Hypothesis highlights a key problem of conflating strength and aggression in reputations. In this chapter, I test the hypothesis at two levels of conflict processes. First, I investigate the role of reputation in the occurrence of militarized disputes between two states. This analysis focuses on the first stage of interstate violence. Using a broad, sweeping sample of international behavior over a long period of history, this analysis indicates that a state's reputation for violence makes it more likely to find itself involved in new militarized disputes with others. A reputation for using force does not decrease a state's propensity for violence; rather, it has precisely the opposite effect.

In a secondary analysis, I investigate whether this dynamic is true as states face the difficult decision of whether to escalate a military dispute to war. This is one of the most important transitions in conflict behavior, as wars involve

---

[1] Brands, 2016, p. 1.

[2] Brands (2016, p. 1–3) characterizes the British, West Germans, and French as highly concerned about MacArthur's control over atomic weapons, and even notes that India was worried enough to work as an intermediary between Communist China and the United States.

tremendous costs in human life and economic well-being. Does a state's reputation for being willing to go to war keep it safe from future wars? The answer is no: states that develop reputations for going to war are more likely to experience war in the future, even when we control for issues such as rivalry, regime type, and borders. At this most salient moment, when we think a reputation for being tough enough to go to war will propel us into some sort of compromise, the opponent is more likely to conclude that the willingness to go to war represents an inability to compromise. The result is an increased likelihood of war.

In the next section, I begin this investigation with a focus on the notion of rivalry and violent historical relationships between states. These relationships are worthy of our attention for two reasons. First, they serve as source material for other states as they perceive reputation. When two countries engage in repeated violent interactions, the rest of the world watches and learns from this behavior. Later on in this chapter I will weave these sources of information into a specific conflict-related version of the reputation model developed in Chapter 2. Second, when it comes to the empirical investigation of reputations and violence, it will be important to control for the presence of historical conflict within the direct interstate relationship. If two countries have fought multiple wars against one another, it makes little sense to blame the next one on reputational information. States that have developed direct historical relationships with one another are less reliant on reputational information when crafting their foreign policy with respect to one another.

After this background discussion, the chapter delves into the technical process of hypothesis testing. This portion might be a bit tedious for readers with less technical training, but the goal is to transparently design a set of empirical tests to evaluate the hypotheses emerging from this new theory of reputation and interstate behavior. I have designed the quantitative analyses to provide an abstract but systematic and externally valid assessment of my arguments. These analyses are a good complement to the historical discussions above. Together, these tests and the historical illustrations throughout the book and demonstrate the plausibility and applicability of this approach.

Reputation and Conflict in International Politics

The role of historical violence between nations in the incidence of militarized conflict is well established. The entire rivalry literature, for example, is built upon the premise that political interactions among nations should be studied as long temporal relationships where multiple conflicts cannot be considered independent from one another.[3] More generally, in work done with Andrew Enterline, I demonstrate that a history of violence between nations is a powerful predictor of future militarized disputes.[4] The argument is fairly intuitive: interstate conflict leaves an indelible mark on the nations involved, and these memories influence foreign policy decision-making in times of crisis. Further, recent research indicates that a reputation for violence, by which I mean indirect historical evidence of violence, may also impact the likelihood of interstate conflict.[5] Together, these two streams of information place crises and crisis behavior in macro-relational and historical contexts.

Historical and reputational contexts are especially salient to the concept of dispute escalation. In international crises, states must react quickly to unfolding events. To do so, they rely upon information obtained from prior interactions and extra-dyadic observation. This information provides a base of knowledge from which states draw when choosing strategies for confronting their crisis partner and anticipating reactions to those strategies.

I am primarily interested in how conflictual histories and reputations affect the propensity of states to resolve their disputes either through peaceful means or war. It is not obvious how the context of conflictual interactions and reputations translate into the willingness of states to negotiate a settlement or escalate to war. Previous research on the subject emphasizes competing logics, creating an unclear image of the relationship between a hostile reputation and the potential for dispute escalation. The Crisis Incompetence Hypothesis suggests that conflict is a signal to others that past crises may have been handled incompetently. As such, states who observe other states in conflict may conclude that they are overly aggressive or otherwise incompetent in times of crisis. Rather than concluding that these aggressive or incompetent states are too dangerous to be reckoned with, states develop an expectation that future crises will be handled as they were in the past and they plan accordingly.

As a result, conflict begets conflict. In other words, in the context of prior hostilities, pressures to escalate conflict outweigh pressures to reach peaceful settlement. In the following pages, I highlight competing pressures that states face in crisis management. I hold that states do, in fact, gain information from one another's historical interactions and reputations that are useful in

---

[3] Diehl and Goertz, 2001; Senese and Vasquez, 2003.

[4] Crescenzi and Enterline, 2001.

[5] Crescenzi, 2007.

resolving crises. Nevertheless, behavioral and reputational histories predicated on conflict create substantially greater pressures to anticipate violence and escalation—pressures that essentially outweigh the willingness of states to resolve their crises peacefully.

Information and Peaceful Settlement

The bargaining and signaling research literatures offer insights on the role of information availability and the potential for dispute onset and escalation. The initial assumption is that war is costly for all combatants, and, given the opportunity, states would prefer to settle disputes peacefully on satisfactory terms rather than invest their resources in an escalation to war for which they cannot know the outcome with certainty.[6] Information about each state's willingness to fight and their relative resolve to win is privately held. Furthermore, each state has an incentive to misrepresent this information in order to achieve more attractive settlement terms.[7] Thus, wars may result from these information asymmetries even when potential settlements exist that both states would prefer to conflict.

Information on an opponent's willingness and resolve is essential if nations are to avoid the costly gamble of war. It is here that rationalist explanations of war often emphasize the importance of audience costs. When states come into dispute, information about one another's preference for settlement or war is gained as the dispute escalates into a public contest, creating audience costs for each crisis participant. The attention of an influential domestic audience can be costly to state leaders, as decision makers may be punished for failed foreign policy. In this sense, the willingness (or reluctance) of decision makers to risk greater audience costs by escalating a crisis provides critical information about each crisis participant's willingness and resolve to escalate a crisis to war.[8] Thus, the more leverage domestic audiences have over the ability of decision makers to remain in office, the more informative (and costly) is the signal of crisis escalation.[9]

However, I argue that judging one another's sensitivity to audience costs is not the only way that states can learn about one another's resolve, willingness to escalate, and other private information. Dyadic interactions do not occur in a

---

[6] See Fearon, 1994, 1995; Schultz, 1998; Werner, 1999; Wagner, 2000.

[7] Fearon, 1995.

[8] Fearon, 1994.

[9] By this intuition, democratic states are more capable of sending credible signals to their crisis partners, since they are more sensitive to their domestic audiences than are decision makers in autocratic states.

vacuum, but rather in the context of historical relationships. States accumulate valuable information about one another through previous interactions and by observing one another's relationships with extra-dyadic states. In this sense, behavioral and reputational histories may act as a source of information from which each state can gain a better understanding of one another's willingness to escalate a dispute to war. Learning from prior interactions with a particular state, or observing its previous interactions with other states, provides important information with regard to the state's military capabilities, the credibility of its diplomatic signaling, and its resilience in pursuing its goals through military confrontation. Armed with this information, states may gain a better understanding of each other's bargaining ranges and reservation points. This knowledge subsequently produces opportunities for achieving peaceful negotiated settlements, as states become more capable of making offers of peaceful resolution that both prefer to war. Consequently, observed behavioral and reputational histories provide information that states can employ in attempting to avoid the costly gamble of war.

Pressures to Escalate

While hostile behavioral and reputational histories provide a wealth of information to states engaged in a dispute, I argue that these effects compete with concurrent pressures on states to escalate their crises to the level of full-blown war. I hold that the presence of conflictual dyadic interactions and extra-dyadic reputations will increase the likelihood of dispute escalation between states, overcoming the potential signaling and bargaining benefits disclosed by the information found in states' behavioral and reputational histories. Below, I discuss the dynamics of the escalation process in which state policymakers and selectorates create pressures toward war that overcome the informational benefits inherent in hostile histories.

Policymakers

As states build hostile behavioral and reputational histories, policymakers in these states come to view one another as enemies. Histories that are characterized by conflict create contexts within which states learn to expect future confrontation, generating pressures to escalate crises to war. Leng provides support for this proposition by arguing that policymakers in states embroiled in a crisis are guided by realpolitik-dominated belief systems.[10] In other words,

[10] Leng, 1983, 1988, 1993, 2000.

states are driven by power and interest, the goal of crisis bargaining is to win, and crisis participants distrust one another's intentions. Thus, decision makers believe that coercive bargaining strategies are their best option in attempting to achieve a successful outcome to the crisis bargaining process. Yet, these very strategies are those that are most likely to lead to conflict onset and escalation. Furthermore, belief systems determine the lessons that policymakers are likely to learn from past events. Since these realpolitik belief systems are highly resistant to change, policymakers learn to employ increasingly coercive bargaining strategies in future crises. More specifically, Leng holds that policymakers believe that international outcomes are a result of the policies that they employ. Policymakers thus learn to repeat successful policies in future crises, while discarding unsuccessful policies in favor of better options. Consistent with this logic, he finds that crisis participants learn from prior interactions by repeating coercive strategies that were successful in past crises, and adopting even more coercive strategies when previously employed coercive tactics prove unsuccessful.

Vasquez highlights a similar role for elites and decision makers in this process.[11] He argues that wars only result after a prolonged history of hostile and tense relations between states. Such a history of conflict increases the influence of hard-line policymakers who promote assertive and confrontational policies directed at the other crisis participant. Additionally, crisis participants become increasingly distrustful of one another's intentions. This leads to a mutual perception within the dyad of a mounting threat, thus making dispute escalation that much more likely. From this perspective, the information inherent in each state's behavioral and reputational history does little to produce opportunities for achieving a peaceful negotiated settlement. Instead, this information contributes to the tension and hostility present in the crisis.

Selectorate

In addition to the role of policymakers in generating increasingly coercive crisis bargaining strategies, a similar phenomenon is likely to manifest itself among the selectorate, be they the general public in more democratic states, or the ruling coalition in more authoritarian states. Previous research has uncovered the tendency of state selectorates to unify their focus on an external enemy when faced with a threat to the state's security.[12] In this sense, selectorates become

---

[11] Vasquez, 1993.

[12] See Coser (1956) for a discussion of group dynamics with regard to external threats, and see Mueller (1970), Kernell (1978), and Brody (1984) for a related discussion of the link between external security threats and the "rally around the flag" effect.

more cohesive in their orientation to the outside threat. Hostile histories are also likely to make the selectorate increasingly averse to compromise and peaceful negotiation with the other crisis participants. A history of disputes and violence created by an external threat challenges the selectorate's sense of national pride, strengthening its preference for military action.

Compromise and negotiation, on the other hand, are likely to be viewed as conciliatory and weak. This aversion to peaceful negotiation among the selectorate then translates into further pressure upon decision makers to pursue ever more coercive crisis bargaining strategies. This increases the possibility that policymaking officials become "locked in" to pursuing escalatory policies, as policymakers are obliged to satisfy the foreign policy interests of the selectorate in order to remain in office.[13]

Under these circumstances, a cycle of coercion results. In the context of behavioral and reputational histories characterized by conflict, policymakers learn from previous experience and extra-dyadic observation to use increasingly coercive strategies in managing crises with their crisis partner. In addition, the selectorate's preference for coercion increases the pressure on policymakers to defend their national pride by using coercive methods in managing the crisis. These pressures produce rising levels of coercion that are increasingly likely to culminate in war between the crisis participants. In this sense, pressures to escalate override the potential benefits of the information inherent in behavioral and reputational histories—benefits that might achieve a suitable, peaceful settlement.

Expectations: Applying the Reputational Learning Model to Empirical Models of Conflict Onset and Escalation

In conjunction with the reputation theory established in Chapter 3, this discussion suggests a set of conflict specific hypotheses to evaluate. The first two are based on the Crisis Incompetence Hypothesis, which argues that states that develop reputations for incompetence in times of crisis are more likely to

---

[13] See Bueno de Mesquita, Siverson, and Woller (1992) and Bueno de Mesquita and Siverson (1995) for a formal account of the relationship between the success or failure of a leader's foreign policy initiatives and her ability to remain in office. See also Dafoe and Caughey (2016) for an analysis of how honor and its preservation can push leaders into going to great lengths to demonstrate resolve, even at the risk of unnecessary violence.

experience future violence. Here I specifically examine the hypotheses that a reputation for using violence in past crises results in an increased likelihood of future militarized conflict with other states, as well as an increased likelihood that such disputes will escalate to war. Moreover, the Direct History Hypothesis suggests that as two states develop their own direct historical knowledge through crisis interactions over time, their reliance on this reputational information lessens. Therefore I expect in the following analysis that a reputation for violence will matter most when a dyad does not have a direct and violent behavioral history. Lastly, I expect reputations for conflict to fade over time (reflecting the Temporal Distance Hypothesis) and to be affected by the relational context from which reputations emerge (reflecting the Spatial Proxy Hypothesis). In other words, conflict and war are more likely when states have conflictual reputations with other nations similar to their dyadic partners.

In the following discussion I lay out a research design intended to empirically test these hypotheses. The behavioral hypotheses dealing with reputation as it affects conflict and the escalation to war, as well as the interaction with direct conflict histories, will be easiest to examine directly, using statistical analysis. The last two hypotheses, concerning temporal and proxy dimensions, are examined indirectly, through the operationalization of the concept of a reputation for violence in world politics.

There are two concepts that are key to applying the reputational learning model to the question of whether reputations affect conflict and war. The third concept requiring explanation is the notion of a behavioral, direct history between the two states that form a dyad. Here I borrow directly from my work with Enterline (2001), particularly our dynamic, conceptual model of interstate interaction. This model defines the behavioral historical relationship between two countries as an evolution of information involving change motivated by shocks and decay. Interstate interactions inform the historical relationship both in conflictual and cooperative directions, and the lack of interaction degrades this information over time. In the absence of activity, the behavioral history between two states is defined as neutrality. The occurrence of conflict shocks this relationship negatively, but the effects of this shock diminish over time. Similar shocks can occur as a result of cooperation. Together, these shocks and the information decay process provide a behavioral historical context within which two states operate.

The fourth and last major concept, *reputation*, is the most subtle. At the heart of this concept is the idea that states observe each other behaving outside their direct dyadic experience. For example, North Korea observes the United

States' behavior toward Iraq, and uses this behavior to inform its direct dyadic relationship with the United States. In effect, Iraq serves as a proxy for North Korea, and there are as many proxies available as there are states in the system outside the immediate dyad. Some proxies are more useful than others, and this utility is driven by similarities between the principal and proxy (North Korea and Iraq) along dimensions such as power and interest. Thus, North Korea assembles a reputational history for the United States that is both dynamic over time and specific to North Korea. A more specific formulation of this reputational history is laid out in the section that follows.

Step One: Modeling Dyadic Conflict History

The first step in modeling conflict reputation is to specify the way in which states develop a dyadic history of conflict behavior. This requires us to view the dyadic behavior as a process over time, embedded in time. The theory laid out in the last chapter provides a foundation for this specific dimension of reputation. Overall, the model follows a process of growth and decay. The occurrence of conflict between states forms a behavioral history, and inaction over time causes that information to decay or fade. When considered in relational pairs, or dyads, we can assign characteristics to these two states within the dyad. Dyads can also be characterized by their two directed components. As such, J's historical behavior toward I can be different than I's historical behavior toward J. Here the focus is on the history of conflict for any two states I and J. Let ρ_{jit} represents J's conflict history at time t with state I.[14] This history, illustrated in Figure 4.1, occurs throughout the population of pairs of states in the system.

Recalling the equation for direct behavioral history that was crafted in Chapter 2, we can formalize this concept thusly:

$$\rho_{jit} = (e^{-\left(\frac{\tau}{\sigma}\right)})\rho_{ji(t-1)} + \left(\frac{\upsilon}{\tau}\right) - \left(\frac{\omega}{\tau}\right). \qquad (4.1)$$

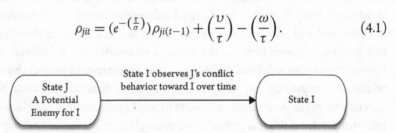

Figure 4.1 The Directed Conflict History: State J's Conflict Behavior Toward State I.

---

[14] I use ρ here consistently with equation 2.1 in Chapter 2.

Here, τ is the amount of time that has past since the last conflict behavior was observed, σ captures the amount of activity that accumulates over time, υ represents the occurrence of new cooperation between J and I, and ω identifies the occurrence of new violence between J and I at time t. The exponential decay model is accelerated by τ, which means the conflict history becomes less informative as time passes without new conflict events. At the same time, information decay slows down as σ increases. This reflects the assumption that a state's historical policy choices have a cumulative impact, and as more and more events take place this history and its memory become closer to permanent. Finally, τ diminishes the impact of the shocks of new violence. This reflects the assumption that events that occur regularly are more informative than events that are infrequent (and thus potentially interpreted as random or mistakes). Time passing without violence may not indicate a real deterioration in enmity, of course, as there are deeper or structural sources of conflict and enmity not represented in this model. Ultimately, I assume that states, their leader and populations approximate perceptions of enmity based on historical behavior. The alternative approach is to assume a constant rate of decay for all states across time, or to eliminate the decay of historical information altogether. Neither alternative offers the richness of this set of assumptions. For simplicity, I bound this function between 1 (J is perfectly in alignment with I, fully cooperative) and -1 (perfect enemies), with 0 representing no information (or a perfect mix of information that cancels itself out) for the $\overrightarrow{JI}$ dyadic conflict relationship.[15]

This formalization of the process simply allows the reader to see that the direct conflict history concept has three qualities. First, it represents the behavioral changes that occur between the states in a dyad. This is a model that privileges action over speech. Second, it is dynamic over time, both in how these new changes translate into historical information and in how inaction matters. Third, the combination of behavior and context combine to create one measure of the direct history within the dyad.

Step Two: Modeling Conflict Reputation

While the direct history between any two states is captured by the previous concept, how do we represent reputation as an indirect, vicarious learning source of information that is constructed by information existing outside the dyad? Figure 4.2 illustrates how states do not limit their evaluations to the direct dyadic

---

[15] See Crescenzi, Enterline, and S. B. Long (2008) for a detailed discussion of the structure of this model as well as the bounding function.

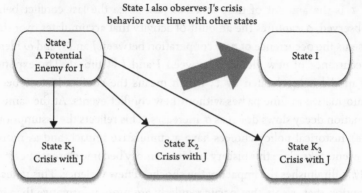

Figure 4.2 Observing a Potential Enemy's Historical Record Toward Others.

history with a potential enemy. Rather, they are able to evaluate the historical behavior of that state toward other states in the system. Figure 4.2 shows three other states as an illustration, but when a government evaluates a potential enemy it considers *all* of that state's dyadic interactions with others.

To model this generic process, think of state I as a security seeker and J as its potential enemy in a population of states (N). To maximize generality, I assume the pool of potential enemies is every state in the international system. Let the other states in the system be labeled K states. In addition to observing J's historical behavior toward I, state I is able to observe J's conflict behavior with the other states in the system, which contributes to J's reputation for using violence. I label this conflict reputation information ψ_{ijt}, which suggests that J's reputation is relative (in the eyes of the beholder, which in this case is I).[16] Indeed, J's reputation is contextual to the way I processes J's conflict histories with the other states in the system. State I learns of J's reputation for violence by observing J's interactions with all other K states in the system.

The process of observing J's conflict reputation has two important components. First, recall that reputation is in the eye of the beholder, meaning that state I will filter J's behavior through its own lens to evaluate previous behavior. Here the quality of the proxy state (state K) becomes important. If state K is similar to I and thus a good proxy for I with which to evaluate J, and state J has a history of violence with K, this translates to a conflictual reputation in the eyes of state I.

[16] ψ is used as the load combination factor in structural engineering, so perhaps it is a good fit here as well.

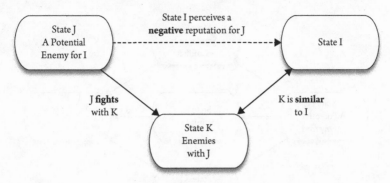

Figure 4.3 Negative Conflict Reputation.

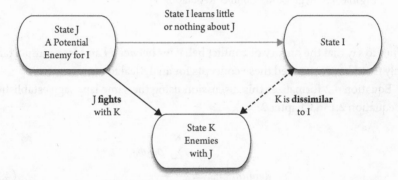

Figure 4.4 Poor Proxy for Conflict Reputation.

Figure 4.3 illustrates this learning process. If, however, K is a bad proxy for I, the information is far less valuable (as illustrated in Figure 4.4).

The second component of modeling this reputation tackles the issue of how to represent how a government aggregates all this information. To keep the model as simple as possible, I assume that any weighting of the information has already occurred when state I determines to what extent each K state is a good proxy from which to learn. Figure 4.5 illustrates this aggregation of information. If ρ_{jkt} represents state J's historical conflict history in each $\overrightarrow{JK}$ dyad, at its most basic, *Reputation*$_{ijt}$ is simply an aggregation of the set of ρ conflict histories at time t that state J has with all the states in the system that are *not I*. It is important to note that the direct history between I and J does not contribute to I's perception of J's *external reputation* for being a historically violent state. That

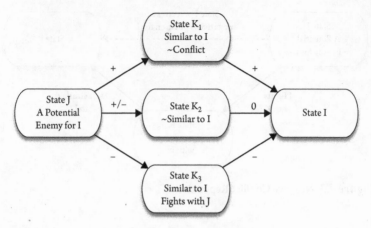

Figure 4.5 Aggregating Conflict Reputation Types.

is not to say that the history of conflict behavior between *I* and *J* is unimportant, only that I have separated these concepts for analytical focus.

Equation 4.2 formalizes this discussion using the same language established in equation 2.1 in Chapter 2:

$$Reputation_{ijt} = \frac{\sum\limits_{k \neq i,j}^{N} \rho_{jkt}\phi_{ikt}}{N-2} \tag{4.2}$$

where N is the size of the system

   ρ_{jkt} is a vector direct conflict history information between j and k at $t, \rho_{jkt} \in (-1, 1)$,

   ϕ_{ikt} is a vector of similarity between i and k at $t, \phi_{ikt} \in (0, 1)$.

Analysis: Does Conflict Reputation Influence Future Violence?

The formalization of these concepts is important because it allows the analysis of reputation and conflict to be grounded in empirical specificity. Reputation is such a complex collection of characteristics and assumptions, meaning many different things to different scholars even within the field of conflict processes. The specific models enable the reader to process how my vision of reputation dynamics jibes with their own.

It is time to return to the original question of how reputation matters. Specifically, does a reputation for using force in past crises affect the likelihood of future conflict, or escalation of conflict to war? To answer these questions, I use a quantitative analysis of a large sample of dyads over time. Large-n analyses, such as those featured in this chapter and the next, are a good way to evaluate hypotheses while maximizing the external validity of the analysis. These benefits come at the price of an abstract treatment of reputation along with the other covariates in the analysis. Hopefully the historical illustrations found elsewhere in the book help ameliorate these drawbacks, and the book as a whole presents a complete evaluation of the role of reputation in world politics.

To analyze the conflict-specific version of the hypotheses from Chapter 3 as laid out above, the next step is to get specific about operationalizing the concepts of reputation and direct conflict history into variables. I then identify and operationalize a set of additional phenomena that influence conflict and war onset to operate as control variables to improve the validity of the analysis without losing the ability to parse out the role of reputation. I then specify the research design and present the findings of the quantitative analyses. For readers that are unfamiliar with these techniques, the essential findings of the analyses are visually represented in the pages that follow.

Operationalizing the Dependent Variables: The Onset of Conflict and the Escalation to War

The two related yet distinct phenomena of militarized conflict and war, are worth identifying clearly at this point, with respect to the analysis that follows. Even though I seek a partial explanation of these phenomena, clear concepts and measurement are appropriate. By partial explanation, I simply mean that I do not attempt here to provide a comprehensive analysis of why states fight. Instead, I endeavor to focus in on the role of reputation, controlling only for the covariates that one would logically expect to interfere with the inference process.

I employ two different samples of the population of dyads in the international system. The first version includes all possible dyads, for the period of 1817 to 2000. The second sample is spatially limited and includes only politically-relevant dyads, 1817 to 2000. This sample allows me to investigate whether my results hold for the most politically active sample of dyads in the system. This two-pronged approach allows me to test the hypothesis that any given result is driven by dyad selection by political relevance and maximizes my ability to compare my results with those of other studies in the literature.

The first phenomenon, militarized conflict, is represented in this analysis using is a discrete variable that captures the onset of a Militarized Interstate Dispute, as measured in Maoz's Dyadic Militarized Interstate Dispute data set.[17] Given the nature of the survival models, dyad-years with ongoing disputes are dropped from the data set.[18] The variable does not discriminate according to the level of hostility incurred during a dispute.[19]

With respect to the concept of war, most of us have an intuitive understanding of this rarest form of conflict, and it is typically operationalized as militarized conflict involving a large number of battle deaths. Here, I am concerned with the factors that lead states to engage in wars generally, and I distinguish between war and the broader concepts of conflict, such as disputes and crises. I do not address the characteristics of severity, intensity, or duration of war in this chapter, although it may be useful to do so in the future. Thus, the dependent variable in this second focus on war is the initiation of an interstate war as measured in Maoz's Dyadic Militarized Interstate Dispute data set.[20] If the dyad in question experiences war at the time in question, this discrete variable takes on a value of 1. At all other times, its value is 0. Wars are defined by the COW project as militarized conflict involving at least 1000 military battle deaths in a calendar year.

Key Independent Variables

With these dependent variables identified, the next step is to specify the variables that will represent state reputation and the direct conflict history within the dyad. I am interested in two key independent variables: one to represent the concept of *reputational history*, and a second to represent the concept of *direct conflictual history* within the dyad. These are the variables that ultimately allow me to test the hypotheses.

---

[17] D. M. Jones, Bremer, and Singer, 1996; Maoz, 1999.

[18] Running the models on data with these dyad years included produces results that are similar in sign and significance.

[19] Russett and Oneal, 2001.

[20] Maoz, 1999.

Operationalizing Reputational History

I operationalize the notion of reputational history into the Reputation variable using my (2007) Relational Interdependence model. This is a model in which states learn about their dyadic partners by observing their behavior outside of the dyad and by judging the relevance of that behavior to their own situation.[21] If state i and state j are the two members of a dyad, this learning model posits that in an environment of incomplete information about other states' intentions, resolve, and other traits, i can learn about its dyadic partner, j, by observing j's interactions with k states outside of the ij dyad and by weighting that information by some relevance criteria. The Reputation variable incorporates three components to represent these streams of information available to states as they try to learn about their interaction partners:

$$Reputation_{ijN} = \frac{\sum_{k \neq i,j}^{N} IIS_{jk} S_{ik} C_{ik}}{N-2} \qquad (4.3)$$

where IIS captures the direct history for the jk dyad, the historical relationship between states j and k. I measure this IIS component using the Interstate Interaction Score,[22] modified to include changes in joint IGO membership as an indicator of cooperative behavior.[23] This measure quantifies the overall tenor of the relationship between j and k, incorporating information about both conflictual and cooperative past interactions. The International Interaction Score (IIS) has a potential range of -1 (maximum historical hostility) to 1 (maximum historical cooperation) and an actual range of -0.94 to 0.42.

The next component, S, is the S-Similarity Score. This component speaks to the relevance of the interactions that i observes between j and k. I measure this using Signorino and Ritter's (1999) S-Similarity Score, which ranges from 1 (completely similar foreign policy portfolios) to -1 (completely opposite foreign policy portfolios).

The final component, ψ_{ikt}, is the power similarity between i and j at time t. This component also speaks to the relevance of the interactions that i observes

---

[21] The description presented here is necessarily brief. For a complete description of the construction and theoretical rationale behind this learning model, see Crescenzi (2007).

[22] Crescenzi and Enterline, 2001.

[23] Crescenzi, Enterline, and Long, 2008.

between j and k. I measure this as $1 - |CINC_i - CINC_k|$, the result of which ranges from 0 to 1, with 1 representing perfect power similarity and 0 representing perfect power dissimilarity. Thus, as k is more similar to i in terms of power, it is a more valuable source of information for i.

The product of these three components, controlling for system size, produces the Reputation variable. Updating occurs at every time period, which in this case is every year.[24] Note that this score is directional, so I take the smaller of the two directional dyadic scores to represent the non-directional score for the dyad. The Reputation variable ranges theoretically from -1 to 1, but in this analysis the actual range is -0.28 to 0.02.

Operationalizing Direct Dyadic History

The second key independent variable of interest in this study is the Direct Conflict History, which operationalizes the concept of a direct dyadic behavioral history. This variable is identical to the Interstate Interaction Score created by Crescenzi and Enterline (2001), and as such it represents the overall tone of a dyadic relationship, here between i and j. Note that this is also a component in the reputation variable, but the direct history score used in the creation of the reputation score represents the relationship between j and k, where all k states are extra-dyadic state. Since I also posit that the direct historical interactions between dyadic partners affect the probability of war onset, I must include a measure of their relationship that is separate from the reputation variable. As noted above, the direct history variable includes information about both past conflict and cooperation between the states in the dyad. Conflictual information is drawn from the Militarized Interstate Disputes data set[25] using a model that incorporates information about the frequency and hostility levels of militarized disputes, decaying over time towards zero influence.[26] Cooperative information is drawn from data on changes in joint IGO membership derived from version 2.1 of the International Governmental Organization data set.[27] As stated above, the actual range of values for the IIS is -0.94 to 0.42.

---

[24] For simplicity of presentation, I have removed the t subscript indicating that the reputation score is updated in each time period.

[25] Jones, Bremer, and Singer, 1996.

[26] See Crescenzi and Enterline (2001) for a more detailed description of the conflict side of the Interstate Interaction Score (the Conflict Interaction Level).

[27] Pevehouse, Nordstrom, and Warnke, 2004.

Additional Independent Variables

A model that includes only these two independent variables runs the risk of attributing causality to variables that have no such influence, or equally dangerous, of failing to show causality where it exists. Only in the context of a set of control variables widely accepted as causes of war onset can I parse out the individual effects of the key independent variables. I employ a set of controls representing some of the most widely confirmed results in the literature on the causes of conflict and war onset, which I describe briefly below.

Contiguity is measured here by Contiguous States, which is a discrete variable that takes on a value of 1 if the states in the dyad have a COW contiguity level of less than 5, meaning that they are contiguous by land or by up to 150 miles of water. If they are non-contiguous or contiguous by more than 150 miles of water, it takes on a value of 0. The second and third control variables, Both Major Powers and Both Minor Powers, represent the power relationship between the states in the dyad. I only include joint major powers in the war analysis, to balance between too many control variables and the desire to replicate the basic models others have crafted in their research.[28] If both have major power status according to the Correlates of War project, Both Major Powers takes on a value of 1 (rather than 0), while if both are minor powers, Both Minor Powers equals 1 (rather than 0).[29]

The remaining control variables address the effects of regime type and alliance similarity. The Minimum Democracy Level variable provides the minimum *polity* score within the dyad and as such it represents the minimum level of domestic constraint present in the dyad.[30,31] I use the Polity IV data for this measure. See Marshall and Jaggers (2000) for details. Finally, the Alliance Similarities variable is the Signorino and Ritter (1999) S-Similarity Score representing foreign policy similarity. This variable controls for the possibility that direct foreign policy similarities and the interactions that these similarities represent are correlated with conflict or war onset and direct and reputational history within the dyad.

---

[28] See Senese and Vasquez, 2003.

[29] I prefer setting up these variables as categorical identifiers, rather than measuring the power differential continuously, but alternative specifications yield similar results.

[30] See Oneal, Russett, and Berbaum, 2003.

[31] Note that the "polity" variable is the result of subtracting each state's "autoc" score from its "democ" score, a widely-adopted but imperfect practice for scholars using the Polity data.

Method

For each set of analyses below, the primary method of investigation is a semi-parametric Cox event-history model, which is used to test the hypotheses. As with all event-history analysis, the focus here is on modeling the hazard rate of an event. In this case, the event, or hazard, is the onset of a militarized dispute. Event history models help us understand the factors that hasten or delay such events.

The Cox model is adept at assessing rare events, such as the incidence of militarized conflict or the onset of war. Recently, the Cox model has emerged as a tool of choice when using event history models, due to its parsimonious demands and flexibility handling time-varying covariates (Box-Steffensmeier and B. S. Jones, 1997). Because it requires fewer assumptions than its cousins (such as Weibull models), it is a useful and robust choice when we do not have expectations of duration dependence (in this case, the notion that the hazard of dispute onset will grow larger or smaller as a function of the age of the dyad). For example, I tested the models examining the onset of war for violations of the proportional hazards assumption using Schoenfeld residuals and found that while several variables appear to violate the assumption, the reputation variable does not. When I interacted each variable with the natural log of the year variable and added those interactions to the models individually, the model remained generally stable. While the addition of each interaction tended to inflate the coefficient for the original variable and sometimes change its significance or sign, the other variables in the model retained their sign, significance, and coefficient magnitude with very few exceptions.

Like all model options, the basic hazard analysis of war that is accomplished by using the Cox model is an imperfect research design for the question of escalation to war. Specifically, previous research has shown that both the key independent variables, as well as the control variables, have an impact on the onset of militarized disputes (a broader, less severe definition of conflict among nations).[32] Without controlling for the factors that influence only the selection into the first stage of conflict (disputes), I run the risk of attributing these influences mistakenly or in overstated fashion to the onset of war. Previous studies of escalation to war.[33] However, the models used to address this possible

[32] Crescenzi, 2007.

[33] Reed (2000) and Kinsella and Russett (2002) have used statistical techniques that account for the possibility that war onset results are biased if the causes of war onset are related to the causes of militarized interstate dispute initiation. The selection model they employ is designed to address problems associated with logistic regression, not event history analyses such as the one estimated

selection bias have come under increasing criticism for their instability, and my own application of such models found no evidence of selection bias; a finding that is in line with the results of Senese and Vasquez's research on war (2003).

Beyond the use of survival models, I re-estimate the full models in each analysis using probit models as a robustness check, and to aid in the visual presentation of the substantive impact of reputation on conflict and war. While probit models and survival models have important similarities, they are also different enough to each have their own strengths and weaknesses. The analyses below are always qualitatively consistent, especially with respect to the Reputation and Direct Conflict History variables, providing confidence in the overall venture. Probit model results are also easier to visualize, which helps convey the essential quality of the findings herein.

Results

Cox Event History Analysis of Reputation and the Onset of Conflict

The results of the initial hazard analysis are reported in Table 4.1. Model 1 simply assesses the null model, which establishes a baseline without the inclusion of reputation in the analysis. on the likelihood of dispute onset across all possible dyads from 1817–2000. Model 2 provides a stark analysis using just the Reputation variable. The coefficient estimate for Reputation is negative and statistically significant, indicating that conflict is more likely when reputation decreases (J has hostile ties with countries similar to I) and less likely when reputation becomes more positive. Model 3 presents a more thorough test, as it includes the control variables into the analysis (again, all dyads, 1817–2000). Even with this inclusion of alternative explanations for the incidence of disputes, the reputation variable has a negative, statistically significant coefficient.

Figure 4.6 visually demonstrates the impact of the Reputation variable on the "survival" of dyads, where survival means the dyad does not experience the onset of a militarized dispute. The graph contains two lines consisting of the predicted survival rates across time. These graphs are produced using the coefficient estimates from Model 3 in Table 4.1. The solid line reflects the survival rate predicted for dyads when at least one state in the dyad has a reputation for using force with other states. The dashed line reflects the predicted

---

in Table 4.2 below. It is unknown to what extent selection problems affect the estimates produced by event history analysis, and I am unaware of a model that allows for event history analysis with selection that can handle time-varying covariates. See Boehmke, Morey, and Shannon, 2004.

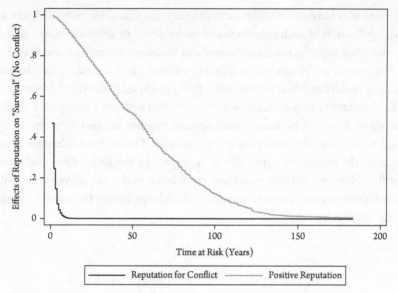

Figure 4.6 The Impact of Reputation on Conflict Onset.

survival rate for dyads when the states have more positive reputations (meaning they avoid conflict with others). Dyads with negative (conflictual) reputations are consistently more vulnerable to disputes than dyads that have neutral or positive (cooperative) reputations. The summary interpretation of Table 4.1 and Figure 4.6 is the conflict specific version of the crisis incompetence hypothesis is supported: dyads with conflictual reputations are at a higher risk for militarized dispute onset.

One drawback to the Cox model is that it assumes all the covariates influence the hazard of conflict consistently across time. This proportional hazards assumption is difficult to maintain over long periods of time (1817-2000 being no exception here). All of the independent variables in Model 3 of Table 4.1 violate this assumption (except *Alliance*). Two additional sets of analyses are used to compensate for the existence of nonproportional hazards. First, note that I treat the key independent variables, Reputation and Conflict History, as time-varying covariates to control for this problem. The results are consistent with or without this model specification. Second, I have re-run Model 3 from 4.1, with each covariate interacted with time to correct for non-proportional hazards (Cleves, Gould, and Gutierrez, 2002).[34] Due to the large proportion of covariates

---

[34] The new variables were generated by interacting the independent variables with the natural log of time.

Table 4.1 **A Survival Analysis of Dispute Onset**

Variable	Model 1 *1817–2000*	Model 2 *1817–2000*	Model 3 *1817–2000*
Reputation		−21.425***	−14.397***
		(1.095)	(2.344)
Direct Conflict History	−3.865***		−4.224***
	(0.217)		(0.220)
Reputation*Direct History			−28.578***
			(4.612)
Contiguous States	2.760***		2.716***
	(0.142)		(0.142)
Both Minor Powers	−1.339***		−1.294***
	(0.128)		(0.127)
Capability Ratio (logged)	−0.113**		−0.121***
	(0.035)		(0.033)
Minimum Democracy Level	−0.003**		−0.003**
	(0.001)		(0.001)
Alliance Similarities (S-Score	0.169		0.101
	(0.296)		(0.293)
Reputation*time(logged)		0.118***	0.023
		(0.013)	(0.024)
Direct History*time(logged)	0.023***		0.020***
	(0.003)		(0.004)
Observations (time at risk)	586,673	660,830	586,673
Failures	1,998	2,386	1,998
Log likelihood	−13,184	−19,616	−13,059
AIC	26,382	39,236	26,138
χ^2 (Wald)	3,400***	452***	4,372***

Coefficients are presented in log-relative hazard format.
Robust std. errors adjusted for clustering on dyad in ( ).
*** = significant at the .001 level, ** = .01, * = .05.

that violate the proportional hazard assumption, I have also estimated one
time-interacted covariate at a time. Including all of the time-interactions at once
runs the risk of imposing multicollinearity in the model. Adding one interacted
variable at a time is a common procedure for coping with nonproportional

hazards (Cleves, Gould, and Gutierrez, 2002, see Ch.11). The results are not reported here, but they are consistent with the results in Table 4.1.

To fully evaluate the hypothesis that reputation matters most when the direct conflict history is absent, I interact Reputation and Direct Conflict History. As such, a complete interpretation of the results is best done visually. Figures 4.7 and 4.8 jointly provide a robust interpretation of the impact of reputation on conflict. To create these figures, I re-estimate Model 3 from the table above using a probit model specification; I then use the results to visualize the substantive impact of reputation including the interaction effects with a direct conflict history. In Figure 4.7 I illustrate the impact of reputation on conflict in two scenarios. In the first scenario the two states in the dyad already have an established history of violence, as illustrated with the solid line and the dark grey shading. In this scenario, reputation does not impact the probability of conflict onset. In the second scenario the two states have no direct conflict history, as illustrated with the dashed line and the lighter grey shading. In this scenario reputation matters quite a bit, with a conflictual reputation for either state generating significantly higher probabilities of conflict onset.

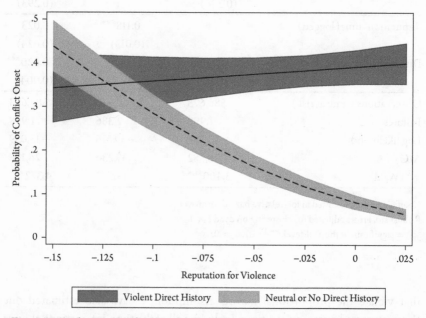

Figure 4.7 The Impact of Reputation on Conflict Onset With and Without Direct Conflict Histories.

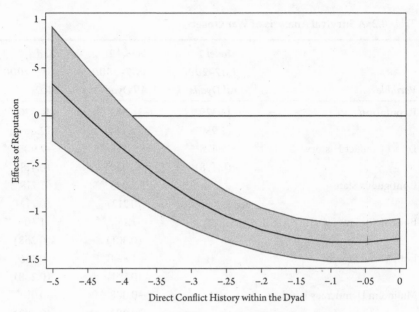

Figure 4.8 Reputation's Effect on Conflict Onset Relative to Direct Conflict History.

Figure 4.8 provides another view of the same analysis, this time examining the effect of reputation on violence across a wide range of scores for the direct conflict history variable. Again, the effect of reputation is greatest when the states in a dyad do not have a strong direct conflict history. This makes perfect sense, and is in line with the fundamental characterization of reputation as information that is used as a substitute for direct interaction. Combined with the survival analysis above, these visualizations present a compelling picture that a state with a reputation for using violence is more likely to experience militarized violence in the future. Conflict begets conflict—even if that conflict comes from other contexts and other dyadic ties.

Cox Event History Analysis of Reputation and Escalation to War

The next set of analyses focuses on the rare but important phenomenon of interstate war. The previous analysis established that reputations can make conflict more likely, but do these reputations also exacerbate the chances of war? Table 4.2 presents the results of the Cox event history analysis of three model specifications to help answer this question. In Model 1, I examine the impact of the two key independent variables on the probability of war onset for all possible

Table 4.2 **A Survival Analysis of War Onset**

Variable	Model 1 1817–2000 All Dyads	Model 2 1817–2000 All Dyads	Model 3 1817–2000[1] PRDs
Reputation	−14.329***	−16.873***	−14.330***
	(2.959)	(2.244)	(2.260)
Direct Conflict History	−5.478***	−3.598***	−2.903***
	(0.478)	(0.428)	(0.418)
Contiguous States		2.045***	1.218***
		(0.212)	(0.219)
Both Major Powers		1.152***	1.406***
		(0.301)	(0.268)
Both Minor Powers		−1.824***	−0.456
		(0.184)	(0.268)
Minimum Democracy Level		−0.008***	−0.010***
		(0.002)	(0.002)
Alliance Similarities (S-Score)		−0.237	−0.499
		(0.355)	(0.364)
Reputation*time(logged)	0.062	0.082*	0.053
	(0.042)	(0.037)	(0.037)
Direct History*time(logged)	0.033***	0.027***	0.017*
	(0.009)	(0.008)	(0.007)
Observations (time at risk)	634,374	639,599	89,219
Failures	275	271	231
Log likelihood	−2,128	−1,825	−1,356
AIC	4,264	3,669	2,730
χ^2 (Wald)	792***	1,446***	470***

Coefficients are presented in log-relative hazard format.
Standard errors adjusted for clustering on dyad in ( ).
*** = significant at the .001 level, ** = .01, * = .1.

dyads between 1817 and 2000. As predicted, the coefficient for reputation is negative and statistically significant at the 0.001 level, meaning that the onset of a war between *i* and *j* is more likely when *j* has hostile historical relationships with countries similar to *i*. War onset is less likely when *j* has cooperative historical relationships with countries similar to *i*. Also as predicted, war onset is more likely when *i* and *j* have a direct history of hostile interactions, but less likely when they have a direct history of cooperative interactions. This finding is also statistically significant (at the 0.001 level).

In Model 2, I estimate a more complete model specification that includes the control variables described above. If the apparent roles of reputation, direct historical interactions, or their interaction are caused by other unmeasured, but possibly correlated, factors, the addition of these variables should remove the appearance of causality. Even controlling for contiguity, relative power, and the effect of regime type, the findings remain statistically significant, and in the expected directions. Both of the key independent variables remain statistically significant, are of magnitudes similar to Model 1, and retain their expected signs.

Are these results a product of the sample selection (that is, all possible dyads)? Some scholars have suggested that a more appropriate research design considers only cases in which dyads are politically relevant, or connected by proximity or major power ties. This dramatically reduces the *n* available to researchers, but may also reduce the risk of attributing peaceful relations to states that simply have no opportunity to engage in conflict, such as small powers separated by large geographic distances. As a robustness check, in Model 3 I re-estimate the full model using only politically relevant dyads (PRDs) as its sample of cases.[35] The central results do not appear to be a result of sample selection, as they remain statistically significant and retain their expected signs. The use of PRDs has mild effects on the control variables, with democracy losing some statistical significance and joint minor-power status approaching insignificance, but these effects could be the result of the drop in observations between Model 2 and Model 3 (from 615,040 to 85,675).

Turning back to the coefficients in Table 4.2, it is clear that Model 2 also provides confirmation of much of the conventional wisdom regarding other causes of war. The results suggest that states that are contiguous are more likely to go to war with each other, as are pairs of major powers, while democracies and pairs of minor powers are less likely to go to war with each other. In other words, this appears to be a stable, consistent platform to evaluate the effects of reputation on war.

Figure 4.9 provides a visual interpretation of the results in Model 2 of Table 1 as they pertain to the reputations among, and direct history between,

[35] Maoz and Russett, 1993.

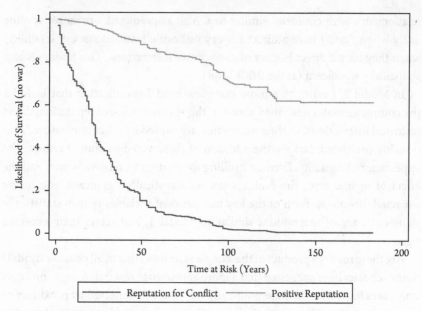

Figure 4.9 The Impact of Conflictual versus Positive Reputation on Escalation to War.

states at the dyadic level. In this illustration, I create survival curves for two reputation scenarios. The solid line represents the likelihood of "survival" over time for the dyad when at least one state has a reputation for using violence. Again, survival here means that the dyad does not experience war. The dashed line represents the survival likelihood for a dyad where neither state has a hostile reputation. Visually it is clear that a reputation for past violence has a significant substantive impact on the ability of states to avoid war. I always caution the reader against placing too much emphasis on the exact predicted survival rates that come out of the Cox model (or any model, for that matter). It is important to remember that these predictions are based on the variables included in Model 2, and the data sample used in the research design. Changes to either dimension of the analysis can yield predictions that are quantitatively, but hopefully not qualitatively, different. As such, I suggest the reader view the information in Figure 4.9 as a rough qualitative assessment. That said, the survival function in Figure 4.9 shows that for cases when the reputational history is negative, the cumulative hazard of war over time is significantly higher than the hazard for cases in which the reputational history is either zero or positive. Overall, these results demonstrate that a conflictual (negative)

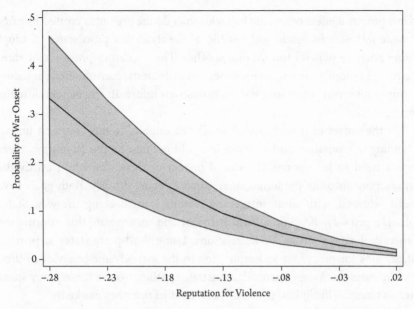

Figure 4.10 The Impact of Reputation on Escalation to War: Probability of War.

reputation within a dyad increases the likelihood that the pair of states will end up fighting a war.

Figure 4.10 provides another look at the substantive effects of reputation on war. For this illustration I use a probit version of the full model of war onset for ease of exposition. The graph allows the reader to see the change in the overall likelihood of war occurring across a range of values for the reputation variable. The solid line in the middle is the predicted probability of war, and the grey area around the line represents a 95 percent confidence interval. As expected, the likelihood of war occurring when at least one state in the dyad has a reputation for using violence is significantly higher than when neither state has a conflictual past. Just as in the analysis of conflict onset, the results in this analysis consistently point to the realization that a reputation for using force in the past makes war more likely, not less.

These results suggest that as states learn from the behavior of their dyadic partner with other states similar to themselves, and as they interact with their dyadic partner directly over time, these interactions create pressures to enter into war, overriding any learning process conducive to peace. Historical interactions inside and outside of the dyad reveal important information about states' intentions, capabilities, and resolve. This information, however, seems to have a less powerful effect on dyadic behavior than do the pressures created by prior hostile interactions inside and outside of the dyad that push states to adopt more coercive policies toward one another. The escalatory pressures of elites learning to adopt more coercive policies and of domestic constituencies equating compromise with policy failure seem to push any informational benefits into the background.

At the outset of this chapter, I sought to establish a more explicit understanding of reputation and violence in world politics. At the same time, there was a need to incorporate the causal impact of this information on dyadic interactions into the predominant research designs of today. Both goals have been achieved, with some interesting lessons learned along the way. States observe extra-dyadic, reputational behavior and incorporate this information when dealing with intra-dyadic relations. Using third-party states as proxies, states look for precedent and reputation in the extra-dyadic behavior of their dyadic partners. As opponents demonstrate hostility toward these proxy states across time, the likelihood of intra-dyadic conflict increases markedly.

This research demonstrates the importance of reputation in the study of international conflict. It also demonstrates the portability of the measure derived from the model, and the accessibility to scholars in the field. The development of this model leads to many new (and renewed) research questions concerning international conflict. Does direct experiential learning outweigh vicarious experiential learning? Do states focus only on congruent foreign policies when identifying useful proxy states to learn from, or does Heider's "the enemy of my enemy is my friend" dimension hold? Given that this vicarious experiential learning influences state decisions to engage in militarized disputes, does it affect the decision to escalate to war?

The broader empirical results suggest that the presence and relevance of reputation (and more broadly, spatial interdependence) to the dependent variable does not necessarily indicate problems of omitted variable bias or other econometric woes. Incorporating the reputation model into standard empirical research on the onset of militarized disputes did not significantly alter the previously established roles of phenomena such as the democratic peace. Instead, the empirical research conducted here suggests that spatial interdependence is an important part of a state's decision calculus regarding conflict, but it is not the only player. Nor does it overlap significantly with other dimensions of this calculus. Its influence on the onset of conflict is unique, and by explicitly modeling it new progress has been made towards a full understanding of what causes conflict to occur.

Conclusion

The basic premise of this chapter is that states learn about their dyadic partners' propensity for violence through observation and experience. I argue that states build behavioral and reputational histories over time, and these traits provide important information with regard to each state's tendency to resolve their disputes through peaceful or violent means. This information is particularly important during times of interstate crisis, as states must make educated decisions and respond promptly to crisis developments. States translate the information inherent in behavioral and reputational histories through a learning process that affects state behavior and consequently affects international outcomes.

The bargaining and signaling literatures[36] give us reason to believe that behavioral and reputational histories characterized by conflict can in fact provide valuable information to states that help them avoid crisis escalation and settle disputes peacefully. Since rationalist explanations emphasize the importance of informational asymmetries to explain war occurrence, one could argue that the information inherent in states' behavioral and reputational histories provide states with a better understanding of each other's preferences and reservations. Such knowledge may produce opportunities for crisis partners to find and agree to diplomatic solutions that both prefer to war, as behavioral and reputational histories reveal otherwise private information.

The possibility that historical interactions reveal information that can help states avoid conflict suggests that states can learn in a way that is conducive to peaceful interactions. Unfortunately, these effects appear to be overpowered by pressures that force states to move into higher and higher levels of escalation, leading eventually to the onset of interstate war. The results indicate that the informational benefits of states' hostile behavioral and reputational histories are overcome by pressures on states to escalate their disputes to war. Policymakers, guided by their realpolitik belief systems, increasingly influenced by political hard-liners, and pressured by progressively more belligerent selectorates, become increasingly likely to escalate disputes to war as their behavioral and reputational history with their dyadic partner is increasingly defined by conflict.

My results are consistent with this proposition. In each model of war onset, I find consistent and strongly significant evidence that as states' international

---

[36] Fearon, 1994, 1995; Schultz, 1998; Werner, 1999; Wagner, 2000.

behavioral and reputational histories of interstate interaction become increasingly characterized by hostility, the likelihood of dispute escalation to war increases, lending strong support to my hypothesized relationship that conflict begets conflict. Although the informational benefits inherent in states' reputational histories may indeed allow crisis participants to gain a better understanding of one another's preferences and resolve, these benefits are not sufficiently strong to outweigh the pressures on states to escalate their crises to war.

The findings also speak to practical issues of interstate negotiations and interactions in times of instability and crisis. While states and their policymakers may believe it fruitful to portray a resolute and coercive posture toward their dyadic crisis partners as a means of achieving more attractive outcomes to their crises, the results indicate that such posturing significantly increases the likelihood that crisis participants will become embroiled in war, even when controlling for regime type. War is a costly gamble that most states would prefer to avoid, but the results suggest that in the context of direct conflict and reputational histories, they nevertheless become reluctant participants in an upward spiral of escalation.

The findings also provide further support for the premise that states in the international system are relationally and temporally interdependent and that these effects, even outside of the dyad, can be salvaged from the error term and measured and tested empirically. States engage in a process of observational and experiential learning, in which they observe the extra-dyadic reputation of and recall their dyadic historical interactions with their crisis partners. This learning process has real effects on international outcomes and need not be seen as an econometric problem in need of an econometric solution. Consistent with other recent work, these results demonstrate the utility of incorporating relational- and time-specific information into models of interstate behavior.

Several avenues for future research arise from these findings. War onset is but one facet of the conflict process to which an understanding of behavioral and reputational histories is likely to be relevant. In particular, issues of war duration and termination are pertinent areas of application, raising several research questions. Are warring dyads with increasingly conflictual histories more likely to experience wars of longer durations? Are hostile behavioral and reputational histories more likely to exacerbate commitment problems, making resolution and peace maintenance more difficult? Are third-party intermediaries essential to conflict resolution as a means of resolving the security dilemma? If so, how do the behavioral and reputational histories of third-party states vis-à-vis the warring states affect its mediation abilities?

With this fundamental analysis of reputation and violence complete, however, the next chapter examines the role reputation can play in international cooperation. Just as reputation can exacerbate mistrust and unravel the ability of states to resolve conflict nonviolently, a reputation for upholding one's agreements can make future agreements and cooperation more likely. The next chapter examines this argument in the context of international alliance behavior.

5

Reputation, Learning, and
the Onset of Alliances

The way to gain a good reputation is to endeavor to be what you desire
to appear.

—Socrates

How do states' reputations for credibility and reliability influence interstate cooperation? The last chapter focused on the role of reputation in the occurrence and escalation of violence; however, states also count on reputations when they engage in cooperative relationships. Therefore, in this chapter I will empirically investigate this link between reputation and cooperation, testing the argument that when states develop reputations for competence in cooperative situations, they are more likely to experience reciprocal cooperation in the future. There are a multitude of cooperative dimensions one could focus on for such an analysis. The focus could be on the phenomena of economic exchange, including trade, foreign direct investment, or bilateral investment treaties (BITs). Or, we might examine compliance with collective agreements designed to ameliorate problems such as environmental degradation, resource scarcities, or global warming. Nevertheless, I have chosen to focus in this chapter on the phenomena of security alliance formation. This focus has been chosen partly to make the analysis of cooperation as analogous as possible with the previous analysis of conflict. My motivation is also driven by the choice to maintain the analyses of this book at the interstate unit of analysis. Security alliances are perhaps the least internally divisive issues in study of cooperation. Trade and investment decisions, for example, nearly always privilege one domestic group at the expense of another, but alliances designed to improve security are beneficial to the entire state. At the very least, this analysis provides a simple baseline from which more complicated dimensions of cooperation can be assessed.

Alliances are also high-stakes decisions with survival consequences for states, and the decision to form an alliance tends to be plagued with the same problems of incomplete information as conflict decisions. Consider, for example, the challenge the British faced in the twilight of the era of Pax Brittanica. In the closing years of the nineteenth century, Britain began to emerge from the "splendid isolation" it had enjoyed during the previous decades. Continued conflicts over colonial boundaries, the mounting costs (both in terms of military expenditures and in reputation) of the Boer War, and particularly the recent completion of the Franco-Russian Alliance illustrated to British leaders a disturbing decline in the state's power and prestige relative to other European states. To many senior British diplomats, strategic alliances represented the most efficient means to re-assert Britain's position in world affairs, and to allow it to more easily defend its vulnerable overseas colonies.[1] British leaders were eager to locate a suitable ally whose military capabilities would complement Britain's, and who likewise shared a desire to check the expanding power of France and Russia, especially in the Far East. Russian expansion to the East was deemed particularly worrisome, and British interests in China and the Pacific required the United Kingdom to shore up its continental defenses while committing greater resources to the Far East. To that end, Britain opened alliance talks with two potential partners in the late nineteenth century: Germany and Japan.

Indeed, the alliance environment was quite malleable at the end of the nineteenth century. Various alliance arrangements were floated among British decision makers. The most popular permutation seems to have been an alliance among Britain, Germany, and Japan, or these three plus the United States. A parallel hypothetical agreement included an alliance with Italy and Austria. At this time, Japan was viewed in many British foreign-policy circles as a progressive, rising power with a shared interest in checking Russian and French power. Germany was likewise a rapidly expanding power with an obvious and acute interest in balancing the Franco–Russian Alliance. Austria and Italy, however, were generally perceived to be weaker, as well as less stable, entities that were less involved in broader geopolitics. The United States was the most powerful of the potential allies, but it was generally perceived as aloof and reluctant to engage in foreign alliances.[2]

---

[1] Monger, 1963; Weitsman, 2004.
[2] Chang, 1931; Kennedy, 1980; Langer, 1935.

As such, the British deliberated internally about whether to seek out an alliance with Germany or Japan. In the first case, British diplomats and foreign policy decision makers viewed Germany as a natural ally for Britain and a strong counterweight to the Franco-Russian alliance.[3] Despite rising economic and military competition between the countries, Germany did not appear to be particularly hostile at the turn of the century; in fact, relations were generally warmer than they had been in decades. Instead, it was Russia, rather than Germany, that was largely viewed as the most proximate threat to British interests. Moreover, the 1894 alliance between France and Russia was seen as a new structural threat to the British realm. This alliance created significant tensions and pressed both states to examine various strategies to balance a growing threat to their interests.[4]

Why didn't the British ultimately decide to form an alliance with Germany? Germany's economic rise was indisputable, and its location perfect for exacerbating France and Russia. The answer lies in the way the British perceived Germany's reputation for being a good ally. Despite the clear value of an Anglo-German military alliance, negotiations between the two ultimately broke down in 1901 in large part due to British skepticism about Germany's ability to uphold its alliance commitments. During the course of Anglo–German negotiations, the United Kingdom came to believe that Germany had failed to fully comply with its treaty commitment terms with Japan and the United Kingdom over Russian incursions into China. Britain believed that Germany had balked at opposing Russia after the Germans had encouraged the United Kingdom to stand up to the Russians.[5]

These perceptions undercut any confidence that Germany could be the kind of ally that lives up to its obligations. Senior British diplomats expressed significant doubt as to the sincerity of the German leadership and mistrusted their intentions in a potential alliance.[6] Some British diplomats pointed to Germany's recent history of unreliability and poor treatment of alliance partners as a possible cue to what Britain might expect.[7] Arguably, British policymakers feared that despite the obvious military advantage of a formal alliance with Germany, such an alliance could become a strategic vulnerability if Germany

[3] Kennedy, 1980, pp. 224, 231; Langer, 1935, pp. 718, 732–33; Monger, 1963, p. 12.

[4] Langer, 1935, pp. 656, 717; Weitsman, 2004, pp. 118–21.

[5] Monger, 1963; Miller, 2004.

[6] Kennedy, 1980, pp. 193, 233–34.

[7] Gooch and Temperley, 1927; Bertie, 1927; Gascoyne-Cecil, 1927; Petty-Fitzmaurice, 1927; Miller, 2004.

were to shirk on its responsibilities to the United Kingdom in any subsequent crisis with Russia.

During roughly the same period as Anglo-German alliance negotiations, a parallel set of discussions were taking place among British and Japanese diplomats. In some ways, Japan was less valuable to the United Kingdom strategically, because British officials perceived that it was still not militarily prepared to weather a significant conflict with European powers, nor would it be able to credibly defend British interests outside of its immediate Far East arena.[8] However, Japan was able to demonstrate certain features that made it a particularly attractive alliance partner. The principal benefit to the United Kingdom offered by Japan was its shared desire to curtail Russian expansion in the Far East. Additionally important was that it aroused less suspicion among British foreign policy elites than Germany did. Like Britain, Japan had not become entangled in alliances in recent years and therefore had not developed a questionable reputation for reliability. It had also demonstrated its resolve and reliability by committing troops to the British effort during the Boxer Rebellion in 1900.[9]

The commitment Japan showed to Britain during the rebellion, coupled with its victory over China in the Sino-Japanese war, demonstrated Japan's potential as a credible alliance partner and contributed to the formation of the Anglo-Japanese alliance in 1902. It is interesting to note that Japan directly examined Britain's past alliance behavior prior to signing the Anglo-Japanese Alliance. During treaty discussion in the fall of 1901, the Japanese Foreign Ministry researched Britain's reputation for fulfilling its alliance obligations. The findings indicated that while Britain had at times violated treaties, it had not abandoned its alliance partners.[10]

Indeed, senior Japanese diplomats also questioned why Britain was considering breaking with its isolationist reputation by pursuing alliances with Japan and Germany and whether this might demonstrate intentions toward Japan and the Far East. Such examinations almost certainly played into Japan's alliance decisions. The general perception among Japanese diplomats was that a formal alliance with England would be both more reliable and less costly than attempting to reach an understanding with Russia over Korea and Manchuria.[11]

[8] Chang, 1931; Langer, 1935.
[9] Chang, 1931; Ion, 2004; Nish, 2004.
[10] Miller, 2004; Nish, 1985.
[11] Langer, 1935, pp. 767, 783.

The twin examples of Anglo-German and Anglo-Japanese alliance formation beg the broader question of how states' reputations for credibility and reliability influence international political phenomena. Specifically, they raise questions regarding the extent to which states value compliance reputations when making their alliance formation decisions. Indeed, from the example above, it appears that reputations for reliability are an important dimension of the alliance formation calculus. While I do not argue that reputation is the only factor in a state's selection of alliance partnerships, the notion that reliability is an important factor when states consider new alliances is intuitively appealing. In other words, while states hope to satisfy a number of interests by carefully considering the characteristics of potential allies, the expected reliability of future partners is also a component of an alliance seeker's decision calculus. Thus, my specific focus in this chapter is on the question of whether a state's historical reputation for alliance reliability influences its likelihood of being sought as an ally by other states.

States form alliances for multiple reasons. Behind these reasons lies an assumption of reliability. That is, states choose to ally with partners when they have some positive expectation that the alliance will hold in the event of conflict. Otherwise the basis for the alliance is undermined. Any alliance in which a partner fails (or is expected to fail) to live up to its commitments is largely devoid of its merit. Moreover, the failure of an alliance likely renders the abandoned partner *more* vulnerable than it was prior to its formation. Indeed, the level of security that a state hopes to achieve by forming an alliance is only relevant to the extent that the alliance-seeker believes its partner will live up to its responsibilities. Consequently, states choose their partners carefully, preferring those likely to honor their agreements.

Based on this intuition, let's examine the idea that reputations for reliability can affect alliance formation choices. The idea isn't to argue that a reputation for reliability is the only, or even the most important, influence on alliance partner choices. Clearly, an ally isn't particularly useful unless it brings security, or trade, or some other policy dimension to the table. But the benefits that another state can bring to an alliance relationship may be mitigated by how trustworthy that ally is when its resources and efforts are actually needed. In this chapter I develop the notion of a reputation for reliability and apply it to the phenomenon of alliance formation. In the process, I'll customize the reputational learning model from Chapter 3 and develop an alliance reputation model. I then operationalize this learning model into a reputation score that reflects the historical reliability of a state, and I use this new variable to test the simple notion that a reputation for being a reliable ally makes a state a more attractive partner for future alliances. The empirical research at the end of this chapter provides support for this reliability hypothesis, suggesting that when states develop reputational identities (in this case for being reliable allies), those identities can provide useful and actionable information for other actors in the international arena.

From these illustrations one can start to piece together a conceptualization of alliance reliability reputation. Perhaps alliance seekers measure one another's reliability by observing how potential partners have performed in upholding their alliance commitments to other states in the system, assigning a reputation for (un)reliability to each of its potential partners. Furthermore, states assess the relevance of this historical information based on how recently past alliance commitments were upheld (or violated) and how similar the affected state is to the alliance seeker. Below I elaborate on the nature of alliance agreements and my theoretical expectations on the importance of reputation in the alliance formation process.

Reputation and Alliance Formation

Alliances are formal agreements made between two or more states to coordinate their multilateral actions. They make plain the commitments between the parties and the conditions under which these commitments are activated. States forming an alliance thus agree to take certain actions when specified conditions arise, certain events occur, or certain actions are taken by outside parties. A variety of benefits motivate decision makers to pursue such agreements. Previous research has indicated that states ally in order to improve their security through capability aggregation and enhanced autonomy of action.[12] Alliance agreements also act as signals of the signatories' intentions to come to one another's aid in times of crisis.[13] These signals, when credibly conveyed, should deter challengers and induce concessions from targets. Ultimately, they may even encourage the settlement of disputes short of war. Efficiency gains are also attractive, as alliances serve to reduce the resource commitments necessary for an effective defense.[14] Alliances produce economies of scale that can allow states to spend less individually while increasing their overall security by pooling resources. Given the

---

[12] Morgenthau, 1967; Waltz, 1979; Walt, 1987; Powell, 1999; Morrow, 1991.

[13] Sorokin, 1994; Smith, 1995; Morrow, 2000.

[14] Altfeld, 1984; Conybeare, 1994; Morrow, 1993.

cost of security for governments, these efficiencies offer the opportunity to achieve security goals without overburdening one's economy. Lastly, the alliance formation process can provide states with an environment that encourages the cultivation of international friendship and cooperation. Research suggests that alliances improve the prospects of peace among treaty signatories.[15]

Clearly, research in this area suggests that there are strong positive motivations to seek out allies. However, few studies have explicitly tapped the underlying intuition that potential allies must exhibit a history of past alliance credibility in order to be considered as viable partners. Scholars often implicitly assume that the present security needs of the state are the sole drivers for alliance formation. No doubt, states form alliances in order to increase their military capabilities, deter a common threat, or advance other mutual goals. Without these primary incentives, there is no reason to seek out alliance partners in the first place. So, if I can assume that these primary motivations are in place, what else matters for states as they seek out partnerships in the global political arena? One additional factor in the decision process is the past performance of potential partners in honoring their commitments. If there is only one alliance partner available to satisfy the primary motivations of alliance formation, then the market dictates that past actions should not matter much. In this case, a state faces the choice between having one possible ally versus going at it alone. But how does that decision process change if and when there is a market of potential allies from which to choose? Multiple possible alliance partners in the system means that states need not settle for any available partner with complementary capabilities and interests. In this situation, state reputation is an important factor in determining who allies with whom. I think the logic of how reputation matters in this context is fairly straightforward. All else being equal, states choose to form alliances with other states that possess a reputation for upholding past agreements, rather than with states that have poor reputations for meeting their obligations.

The reason reputation matters is that all the advantages of an alliance depend on a state's willingness to follow through with its agreement. Regardless of the primary motivations, an underlying issue remains: the aforementioned benefits from alliances only materialize if an ally upholds (or is expected to uphold) its commitments. Unreliable allies are unlikely to add to a state's security regardless of the additional capability offered. To the extent that the existence and terms of the formal agreement are public knowledge, an alliance member's failure

[15] Long, Nordstrom, and Baek, 2007.

to fulfill its obligations is observable to all states in the international system. As a consequence, for instance, a potential adversary is less likely be deterred by the combined strength of a coalition if either alliance partner is perceived as unreliable.[16] Furthermore, the calculus of a state contemplating conflict initiation is made more tenuous if it cannot be assured that its partners will aid it in this endeavor. Similarly, the bargaining strength of a state embroiled in a crisis is determined at least in part by its allies and the perceived reliability that they bring to the bargaining table.

Problems with credibility affect more than just state security during a crisis. If the credibility of alliance commitments is compromised, so will be the alliance seeker's gains in bargaining power arising from the alliance. In other words, an ally with a reputation for shirking its responsibilities can erode the very power gains that motivate the alliance in the first place. Finally, efficiency gains can completely unravel when reputations erode trust. When states are stuck with untrustworthy allies, they will feel the need to duplicate security contributions, develop contingency plans, and rely less on the partnership. Unreliable alliances make any attempt to realize economies of scale-type gains in security provisions a risky proposition, and they increase security costs for the alliance seeker.

Alliances are expensive partnerships for states, imposing costs upon their signatories. The literal costs, such as the expense of coordination (including training and infrastructure changes) or the costs associated with the implementation of an agreement in times of crisis, are the easiest to observe. For example, the involvement of NATO forces in the 2011 campaign in Libya cost each NATO member billions of dollars. Already committed to military campaigns in Iraq and Afghanistan, the states' additional expenses in Libya are generating domestic political disagreements as well. But I can also think of costs in terms of the loss of autonomy that comes with an alliance obligation. These costs can be thought of as a tradeoff between security and autonomy because all alliances require some degree of foreign policy coordination between partners.[17] Such coordination may mean that one or both allies must abandon some preferred policies. Military coordination may limit the tactical flexibility of each ally if war should come, and the specialization of forces may leave an ally exposed to other threats.[18]

---

[16] In fact, previous research suggests that states consider the credibility of their target's alliances before attacking (Gartner and Siverson, 1996; Smith, 1996).

[17] Altfeld, 1984; Morrow, 1987, 1991, 2000.

[18] Morrow, 1994.

The costs of an alliance are well known to states in advance (albeit with varying degrees of uncertainty with respect to implementation), so we can assume that states only enter into such agreements when the expected benefits outweigh the expected costs. States are loath to incur these costs, however, if the benefits from an alliance are uncertain due to fears that an ally will be unreliable in a future crisis. Such uncertainty generates risks that states wish to avoid. The very nature of an alliance is meant to condition a state's expectation of its partner's future actions. Yet alliances are essentially unenforceable contracts. While technically binding, there typically exists limited recourse for states whose partners breach the terms. Consequently, the abandoned partner absorbs the high cost of defection.

Since alliances operate "in the shadow of war,"[19] the losses incurred from defection are likely to be quite large indeed, potentially resulting in a military defeat or, at minimum, a reduced capability to negotiate a satisfactory outcome. This suggests that reliability is a characteristic of state behavior that is crucial to the calculations of potential alliance partners. When we think about the character of a state with respect to reliability, there is no reason to assume that the perception of that character is limited to direct interactions with the state.

Of course, reliability isn't always easy to identify. Firms devote significant resources to manipulating their reputations using marketing tactics instead of behaviorial characteristics, leaving the consumers and other firms to separate fact from wishful thinking. States in an anarchical international system face a similar obstacle. The intentions of states and the credibility of their commitments function as private information. The ability to keep information private means that states likely to renege on their commitments have an incentive to mask this quality in order to persuade other states to ally with them, thereby accruing the benefits outlined above at little cost. Indicating one's true intention to honor one's commitments relies on the credibility of such claims, as states lack the institutional framework necessary to enforce cooperation. Consequently, states seeking alliance partners must, by some mechanism, assess the likely reliability of potential partners beyond simple assurances given that such assurances may evaporate in a crisis. One way states achieve this objective is by observing one another's compliance with past obligations. States use this information to form expectations about the future reliability of potential alliance partners.

[19] Morrow, 2000, p. 63.

It is worth asking where this incentive to misrepresent comes from. After all, why would a state wish to enter an alliance with no intention to fulfill its obligations in the event of a crisis? The biggest reason lies in the deterrent effect of an alliance. With intentions private both from allies and potential enemies, the classic conundrum emerges for challengers who must decided whether and how much to demand from a target government. If that target government can enhance its perceived power position through alliance commitments, then challengers will be less likely to issue demands in the first place. Alastair Smith explored the strategic implications of this type of private information, finding that when potential challengers are sufficiently convinced that an ally will defend a target, demands are not made and crises fail to materialize.[20] This logical structure to the strategic problem is well suited for understanding the importance of alliance commitments, but it also highlights the importance of the challenger's expectation that the defender is reliable.

It is possible that expectations of reliability are so important that they can become policy goals in their own right. I assume here that states are aware of their own ability and willingness to abide by various alliance terms, at least at the time of alliance formation. Further, let us assume that states understand the risks of forming alliances strategically but insincerely. Due to the risks involved, states form alliances when they believe there is a reasonable probability of successful cooperation.[21] Indeed, Leeds shows that the majority of alliance commitments are honored.[22] This finding prompts questions regarding the nature of alliance formation: if abiding by alliance commitments is costly, what drives states to so often fulfill their obligations despite incentives to shirk? One answer is that by limiting their commitments to those they expect to fulfill, states help ensure that they will not have to renege on their promises at a later date thus negatively affecting their reputation for reliability. States that preserve positive reputations put themselves in a position for obtaining future rents. In this sense, the maintenance of a reputation for reliability plays an integral role in the alliance formation process. In short, policymakers understand that when alliance obligations go unfulfilled in a time of crisis, the resulting reputational costs can be damaging.

Despite the intuitive nature of the reliability argument, existing research has focused largely on common interests and regime characteristics to explain the

[20] Smith, 1995.
[21] Downs, Rocke, and Barsoom, 1996; Leeds, 1999.
[22] Leeds, 2000, 2003.

credibility of alliances. Research on regime characteristics hints at the reliability thesis.[23] For example, B. Ashley Leeds suggests that the commitments of democracies are more credible because democratic executives are held accountable at home for breaking foreign commitments.[24] However, this should not be taken to mean that nondemocratic regimes lack the ability form reliable alliances. In fact, the literature on this topic has come to somewhat different conclusions.[25] Also, capability aggregation models often take reliability as given. When alliances form on the basis of a common security interest, reliability is assumed to flow from a common goal. However, the temptation to shirk makes collective action on any common interest difficult.[26]

Thus, states must use some credibility assessment criteria in order to choose among potential alliance partners. Reputations for reliability serve as one such factor. States have access to readily available information about a prospective ally's future reliability: historical behavior. States prefer to choose partners that possess reputations for upholding their prior alliance commitments. By picking allies on the basis of their reputations, states are more likely to realize the benefits of an alliance while limiting their risk of abandonment. As such, perhaps the way in which alliance seekers calculate one another's reliability is by observing (1) how potential partners have performed in upholding their alliance commitments to other states in the system by assigning a reputation for (un)reliability to each of its potential alliance partners, and (2) determining the relative significance of that historical information based on the similarity between the alliance seeker and the potential ally's previous partners.

The arguments made above can thus be summarized in the following simple hypothesis: *A state is more likely to select an alliance partner that has a reputation for honoring its alliances.* This hypothesis indicates how historical information is processed by states as they choose alliance partners. It is important to note that I am not arguing that reputation is the only factor governing alliance formation. Reputation is simply one factor in the decision calculus. Moreover, I suspect reputation becomes a consideration only after potential allies are identified based on their power contributions. But just because reputation matters later in the decision-making process does not mean it is unimportant.

---

[23] Lai and Reiter, 2000.

[24] Leeds, 1999.

[25] Simon and Gartzke, 1996; Siverson and Emmons, 1991.

[26] Olson, 1965.

In order to evaluate this hypothesis, we need to get more specific about a few terms. Much has been written recently about the subtle but important dimensions of alliance commitments, particularly in conjunction with the Alliance Treaty Obligations Project (ATOP). Later in this book, I will draw from this research to focus in on the notion of a state upholding (or failing to) its alliance obligations. But first, I need to get more specific about how a state might develop a reputation for being a good (or bad) ally. For this process, the model of reputation I developed in the last chapter will anchor the development of my conceptualization of alliance reputation.

Conceptualizing A Reputation for Honoring Alliances

Before I can empirically evaluate the above hypothesis, I first need to offer a justification for conceptualizing reputation. I choose to conceptualize reputation at the state level, rather than focusing on individual leaders. This assumption raises the question, however, of whether states or their leaders are the true owners of a reputation. Are alliance agreements the product of state decisions or policymaker decisions? Do states form reputations for alliance reliability, or are these reputations assigned to heads of state? The answer to these questions is inevitably both. While others have successfully focused on the reputations formed by state executives,[27] I model alliance reputations as a state characteristic for three reasons.

First, alliance agreements are sticky, often surviving the tenure of individual leaders. Decisions by executives to fulfill or violate treaties are often made on agreements that were formalized under previous regimes. Yet honoring agreements made by previous leaders are still observed by other states in the system when calculating reputation. While foreign policies may be influenced by the opinions of individuals, the realm of possibilities is constrained by state-related factors, including the nation's capability, geopolitical stature, existing relationships with other states, and the similarity of its national interests with others in the system.

Second, leadership turnover occurs regularly in many states, especially in democracies. Therefore many leaders have little time and opportunity to form reputations. Leadership reputations need to be reset with each new administration, reflecting a recurrence of valueless reputations and providing no information about the state's historical behavior. Theoretically, this practice requires

---

[27] Gibler, 2008.

a peculiar assumption about the way in which information is processed for a resetting of leadership reputations to reflect reality. Such a practice requires states and their leaders to know nothing about their historical relationships as soon as leadership changes occur. Do states erase their knowledge of prior interactions with changes of administrations? This seems unlikely. For example, consider the leadership change in the United States from President Bush to President Obama in 2009. To many observers, this change appeared to indicate a dramatic shift in foreign policy direction. Yet the pre-existing commitments of the United States remained largely unchanged. My conceptualization of reputation attempts to account for the decaying effect on information as time passes, yet allowing this information to persist across changes in leadership within states.[28]

Third, the process by which states choose to honor or violate their agreements is the product of domestic processes that vary widely. In some autocracies, this may indeed be the consequence of a single policymaker's unilateral decision, which is then implemented by the state apparatus without other internal influences or objections. This may be true in those states in which power is highly concentrated, although this need not be true in all autocracies. Ultimately, the entire state is held responsible for the consequences of honoring (or not) an agreement. Another way to frame this question is to ask whether states or their leaders join and maintain alliances. Consider the United States as an example. In the United States the executive office negotiates treaties and alliances, but the US Senate must ratify each agreement with a two-thirds majority vote. If the alliance is a defense pact and that ally happens to be attacked, it is Congress, not the president, that has the formal responsibility to declare war on a foreign opponent. The process is just complex enough to dilute the focus of the reputation from presidential to governmental.

In democracies, the process of signing and fulfilling agreements is far less individualized. Indeed, a common characteristic of democracies is that separate branches of government have institutional checks on one another in making important decisions. Alliance reliability may not be easily assigned to individuals, as alliance formation and compliance decisions are accurately described as the product of a political bargaining process between individuals or institutions.

---

[28] Gibler (2008) offers an interesting tool to account for the persistence of leadership reputation beyond regime transitions. In a robustness check, he includes a reputation variable that allows leader reputations to persist for ten years beyond the end of each leader's tenure, and his results remain consistent. My approach is similar. However, I prefer to conceptualize the fading of information with time by using an exponential decay function. I specify this function in the next section.

For these reasons, the model delineated below focuses on state reputations, leaving aside the effect of leadership reputation for additional research that may build off of this basic platform model. This is not to say that research focusing on leadership reputation is unwise; that is hardly the case. Indeed, valuable research is being conducted on leadership reputation and alliance phenomena.[29] The dual approaches can be considered complementary, with each addressing the problem from a slightly different perspective to triangulate on a valid concept. If my analysis proves to be similar to those reported on leadership reputation, then I can be more confident that this research vein has produced consistent knowledge that points to the importance of reputation in affecting the formation of alliances.

Alliance Reputations: Applying Reputational Learning to Alliance Behavior

Modeling alliance reputation requires answering questions about how images of good and bad allies are constructed over time. If a state opts to abandon its ally in a time of need, how do other states process this shock and incorporate it into an overall notion of reliability? One option is to argue that evidence of any past agreement violation should condemn an ally as wholly unreliable. This would be analogous to a "Grim Trigger" approach.[30] However, assessments of reliability can be more complex than this, as states process information within a dynamic and diverse environment of world politics. A measure of ally reputation should account for the observed behavior of the potential ally within the context of recent history as well as other observations. Some states may have a perfect record for (un)reliability, although an image of a completely unreliable state is difficult to fathom. More likely is a scenario where states may have fulfilled some past commitments but not others, causing them to acquire a mixed record in the eyes of future allies. A more realistic model of alliance reputation should be able to process this mixed record and deal with the effects of time.

Not all observations of past alliance behavior may be equally relevant to current alliance seekers. As time passes, the relevance of older observations fades. This "time heals all wounds" approach may be overly optimistic, but it is an elegant way to allow past mistakes to diminish in importance over time. It also imposes a need for states to maintain a good reputation with repeated positive

[29] Gibler, 2008.
[30] See Axelrod (1984).

behavior. There are thus two main components to the model of each state's reliability reputation: *information* about a state's alliance reliability and the *relevance* of that information to potential allies. The goal is to approximate the information used by states when crafting new alliances. By crafting an explicit model of the nature and dynamics of this information, I have undoubtedly simplified this process. Clearly, a state's reputation is highly contextual, perception based, and undoubtedly biased by emotions, identity, domestic politics, and idiosyncratic factors unique to each state. I do not claim to be able to fully model a state's reputation as it is perceived by every individual state at each moment in time. I can, however, capture a dynamic and contextual representation of reputation that is applicable to any state in the international system at any time in modern state history. Moreover, this approach is transparent and customizable, which allows future scholars to customize the model to focus on specific countries, or to manipulate the model to test particular assumptions about they spatial and temporal dynamics of reputation.

The Reputational Learning theory developed in Chapter 3 provides the roadmap for understanding the evolution of alliance reputations. Behavior forms the core of any reputational image, but the relevance and perception of that behavior can be just as important to the audience. In this case, alliance behavior forms the core of alliance reputation. Just as with the general theory, however, the dynamics and relevance of this behavior across time and space help me craft a model of alliance reputation that is contextual to potential alliance seekers. Thus, I am able to recreate the reputational learning model here in a customized alliance form, starting with a dynamic model of alliance behavior and then showing how these histories form reputations.

Step One: Modeling Dyadic Alliance History

The first step in modeling alliance reputation is to specify the way states develop a dyadic history of alliance behavior. The approach here is to view the dyadic behavior as a process over time, embedded in time. The theory laid out in Chapter 3 is easily adaptable for this purpose. New alliance events inform an alliance history between states, and inaction over time causes that information to diminish. I begin with a direct alliance history concept that is directed-dyadic. Recall that a dyad is a term that is meant to represent interactions across two actors (in this case, countries). A *directed dyad* is slightly more specific, referring to the behavior of one country towards the other in the dyad. Thus, J's historical behavior toward I can be different than I's historical behavior toward J. In this

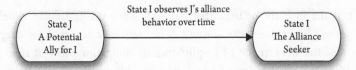

Figure 5.1 The Directed Alliance History: State J's Alliance Behavior Toward State I.

chapter, I am interested in how one country behaves toward the other with respect to its alliance commitments. For any two states I and J, γ_{jit} represents J's history at time t of upholding or reneging on its alliance obligations with I. This history, illustrated in Figure 5.1, occurs throughout the population of pairs of states in the system. Even when we consider the importance of multilateral alliances (e.g., NATO), we should notice that when any member state acts on its alliance commitments, the other member states update their impression of that state's reliability accordingly.

States develop these specific alliance histories with other states based on the actions of those states in the past. Each state in the international system has a history of its actions when called to act in accordance of its alliance obligations. Upholding one's alliance obligations creates a positive change to the alliance history, violating obligations imparts a negative change. These events have an immediate impact, which diminishes over time. If a state has never had to uphold or violate its obligations, even this information has meaning to others. At any moment in time that the state is not acting on its alliance obligations (either by upholding or walking away from commitments), the absence of new information means other states only have history to rely upon. Memories of past actions weakens over time, so I assume that the alliance relationship gradually becomes less informed by its history. Just as is the case with reputational learning, this information decays in different ways for different situations. A state with an alliance history with very few alliance events will find that its reputation diminishes quickly. At the same time, states with a lot of alliance behavior opportunities (both positive and negative) generate histories that are more permanent. This speed of information decay is endogenous to the model: as a dyad experiences more and more alliance events, the rate of decay of old information slows down. This set of assumptions can be formalized in Equation 5.1 as follows:

$$\gamma_{jit} = (e^{-\left(\frac{\tau}{\sigma}\right)})\gamma_{ji(t-1)} + \left(\frac{\upsilon}{\tau}\right) - \left(\frac{\omega}{\tau}\right). \qquad (5.1)$$

Here, τ is the amount of time that has past since the last alliance behavior was observed, σ captures the amount of activity that accumulates over time, υ identifies the occurrence of J upholding its obligations to I at time t, and ω identifies the occurrence of J violating its obligations to I at time t. The exponential decay model is accelerated by τ, which means the alliance history becomes less informative as time passes without upholding/violating events. At the same time, information decay slows down as σ increases. This reflects the assumption that a state's historical policy choices have a cumulative impact. Finally, τ diminishes the impact of the shocks of upholding or reneging on alliance commitments. This reflects the assumption that events that occur regularly are more informative than events that are infrequent (and thus potentially interpreted as random or mistakes). I recognize that time passing without the opportunity to uphold an agreement may not indicate a real deterioration in resolve. The question of whether or not this information is fully public, however, is important as well. Ultimately, I assume that states approximate perceptions of reliability based on historical behavior. The alternative approach is to assume a constant rate of decay for all states across time, or to eliminate the decay of historical information all together. Neither alternative offers the richness of this set of assumptions. For simplicity, I bound this function between 1 (J perfectly upholds its obligations to I) and -1 (J perfectly fails to uphold its obligations to I), with 0 representing no information (or a perfect mix of information that cancels itself out) about the $\overrightarrow{ji}$ dyadic alliance relationship.[31]

The model allows the researcher considerable flexibility. For instance, one could weight the relevance of positive versus negative alliance behavior by altering the beta constants, perhaps to test an argument about the psychological impacts of the two qualitatively different types of events. The speed at which information from old events diminish can be customized by changing the alpha constant, perhaps matching unique constants to types of governments (democracies v. autocracies) or leadership tenure.

Step Two: Modeling Alliance Reputation

The direct relationship between any two actors in the system is fairly easy to represent, and I am certainly not the first to do so. But is that all the information that a government needs when it is evaluating a potential alliance with another

---

[31] See Crescenzi, Enterline, and S. B. Long (2008) for a detailed discussion of the structure of this model as well as the bounding function.

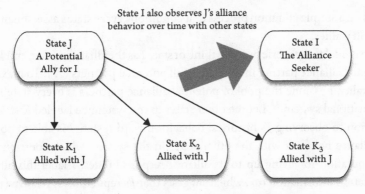

Figure 5.2 Observing a Potential Ally's Historical Record Toward
Others.

state? It seems unreasonable to assume that governments do not incorporate the
behavior of potential allies toward *others*. Figure 5.2 illustrates how states do not
limit their evaluations to the direct dyadic history with a potential ally. Rather,
they are able to evaluate the historical behavior of that potential ally toward other
states in the system. Figure 5.2 shows three other states as an illustration, but I
assume that when a government evaluates a potential ally it considers *all* of the
historical behavior of that potential ally.

Modeling how one state perceives the reputations of its potential allies is the
objective here, but how does one extrapolate from these individual directed dyad
histories? The key is to focus on how state I perceives the alliance reputation of
potential ally J. The foundation of I's perception of J lies in J's alliance history
with the other states in the international system (I refer to these as K states,
defined as states that are neither I nor J). States perceive the reputation of a
potential ally by observing its historic behavior toward other states. Moreover,
some K states are more useful proxies than others, and I assume that similarities
between I and K are a useful way to approximate the relevance of any alliance
activity between J and K. State I observes J's alliance behavior with all the other
K states in the system. The question then becomes, what does state I do with this
information? The first step to answering that question fully is to understand how
all these observations translate into one perception of state J's alliance reputation.
State I aggregates and processes this extra-dyadic information to observe an
overall reputation for J's alliance behavior. In reality, this process is going to be
in part an idiosyncratic reflection of the norms, regimes, and bureaucracy of
the alliance seeking state. But it is possible to set these idiosyncrasies aside and

focus on a simple common process that conditions every state's assessment of its potential allies.[32]

To model this generic process, think of state I as the alliance seeker, and J as its potential alliance partner in the pool of all potential partners (N). To maximize generality, I assume the pool of potential alliance partners is every state in the international system.[33] Let the other states in the system be labeled K states. In addition to observing J's historical behavior toward I, state I is able to observe J's alliance behavior with the other states in the system, which contributes to J's reputation for living up to its alliance responsibilities. I label this alliance reputation information α_{ijt}, which suggests that J's reputation is relative (in the eyes of the beholder, which in this case is I). Indeed, J's reputation is contextual to the way I processes J's alliance histories with the other states in the system. State I learns of J's reputation for reliability by observing J's interactions with all other K states in the system with whom J has shared an alliance.

The process of observing J's alliance reputation has two important components. First, recall that reputation is in the eye of the beholder, meaning that state I will filter J's behavior through its own lens to evaluate previous alliance behavior. Here the quality of the proxy state (state K) becomes important. If state K is similar to I and thus a good proxy for I with which to evaluate J, and state J has a history of upholding its commitments to K, this translates to a positive reputation in the eyes of state I. Figure 5.3 illustrates this learning process. What happens if a K state is a good proxy for I, but state J has a history of violating its commitments to K? In this case, I uses this information to form negative expectations about J as a potential ally (as illustrated in Figure 5.4). Finally, if state J honors (or violates) its alliance commitments with a state K that is a poor proxy for I, this information is discounted by I because of the incongruence between the alliance seeker and its proxy (see Figure 5.5).

The second component of modeling this reputation is to represent how a government aggregates all this information. To keep the model simple, I

---

[32] Note that I do not include a component to "reset" reputation through regime change. Some have argued that regime changes can bring changes in type or reputation, and these transitions to new leadership impact alliance reliability (Gartzke and Gleditsch, 2004) or disputes between allies (Chiozza and Choi, 2003). I am skeptical that these events reset reputation completely and instantly, and am thus unsure about how to integrate them into the model. Thus, this baseline model proceeds without the regime change dimension. If regime changes do in fact alter reputations of states, then the subsequent analysis should be biased against confirming the hypotheses.

[33] One can easily customize this model to focus only on neighborhoods or communities of states as the potential population of allies.

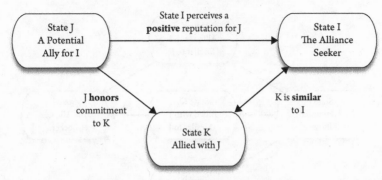

Figure 5.3 Positive Alliance Reputation Information.

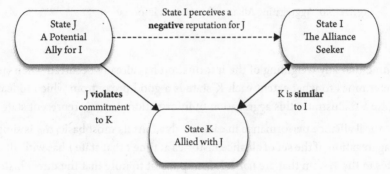

Figure 5.4 Negative Alliance Reputation Information.

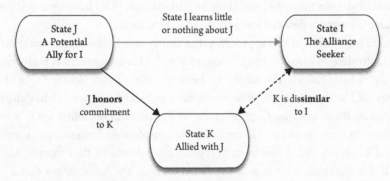

Figure 5.5 Poor Proxy Alliance Reputation Information.

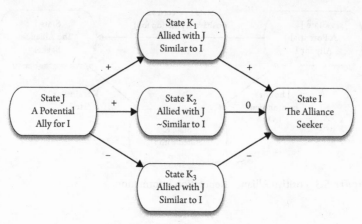

Figure 5.6 Aggregating Alliance Reputation Information.

assume that any weighting of the information has already occurred when state I determines to what extent each K state is a good proxy from which to learn. Figure 5.6 illustrates this aggregation of information. Let γ_{jkt} represent state J's historical alliance performance in each $\overrightarrow{jk}$ dyad. At its most basic, α_{ijt} is simply an aggregation of the set of alliance histories at time t that state J has with all the states in the system that are *not* I. It is important to note that the direct history between I and J does not contribute to I's perception of J's external reputation for being a reliable (or unreliable) ally. That is not to say that the history of alliance behavior between I and J is unimportant, only that I have separated these concepts for more detailed and precise analytical focus.

One innovation of this approach is the ability to introduce a relevance criterion into state I's calculation of J's reputation.[34] This component is represented by ϕ_{ik}, which reflects the similarity between the alliance seeker (I) and all states (K) with whom the alliance seeker's potential partner (J) has already shared an alliance. Thus, I's observation of J's historical reliability for K is only relevant to I insofar as I and K are similar to one another. For example, suppose that I observes that J has been exceptionally reliable in its commitment to K. If I is different from K in a fundamental way, the information that I can glean from the $J-K$ relationship is fundamentally limited with regard to I's

---

[34] This additional nuance to the model is optional, although it is supported by the conceptual discussion above. One could easily model α_{ijt} without weights on the individual extra-dyadic streams of information.

expectation of *J*'s reliability in a potential *I*—*J* alliance. However, if states *I* and *K* are very similar to one another, the fact that *J* has been a reliable partner to *K* will lead *I* to assign *J* with a positive reputation, as *I* will expect *J* to be a dependable partner in a potential *I*—*J* alliance. Both the *J*—*K* alliance history component and the *I*—*K* similarity component are represented in the full model below, where *J*'s dependability in the *J*—*K* alliance is observed as ranging from completely unreliable (−1) to fully reliable (1), and where the similarity between states *I* and *K* can range from entirely dissimilar (0) to identical (1). The combination of components is then normalized by the size of the system.

Putting the pieces together, Equation 5.2 formalizes this discussion:

$$\alpha_{ijt} = \frac{\displaystyle\sum_{\substack{k \neq i,j}}^{N} \gamma_{jkt}\phi_{ikt}}{N-2} \tag{5.2}$$

where N is the size of the system

    γ_{jkt} is the alliance relationship between *j* and *k* at *t*, $\gamma_{jkt} \in (-1,1)$,

    ϕ_{ikt} is the similarity between *i* and *k* at *t*, $\phi_{ikt} \in (0,1)$.

With this model in place, I can now return to the original question of how reputation matters. In this case, the specific question is, does a reputation for being a good (or bad) ally have an impact on whether or not a state will be sought out as an ally in the future? Or does past alliance behavior fade into history, as states view only the here and now when organizing against a foe or competitor? Now that I have a clear model of how these reputations form within the context of the alliance seeker, the next step is to determine whether alliance seekers use reputational information when forming new alliances.

Does Alliance Reputation Influence Future Alliance Formation?

To test the argument that a positive alliance reputation makes a state more sought after in the future by other potential allies, I turn next to the idea of alliance formation, or alliance onset. I employ data that identifies the onset of an alliance between each pair of states. This dependent variable, which I call Alliance Onset, takes on a value of 1 for the first year of an alliance and 0 otherwise, meaning it is a simple marker for when two countries join an alliance. I use the Alliance Treaty Obligations and Provisions (ATOP) project for this dependent variable of alliance onset.[35] Attention to agreement terms increases the accuracy in the coding of instances in which states either honor or violate these provisions. Importantly, arguments about learning from the experiences of others require that alliance compliance be based in observable events. The ATOP data do not code secret agreements. I am therefore reasonably confident that states are indeed able to observe the alliance behavior of others, thus allowing for the creation and observation of state reputations for reliability.[36]

Note that α_{ijt} contains information that is directional, meaning I's reputation for reliability as viewed by country J is conceptually distinct from J's reputation as perceived by I. As a result, I conduct my analysis at the directed–dyad–year level.[37] My method of analysis is a standard probit model with robust standard errors clustered on each directed dyad.

Operationalizing Alliance Reputation

To keep the labels of my concept of alliance reputation distinct from its empirical measurement, let Alliance History represent a measure of γ_{jit}, and let Alliance Reputation represent a measure of α_{ijt}. To operationalize this model, I represent γ_{jkt} and ϕ_{ikt} with measures of J's historical commitment to the $\overrightarrow{jk}$ alliance and the similarity between I and K, respectively. I operationalize α_{ijt} to reflect J's commitment to all of its alliance partners except I.

---

[35] Leeds, 2003; Leeds and Savun, 2007.

[36] While I use the ATOP data for my analyses, as a robustness check I replicated the work by Lai and Reiter (2000) using a dependent variable generated from COW Alliance Data (Small and Singer, 1991; Gibler and Sarkees, 2004). I adjusted their dependent variable slightly to reflect alliance formation and included each of the predictors from their primary model. The results produced by the reputation variable were consistent with the direction and significance of the findings reported below.

[37] Employing the directed-dyad-year format is useful given that each state has a distinct reputation. My emphasis on alliance seekers asks that I focus on the decisions of each potential partner. Ideally I would prefer to use data delimiting those states that were the initiators of agreements. Lacking data at this level, the directed–dyad–year data format provides the necessary design to account for individual state decisions. However, a potential issue arises when state I is deemed reliable while J is considered unreliable. If in this case I and J were to ally, the J-I dyad would support the hypothesis while I-J would not. Such a scenario should bias against supportive findings. Thus support found for the hypothesis should be considered more, rather than less, dependable.

Measuring Dyadic Alliance History

The premise of the Alliance History variable is that historical relationships between states evolve or shift in two ways. First, the relationship is affected by change, or the occurrence of new information relevant to the dimension of history being measured. In the previous chapter that focuses on reputation and conflict, I am interested in understanding how dyadic histories for conflict and cooperation affect the present likelihood of hostile or peaceful interactions between states. I therefore conceptualize instances of prior conflict as a negative shock to the dyad's historical relationship, whereas prior cooperative events represent positive shocks. Relative to my interest in accounting for a direct alliance reliability history between states, I identify change in an alliance history when an ally is obligated by the terms of its treaty to act in fulfillment of those terms. Two types of events are parsed into separate streams: one stream of information reflects whether an alliance was upheld in a given year (a positive change); and one stream reflects whether the alliance was violated (a negative change).

In constructing this measure, I draw from decisions states make to honor or violate their treaties as they are coded in the ATOP dataset.[38] The ATOP data is the most comprehensive data available on the honoring or violating of alliances. The reputation model requires the ability to observe alliance behavior in action. In this case, I focus on instances in which a state is obligated by its alliance agreements to come to the aid of its partner, and subsequently decide to either honor its commitment or shirk its duty. The ATOP project codes this data with a specific emphasis on the actual terms under which each alliance member is obligated to fulfill its commitments. If more than one alliance obligation is met or violated in a directed–dyad–year, these components aggregate the number of events per year. If in a directed–dyad–year there are no violations or fulfilled obligations, there are simply no shocks to the historical measure.

Second, like in the reputation model in Chapter 3, I assume historical information becomes less useful over time. As events slip into the past, their impact on one's present decision calculus diminishes. I represent this effect by applying a decay function to the temporal record of J's alliance behavior toward K. In the absence of change, the alliance relationship decays toward no information, which I characterize with a value of zero. The speed of decay depends on how long it has been since the last alliance event and the number of events within the dyad. Long

---

[38] Leeds et al., 2002.

time spans during which no activity occurs increase the decay rate, but as more events occur, the rate slows. This conceptualization of direct historical alliance reliability produces a measure that varies in its unbounded state from -0.2 to almost 3.1.

The Alliance History measure can range between -1 and 1; actual values range from -0.33 to 0.68. Negative values reflect a net history of violation, and positive values reflect a history of upholding obligations. The measure thus provides an assessment of direct alliance reliability, processing obligations that were both honored and violated. Therefore, the γ_{jkt} component represents the alliance seeker's (I) observation of its potential ally's (j) historical behavior toward all of its past and current alliance partners (k). Otherwise, the model operates in the same fashion as described above, where alliance commitments that are upheld are considered positive shocks, violated commitments represent negative shocks, and these shocks decay as the amount of time increases between instances in which allies are obligated to act. When state J's alliance partner is faced with a crisis in which the terms of the alliance agreement obligate J to come to its partner's aid, a decision by J to live up to its alliance obligations will positively affect its perceived reliability, whereas a decision by J to shirk on its obligations will negatively affect its perceived reliability to its alliance partners. These historical alliance reliability values then decay to neutrality as the amount of time increases since the last crisis in which J was called upon to fulfill its alliance obligations. The values produced by the model define the nature of the alliance relationship between J and K.

$$Alliance\ Reputation_{ijN} = \frac{\sum\limits_{k \neq i,j}^{N} AH_{jk}S_{ik}}{N-2} \qquad (5.3)$$

where N is the size of the system

           AH_{jk} is the Alliance History score between j and k,

           S_{ik} is the similarity between i and k.

Measuring Alliance Reputation

With this measure of direct alliance history in place, the next step is to generate a variable that represents the aggregation of the $\overrightarrow{jk}$ dyadic alliance histories into a reputation variable for J: Alliance Reputation. To do this, I first apply a similarity weight to each dyadic Alliance History observation to represent how valuable this information is to I, then I simply sum the weighted histories, normalized by the number of states in the international system. To capture the dimension of state K's proxy relevance to state I, I use Signorino and Ritter's (1999) S–Similarity Score.[39] This measure captures the foreign policy similarity of I and K. Similarity of foreign policies is important to I's calculation. If the foreign policies of I and K were to be divergent, I would be unlikely to gain useful information from its observation of J's (un)reliability to K. Therefore, although the S–Similarity Score ranges from -1 to 1, I constrain the measure to values that fall between 0 and 1 by changing all negative values to zero. In this way, I am able to show that as the foreign policies of I and K become increasingly similar, I can intuit that J is likely to treat I similarly to the way it has historically treated K in the $J-K$ alliance. As the foreign policies of I and K become increasingly divergent, the value of K as a proxy for I decreases toward zero. In the empirical model, S_{ikt} is used to represent the ϕ_{ikt} component.[40]

State I's calculation of J's reputation for reliability is thus represented by Alliance Reputation. State I updates this assessment at each time point, which in the measure occurs every year. This reputation variable is generated for three samples to determine the robustness of my argument across different alliance types. As such, Alliance Reputation is generated for (1) all alliance types, including multilateral and bilateral alliances, (2) all bilateral alliance types,

---

[39] I have also generated alternate measures of Alliance Reputation using both the S-Score and a CINC similarity score, in order to capture both policy and power similarity. I have also measured Alliance Reputation weighting only by a CINC similarity score. I then ran robustness checks on the regression analyses using these alternative measures. The results are consistent with what I present here, and thus I use only the single representative measure here for parsimony.

[40] There are two important concerns with this approach. First, it may be argued that modeling reputation in this way may not account for situational aspects of compliance events. But, I would argue, features of compliance situations are captured by the foreign policy similarity relevance criterion. If states I and K have very similar foreign policy orientations, they are likely to have similar interests in the outcomes of crises in which alliance partners are obligated to act. Increasing the complexity of the model to reflect the specific characteristics of each compliance situation unnecessarily complicates the model without adding a great deal of additional traction. Second, it may be argued that various other similarity characteristics may be used to represent the ϕ_{ik} component. Given the centrality of security concerns in forming alliances, power similarity may be an important component of a properly constructed reputation model. In the subsequent discussion of the results I include a robustness check that accounts for power similarity between state I and K. However, the results do not change substantially. The similarity of foreign policies between I and K is the primary relevance criterion used by states in judging one another's reputations, as the foreign policy interests of states are central to their alliance formation and compliance calculi.

and (3) multilateral and bilateral defensive alliances. My expectations do not change across samples, as there is no theoretical reason to expect differences. Consistent results for each should indicate that the findings are not driven by a particular alliance type. Each operationalization theoretically ranges from -1 to 1, i.e., a completely unreliable reputation to one that is fully reliable, with actual values of the most inclusive reputation variable varying from -0.318 to 0.611.

Controlling for Other Causes of Alliance Formation

This chapter is about the role of alliance reputation on alliance formation, but it would be silly to claim that this reputation stands alone as a predictor of all alliances. To account for other explanations of alliance formation, I include a number of control variables, in an effort to be sure that the models do not suffer from omitted variable bias. Several of the variables are taken from Lai and Reiter (2000), where a complete description of the variables can be found.[41] My dependent variable differs from Lai and Reiter's in that I focus on alliance formation, whereas Lai and Reiter analyze the yearly presence of an alliance. Still, the results on the control variables match rather well with these previous studies. I use two variables to evaluate how the regime type of the states within a dyad may influence alliance onset. Both measures are constructed using Polity IV data.[42] Joint Democracy is a dummy variable that codes whether or not both states in the dyad are democratic. Each state must have a score of 5 or above on the Polity scale for this variable to gain a value of 1.[43] Polity Difference measures the similarity of regime types between states in each dyad. This variable is coded by taking the absolute value of the difference between the regime scores of each state in the dyad. As this value increases, the dyadic regime types become increasingly dissimilar. Also, I control for whether both states in the dyad face a shared threat. Joint Enemy is a dichotomous variable reflecting whether or not both states have engaged in a dispute with the same country over the last ten years. The variable is coded using the Militarized Interstate Dispute (MID) dataset (Jones, Bremer, and Singer, 1996). Distance measures the number of miles between capital cities of each state in the dyad. In line with Lai and Reiter, I take the

---

[41] See also Gibler and Wolford, 2006; Gibler, 2008.

[42] Jaggers and Gurr, 1995.

[43] This specification is used in order to maintain consistency with the Lai and Reiter (2000) research design. I have performed sensitivity analyses using 7 as a cutoff instead of 5, with similar results.

square root of the total distance between capitals. If the states are contiguous, the distance is measured as zero. Major Power Status is a dichotomous variable coding whether at least one of the states in the dyad is a global power. Both Distance and Major Power Status are drawn from COW data. Each of the Lai and Reiter variables is updated from 1992 to 2000.

Three other controls not addressed in Lai and Reiter's work are included here, in an effort to round out the alternative explanations that might be driving alliance onset. First, I account for the direct historical alliance behavior between the two states in the dyad. Alliance History is constructed using a component similar to the reputation model described above. However, whereas reputation refers to extra-dyadic information that state I gains about J through J's historical treatment of all other states K, Alliance History considers *only* the historical alliance information within the $I-J$ dyad. In other words, I learns from the way that J has treated I over time. I expect that the more positively I is treated by J, the more likely it will be that further alliance ties will be formalized in the dyad. While the alliance reputation variable accounts for all the extra-dyadic learning that can occur, it fails to account for direct learning within the dyad. The Alliance History variable picks up that direct historical information. Second, Portfolio Similarity judges the level of similarity between the alliance portfolios of each pair of countries.[44] Where states share a number mutual alliance partners, their likelihood of allying with one another should increase given the overlap of their foreign policy preferences. Lastly, the Interstate Interaction Score (*IIS*) measures past conflict and cooperation more broadly.[45] Rather than assessing alliance behavior, the *IIS* assesses the overall tenor of the conflictual or cooperative relationship between I and J. The *IIS* model records militarized disputes to represent conflictual interactions and new joint IGO memberships to represent cooperative interactions. The *IIS* is a useful control because it simultaneously identifies rivalrous dyads along with friendly dyads.[46]

These controls account for several broader categories of alliance formation explanations including shared interests, interstate similarities, capability aggregation, and threat approximation. Therefore, a significant finding for the reputation variables should provide evidence in support of the theoretical propositions that

---

[44] Signorino and Ritter (1999).

[45] Crescenzi, Enterline, and Long (2008).

[46] The models were also analyzed with a Bilateral Trade variable (Trade/GDP), with no change in the sign/significance of the Alliance Reputation variable. I omit the trade variable from the published results because trade is so highly correlated with some of the other controls

reputation influences alliance onset. The inclusion of the independent variables yields a dataset for all directed dyads from 1816 to 2000.

Findings: Alliance Reputation and the Onset of Alliances

The results of the analyses are reported in Table 5.1 and Table 5.2. In order to conduct a comprehensive evaluation, each of the six models addresses a separate sample of alliance formation. Table 5.1 contains three empirical models that analyze the effect of alliance reputation information on alliance onset. Model 1 is the most inclusive, testing the alliance reputation hypothesis using all types of alliances for the entire history of the modern state system. The analysis indicates that states with a reputation for upholding past alliance commitments are more likely to be chosen as allies by other states in the future. I then disaggregate the analysis based on the type of alliance being considered. I am particularly interested in disaggregating the information that states glean from observing other states in multilateral alliances versus bilateral alliances. Multilateral alliances are complex and often involve disproportionate influence by hegemonic or large states, and these complexities might mitigate or obfuscate state reputations. To test this influence bias, I reanalyze the data using only bilateral alliances to inform the alliance reputation score. Model 2 in Table 5.1 contains the results of this test. Perhaps the best way to interpret the results of this test is to conclude that when states consider potential allies for bilateral alliances they pay attention to state reputations for bilateral alliances. That is not to say that multilateral alliance information is meaningless, only that the bilateral reputation information is useful on its own when considering alliance formation.

As a second robustness test, I then reanalyze the reputation hypothesis to determine whether the type of the alliance commitment matters when evaluating past behavior. To do this, I again re-operationalized the alliance reputation score using only information generated from defense pacts. I then analyzed the effect of reputation for behavior in defense pacts on the onset of new defense pacts, as summarized in Model 3 of Table 5.1. Once again, the analysis indicates that a reputation for upholding one's commitments has a positive and significant impact on a state's attractiveness as a future ally.[47] Whether states

---

[47] In addition to Model 3, I analyzed a subsequent model that judged state reputations for honoring/violating offensive alliance agreements on a dependent variable that only coded offensive agreements. Again, states with positive reputations for offensive alliance reliability had an increased

Table 5.1 **Analysis of Alliance Onset**

Variable	Model 1 All Alliances 1816–2000	Model 2 Bilateral Alliances 1816–2000	Model 3 Defense Pacts 1816–2000
Alliance Reputation	1.44***	1.52***	0.56**
	(.20)	(.23)	(.19)
Alliance History	0.62	0.63	1.00
	(.61)	(.61)	(.61)
Portfolio Similarity	0.62***	0.62***	0.79***
	(.04)	(.04)	(.06)
Interaction Score (IIS)	0.20**	0.20**	0.45***
	(.06)	(.06)	(.10)
Joint Enemy	0.55***	0.55***	0.80***
	(.01)	(.01)	(.01)
Distance	−0.01***	−0.01***	−0.01***
	(.00)	(.00)	(.00)
Major Power Status	0.12***	0.12***	0.04*
	(.01)	(.01)	(.02)
Polity Difference	−0.001	−0.001	−0.01***
	(.00)	(.00)	(.00)
Joint Democracy	0.21***	0.21***	−0.05**
	(.01)	(.01)	(.02)
Constant	−2.54***	−2.54***	−3.00***
	(.04)	(.04)	(.06)
Observations	1,045,707	1,045,707	1,045,707
Wald χ^2 (9)	10,226.43***	10,242.20***	9,012.84***
Pseudo R^2	.14	.14	.16
Log-likelihood	−36816.32	−36817.63	−24247.92

*** = significant at the .001 level, ** = .01, * = .05
Robust standard errors clustered by directed dyad in parentheses

assign reputations to one another based strictly on the type of alliance considered is still an open question, but these three empirical analyses point to two clear

likelihood of being sought for future offensive alliances. The consistency of results across different alliance types indicates that no single alliance type is driving the results of the more inclusive samples.

Table 5.2 **Analysis of Alliance Onset Before, During, and After the World Wars**

Variable	Model 4 All Alliances 1816–1913	Model 5 All Alliances 1914–1945	Model 6 All Alliances 1946–2000
Alliance Reputation	13.38***	−1.08***	2.82***
	(4.19)	(.30)	(.48)
Alliance History	−1.33	0.26	1.20
	(6.56)	(.67)	(2.43)
Portfolio Similarity	2.28***	−1.31***	1.30***
	(.46)	(.07)	(.06)
Interaction Score (IIS)	−0.27	0.15	0.22*
	(.15)	(.12)	(.09)
Joint Enemy	0.74***	1.10***	0.17***
	(.05)	(.03)	(.02)
Distance	−0.02***	−0.007***	−0.02***
	(.00)	(.00)	(.00)
Major Power Status	0.67***	−0.15***	0.38***
	(.06)	(.03)	(.02)
Polity Difference	−0.02***	−0.005*	0.001
	(.01)	(.00)	(.00)
Joint Democracy	−0.22*	−0.49***	0.30***
	(.11)	(.06)	(.02)
Constant	−4.64***	−1.08***	−2.91***
	(.42)	(.09)	(.05)
Observations	104,360	99,098	842,249
Wald χ^2 (9)	955.99***	2,895.49***	7,033.80***
Pseudo R^2	.31	.20	.18
Log-likelihood	−1304.38	−7566.24	−24950.54

*** = significant at the .001 level, ** = .01,* = .05
Robust standard errors clustered by directed dyad in parentheses

conclusions. First, alliance reputations influence alliance onset in positive ways. When states develop a reputation for upholding their agreements, that historical behavior attracts future allies. Second, the specific type of alliance being formed in the present may cause states to pay attention primarily to reputations with respect to that type of alliance.

However, I find somewhat surprising results when the model is constrained to the 1914–1945 period. Lastly, the presence of at least one global power in the dyad increases the potential for an alliance formation. Given the global interests of major powers, these states tend to form more alliance ties, in an effort to fulfill their global ambitions. Again, the 1914–1945 period produces a contradictory result. Model 3 thus produces a number of confounding results, which, as I argue below, is likely due to the special circumstances of the time period, which appear to wreak havoc on standard alliance formation dynamics.[48]

Across the models, there is considerable consistency among the results produced by the control variables. In general, there are no surprises. Judging from Table 5.1, a number of conclusions can be drawn. First, in several models, regime type appears to be related to alliance formation. States that are increasingly divergent in their regime types are less likely to form partnerships.[49] Furthermore, conflict histories play an important role in the forming of alliance ties. When states share a common enemy (represented by Joint Enemy), an alliance is more likely to form, regardless of the time period or alliance type addressed. Furthermore, with the exception of insignificant findings in the pre–WWI, WWI, and WWII eras, the Interaction Interaction (IIS) variable produces a positive coefficient. In other words, the more cooperative and less conflictual states are with one another in other areas of their foreign relations, the more likely they are to ally.

An increasing difference of philosophy and focus between two states also has a negative effect on the likelihood of alliance formation, as the efficacy of an alliance is inversely related to differences of focus and concern. Similarly, as the

[48] While there may be a number of explanations, the somewhat unstable results noted in Model 2 relative to the others may be due to the drastic decrease in observations that is a consequence of restraining the time period under analysis. Also, Model 6 is the only other model that shows some inconsistency, and this may be the result of a lack of 1s on the dependent variable as offensive pacts are the least common alliance type among the types analyzed. The fact that Alliance Reputation remains consistently positive and significant across each model type should thus provide robust evidence for the reputation arguments.

[49] However, these results do not appear to be highly robust to alternative specifications, noted by the insignificant findings in the other models. Also, jointly democratic dyads display some inconsistency, showing both positive and negative relationships on alliance formation depending upon the time period analyzed and the type of alliance considered. These results thus provide some support for contradicting arguments contending that either states of similar regime types are likely to align with one another (Siverson and Emmons, 1991) or that the alignment of like states is a post–WWII phenomenon (Simon and Gartzke, 1996).

distance between states' foreign-policy interests decreases, their likelihood of forming an alliance increases, indicated by the Portfolio Similarity variable.

Lastly, Alliance History is insignificant across each model, and little of substance can be said about its effect. Still, other than that this result may not be terribly surprising. This variable captures the historical reliability of states by measuring how reliable state I has been toward its partner J. For this variable to be positive and significant, state I would need to attract additional alliance ties from J on top of its existing agreement as a consequence of I's reliability in past performance opportunities within the dyad. Formalizing additional alliance ties on top of those that already exist occurs less frequently, and the continued addition of alliance ties would likely be unnecessary. Rather, one should more reasonably expect that the information produced by I's performance toward its partner J would be more important to other states K in the system that are seeking alliance partners. It is to these reputational expectations that I now turn.

Models 2 through 4 attempt to determine whether the result in Model 1 is a product of different time periods. Thus, I run separate models to address the years leading up to World War I, the world wars themselves, the interwar period, and the years following World War II. The results from Model 1 remain unchanged in Models 2 and 4, providing further support for my reputation argument. However, Model 3 reports a negative relationship. This is a peculiar finding. However, the context of this particular time period may assist in more fully comprehending this result. Note that this time period produces somewhat inconsistent results for several variables relative to the other models. The years of both global conflicts and the brief interim between them were a period of extreme systemic instability. The rapidly changing power relationships among the major power states likely had a special effect on explanations of alliance formation. With regard to the role of reputation, it appears that during times of great systemic upheaval, alliance seekers may sacrifice their interests in reliability for tactical concerns like countering a powerful and threatening common enemy or allying with proximate states that offer practical geographic opportunities to collaborate militarily. While it may seem that such an unstable time period would be a relevant circumstance under which states would seek partners with strong compliance reputations, this does not appear to be the case.

Instead, the result in Model 3 points to different explanations. For example, it may be that when an extreme international threat to system stability and state survival exists, countries deemphasize the importance of reputation in exchange for commitments from states that can offer substantial capability in defending against what comes to be recognized as a common and ubiquitous threat.

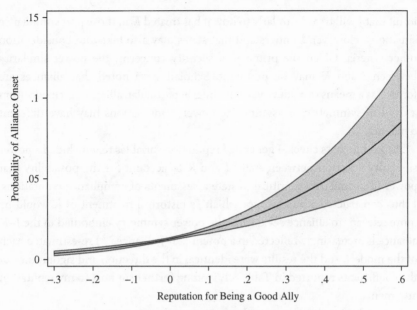

Figure 5.7 Predicted Likelihood of Alliance Formation, 1816–2000.

Except during the 1914 to 1945 period, the remaining models are supportive of my reputation hypothesis. The effects of reputation on alliance formation are consistent and stable. The interwar period tells a different story—as it should. After World War I, the fundamental building blocks of alliances in Europe were demolished, and the reverberations were felt across the globe, as isolationism set in, followed by the Great Depression.

In Figure 5.7, I present a visualization of the substantive effects of alliance reputation as analyzed in Model 1. The vertical axis represents the likelihood of a state enjoying a new alliance. The horizontal axis represents that state's reputation for being a good or bad ally, with negative numbers indicating a reputation for violating agreements and positive numbers indicating a reputation for upholding agreements. Figure 5.7 clearly shows a meaningful increase in the probability of new alliances for states with positive alliance reputations.

In addition to the models reported, I conducted several robustness checks of the results. First, I believe that foreign policy similarity is the primary relevance criterion considered by states when judging another state's reputation. Not only should foreign policy similarity act as a reflection of similar preferences, but it should also account for situational aspects of compliance events. In other words, when states I and K have similar foreign policy orientations, alliance seeker I can intuit that J will treat I similarly to how it has treated K in those past compliance situations. However, I understand that states may also take into consideration other criteria. Given the primacy of security concerns, the power similarity between I and K may be pertinent. Scholars have noted that alliances are formed as a means to achieve various ends; in particular, alliances formed within a dyad of symmetric or asymmetric power combinations may have different dynamics.

As a robustness check, I generated reputation variables that included a power similarity criterion between states I and K to account for the possibility that power (dis)similarity is critical to state assessments of compliance reputations. I thus constructed a measure for which J's historical treatment of K would be more relevant to alliance seeker I as the power symmetry embodied in the $J–K$ alliance is increasingly reflected in a potential $I–J$ alliance.[50] I re-estimated each of the models, and the results were identical in the direction and significance of the coefficients reported in Table 5.1, lending further support to my reputation arguments.

In an additional robustness check, I ran analyses on two samples: potential allies (J states) that are minor powers, vs. major powers. This more focused analysis enables us to roughly view how important reputation is versus the most dominant motivation for alliance formation: power. My results are intuitive: alliance reputations matter more for smaller states than they do for major powers. The coefficient for the Alliance Reputation variable remains positive and significant for the minor power sample, but loses statistical significance when I only sample major powers. The analysis confirms my suspicion that the more powerful a potential ally, the smaller the market for potential allies, and the more that dimension of the calculations dominate foreign policy decisions. On the flip side, when states primarily bring legitimacy, location, or other non-power qualities to an alliance, and when there are multiple states as potential allies, reputation matters more.

I also examine whether my approach of weighting historical information with relevance criteria obscures simpler means by which states judge reputation. In this line of argument, states simply observe how potential partners performed in upholding past agreements, without concern for relevance criteria. If this is the case, an "irrelevant" foreign policy similarity criterion may be driving my results.

---

[50] The power similarity weights between I and K were generated using Composite Index of National Capabilities scores from Singer and Small (1972). Power similarity ranged from 0 to 1, with 0 representing complete dissimilarity of power between I and K and 1 indicating perfect similarity.

I thus removed all relevance criteria from my measures and re-estimated each model. Again, the results were consistent with those reported in Table 5.1.[51]

Next, given that I am attempting to explain alliance formation, there is little reason to include a lagged dependent variable in the analysis, as might be more appropriate for analyses of alliance prevalence. Yet, I have noted this practice in previous work,[52] and for consistency, I replicated each model by including the lagged presence of an alliance within each dyad. However, this did not change the direction or significance of the reputation variable. Also, noting the prevalence of zeros and the small number of ones on the dependent variable, I reconsidered each of my reported models using a rare events logit. Again, the results for my reputation variable remained consistent with the results reported.

Lastly, given the dispersion of the variables of interest, and the large number of standard deviations necessary to encompass the full range of observations, I generated new reputation variables that dropped all extreme outliers which included any observation that fell outside of five standard deviations from the mean. Once again, the results were very similar to those presented in Table 5.1. The one exception was that upon dropping the outliers, the reputation variable produced a positive and significant effect on alliance formation during the 1914–1945 period. This change, however, is actually in line with my theorized expectation, and is thus more supportive of my theory than the result reported in Model 3 of Table 5.1. With this exception, the analyses indicated that the results were not being driven by outliers.

Discussion and Conclusion

Overall, these findings provide support for the idea that when nations seek alliance partners, they pay close attention to the past alliance behavior of their potential partners. While this may seem like an intuitive conclusion to an intuitive discussion about the role of history in foreign policy, it is worth pointing out that scholars have often questioned the relevance of reputation and history in determining the foreign policy choices of governments.[53] My results point to the value of the reputations that states form by their actions toward others over time, providing further support for work in the literature that highlights the

---

[51] Given my theoretical expectations with regard to the value of relevance criteria and the importance of interstate (dis)similarities, I report the results produced by the original models.

[52] Gibler and Wolford, 2006.

[53] Mercer, 1996; Press, 2005.

importance of historical information.[54] My analysis suggests that the dismissal of past actions is premature, at least with respect to states' pursuit of alliance partners.

In fact, my analysis notes that state reputations can weigh rather heavily in the decision-making process. Looking more closely at the results produced in Model 1, I generated the predicted probabilities of forming an alliance when Alliance Reputation is varied from low to high values, while simultaneously holding all of the continuous control variables at their means and all dichotomous controls at their modal values.[55] Substantively, varying Alliance Reputation from its lower to upper extremes produces an increase in the likelihood of alliance formation, increasing the probability of an alliance from nearly zero to over 2.64 percent. Given the low ex ante likelihood of any two states joining in an alliance with one another (.2 percent), which results from the high prevalence of zeros and the small number of ones in the data set, this increase is substantial. However, the range of the reputation variable is rather dispersed, suggesting this substantive illustration is unrealistic. Therefore, I also generated predicted probabilities that moved the values of Alliance Reputation from three standard deviations below to three standard deviations above the mean value. This increase in alliance reliability reputation increased the likelihood of an alliance formation by approximately 38 percent—a substantial rise in the likelihood that states will be sought for alliance relationships. Thus, even when controlling for a number of other relevant explanations, state reputation plays an important role in the process of alliance formation.[56]

---

[54] For example, work on interstate rivalry (Diehl and Goertz, 2001) and state learning (Leng, 2000), and recent research on historic information and state reputations (Crescenzi, 2007; Crescenzi, Kathman, and Long, 2007) all point to the importance of past events in shaping future phenomena.

[55] Predicted probabilities were computed using Clarify Software (Tomz, Wittenberg, and King, 2001).

[56] Scholars often report changes in predicted probabilities by varying the values of individual variables from their minimum to their maximum values while holding all other variables in the model constant. The following list reports a percentage change in the predicted probability of alliance formation for each variable using the results reported in Model 1. In generating these values, each variable is moved from its minimum to its maximum while holding all other continuous variables at their means and all other categorical variables at their modal values: Alliance Reputation=+4,988%; Alliance History=+795%; Portfolio Similarity=+1,149%; Interaction Score (IIS)=+131%; Joint Enemy=+383%; Distance=−98%; Major Power Status=+45%; Polity Difference=−6%; Joint Democracy=+90%. These calculations offer one way to consider the relative strength of each variable.

On further investigation, I also note that the effect of a state's reputation appears to have an increasingly notable effect on the likelihood of alliance formation in more recent time periods. In two additional analyses, the predicted probabilities of alliance formation were conducted for the Cold War and the post–Cold War eras, again using a range of three standard deviations above and below the mean for Alliance Reputation. The calculation for the Cold War era revealed an increase of 60 percent, while the post–Cold War period produced a massive 389 percent increase in the likelihood of alliance formation.[57] This percent increase thus provides initial evidence that state reputations have become increasingly important in informing alliance formation decisions.

This is an interesting finding with regard to broader theories of international relations. For one, realist balance of power theories argue that the world is least stable during periods of multipolar competition. The model analyzing the 1914 to 1945 period addresses one such period. A multipolar system lacks a clear power hierarchy and is highly complex, and thus tends toward instability. One might think that state reputations for reliability would be most valuable during these periods, given system complexity and the potential for costly conflict. However, many of the variables in this model produce unexpected results, as does Alliance Reputation. Although the result for Alliance Reputation is driven by extreme outliers, it does appear that our understanding of alliance dynamics during periods of highly unstable major-power relations may be under-informed. In more stable eras, however, states appear to rely heavily upon historical reputations when making national security decisions. This is interesting because the Cold War and post–Cold War systems are quite dissimilar in terms of major power competition. During the Cold War, East–West bloc politics tended to make alliance systems rather rigid, as a result of states' shared threats. Yet, even in this period, state reputations were critically relevant to alliance decision making. Thus, even the ubiquitous and unifying threat posed by contending blocs does not reduce reputation to an immaterial issue.

Indeed, the results point to the weighty importance of reputation during such periods. Even though a bipolar system may be expected to tend toward stability, the value that states place on the historical reliability of their partners may be particularly important to their balancing calculus. Similarly, in the post–Cold

---

[57] The Cold War was coded as occurring between 1950 and 1989. The post–Cold War era was coded as all years beyond 1989. Although these models are not reported, the coefficient signs and significance levels produced by the models are very similar for each of the variables to those reported in Table 5.1.

War period, when bloc competition has receded, and when great powers are not posed with a unifying threat to their survival, state reputations appear to be most relevant. In this line of thinking, when no omnipresent shared enemy exists, reputations may serve as one of very few tools by which states can punish shirking behavior. While rigid bloc politics may act to limit the ability and willingness of states to violate alliance terms, in the post–Cold War world, such unified positions need not necessarily exist. As a result, reputation becomes increasingly important as an informational tool used by states in selecting reliable partners, since the fear of subjugation by an opposing bloc is no longer present.

A similar effect was produced for subsequent models, even as the subset of alliance types changed. In the period preceding the end of WWII, varying Alliance Reputation from its minimum to its maximum increased the likelihood of alliance formation by 503 percent. In the post–WWII period, the increase rose to 17,875 percent. In Model 4, varying the bilateral reputation score yielded an increase in the probability of alliance formation by 2,720 percent. Moving defensive alliance reputation from its lowest to highest value produced a 951 percent fold increase. Finally, the increase in the probability of offensive alliance formation rose by 3,168 percent.

Interestingly, relative to each of the control variables, Alliance Reputation produced one of the most substantial effects on the likelihood of an alliance forming within the dyad, second only to Portfolio Similarity. Figure 5.7 displays the substantive effects of each variable analyzed in Model 1. Notably, Interaction History, Joint Enemy, and Direct Alliance History also have a substantial effect on the likelihood that a state will be sought as an alliance partner, although Direct Alliance History was insignificant in the model. This is not particularly surprising, given the theoretical and empirical evidence provided by the extant literature on the topic. What is interesting, however, is that even given the strong effect of these and other variables, Alliance Reputation nevertheless produces a powerful effect on the likelihood of alliance formation.

The results presented above indicate that a state's reputation for honoring or violating its prior alliance commitments is an important (but not the only) predictor of that state's ability to attract alliance partners in the future. My findings are indicative of the calculations states make when selecting their allies. The formalization of an alliance agreement may fulfill a number of essential state requirements. Alliances may improve the strength and security of a state, offer more autonomy of action, resolve collective action problems, or reduce the resource burden of maintaining self-sufficient forces. However, these benefits that accrue to states only obtain when the agreements are upheld. As such, states are particularly interested in formalizing agreements that they expect to be honored when the terms obligate.

Yet, the information available to states regarding future compliance is necessarily limited, as no state can perfectly predict the future circumstances under which alliance partners will be obligated to act. A state's reputation for (non)compliance is an important factor that shapes state expectations of a potential alliance partner's willingness and ability to uphold its promises. When a potential partner has shown little willingness to honor its prior commitments, alliance seekers will likewise have little faith in the potential partner's likelihood of respecting a prospective future agreement. As such, states with negative reputations find it more difficult to obtain allies. Those with positive reputations, on the other hand, are far more capable of securing the agreements that they require, because their reputations as historically compliant partners are observed by and appeal to other alliance seekers in the international system.

These results point to future research avenues yet to be explored. Indeed, our conceptualization of alliance reliability reputation need not be limited to an explanation of alliance formation; rather, successfully accounting for reputations for compliance with alliance terms may be relevant to explanations of various alliance phenomena. For example, formal alliance commitments vary in the specificity of their terms. Existing scholarship suggests that states will seek to design these commitments in a way that best serves their own needs.[58] As such, due to various factors, states may be faced with a limited pool of potential alliance partners. Indeed, there may be instances in which states choose to form alliances with partners whose compliance reputations are rather suspect. In these situations, alliance seekers may choose to design obligation terms that are more fully institutionalized and create tangible incentives for historically unreliable partners to honor their future commitments when called upon to do so. Alternatively, more reliable allies likely achieve more flexibility as a result of their dependability. In this sense, successfully conceptualizing and accounting for treaty compliance reputations may not simply be relevant to alliance formation. Rather, a range of alliance phenomena may be reliant upon reputations for reliability, and I expect future research on these issues will yield interesting theoretical and empirical insights into alliance dynamics.

My theoretical and empirical analysis is limited here to a single issue area. It may also be likely that foreign policymakers take care to manage their reputations within a broader realm of issues. This may already be the case, of course, and

[58] Koremenos, Lipson, and Snidal, 2001.

we need only to return to the discussion of recent Polish foreign policy choices to underscore this point. Poland had carved out a new reputation for being a staunch, reliable ally of the United States, possibly in the hope that this reputation will translate into political and economic benefits in dimensions of international relations beyond alliance behavior. One valuable course of future research, it seems, would be to examine how a state's reputation for behavior in one dimension of politics (i.e. alliance behavior) translates into political or economic opportunities along additional dimensions, such as economic organization membership, trade agreements, or capital flows. Such research would improve our understanding of the effects that historical events and state reputations have in manipulating future expectations.

The historic alliance negotiations of the early twentieth century, discussed earlier, also underscore the point further. Germany had carved out a new reputation for lacking the willingness to uphold its agreements, causing negotiations between it and the United Kingdom to break down. However, Japan was simultaneously in search of a partner for protection against Russian expansionism in the Far East. Britain was considered an excellent potential ally, and this was not lost on Japan. As Miller states, "When Komura Jutaro became foreign minister in September 1901...one of his first acts was to have the Foreign Ministry determine whether Britain had ever violated her obligations under an alliance. The response...was that it had never abandoned an ally."[59] For Japan, the subsequent Anglo–Japanese alliance that materialized offered a balance of power against Russian advances in Asia. For the British, other issues were addressed, including colonial interests and the maintenance of secure and open trade routes. It thus may be reasonable to argue that states also value their reputations in one area of interstate relations because they translate to payoffs in other issue areas. One valuable course of future research, it seems, would be to examine how a state's reputation for behavior in one dimension of politics (i.e. alliance behavior) translates into political or economic opportunities along additional international dimensions. Such research would improve our understanding of the effects of historical events and state reputations upon the manipulation of future expectations.

[59] Miller, 2004, p. 119.

6

Implications and Conclusions

"I should of knew," George said hopelessly. "I guess maybe way back in my head I did."

—John Steinbeck, *Of Mice and Men*

A Reputation Revival?

Stepping back from the big-picture empirical analyses in the previous chapters, what are the lessons to be learned from this study of reputation? Is it time for scholars of world politics to renew their focus on reputation as a key causative factor in political behavior? Do state leaders learn from the behavior of other states in the international system? Hopefully I have convinced you that this is indeed the case, and that the best way to move forward with the study of reputation is to remember the informational role that reputation plays in global relations.

In this book I have chosen to focus on the competence dimension of reputation. The importance of competence is contextual, but also consistent and systematic. The criteria states employ to determine one another's competence based on reputational information varies both across and within types of interstate behavior. In other words, actions that illustrate competence in a crisis situation are most likely different than those actions that show competence in contracting, or institutional compliance. Despite these differences, however, the issue of competence is at the heart of the role reputation plays in influencing world politics. This is because states use reputational information to form expectations about future behavior, and competence is a cornerstone for building those expectations.

In this chapter, I review the role of reputation and competence in the phenomena of conflict and cooperation, broadly construed. I then briefly discuss some possible extensions of the basic reputation model developed herein, as well as the possibility of extending the use of the reputation model to study reputation in other dimensions of world politics. This includes a focus on non-state actors, in both cooperative and conflictual contexts. Finally, I delve into the policy implications that emerge when we focus on reputation and learning as suggested throughout this book. Ultimately, this research suggests that shifting perceptions in policy-making from aggressive strength to crisis competence can lead to greater peace and security throughout the international system.

Reputation and Conflict

Perhaps the most controversial result of this research is the suggestion that a state with a reputation for participating in militarized disputes and wars is more likely to experience this kind of conflict in the future with other states. Like everyone of my generation, I grew up during the Cold War, and the mantra of "peace through strength" was never far from our minds. The core finding of this book with respect to conflict, however, is that conflict is too highly correlated with incompetence in crisis management, and thus attempts to project a reputation of strength often end up translating into reputations for aggression. This finding is consistent with much of the current research on recurrent conflict, adding a reputational dimension to what we already know about direct repeated violence. Thus, peace through strength can easily degrade into failed policy that leads to more war.[1]

The notion that engaging in violence leads to a reputation for aggression, rather than one for strength, is corroborated throughout history. Alexander observed Napoleon's unceasing drive to conquer new lands, and correctly surmised that despite their agreements, Napoleon would soon attempt to conquer Russia as well. Had Napoleon been able to convince Alexander that he would competently adhere to the Treaty of Tilsit, Alexander might not have been prepared for the impending French invasion. Because Napoleon conveyed a reputation for aggression and disdain for promises, Alexander could not see a way to comply with Napoleon's ultimate demands. As such, he saw no choice but to prepare for war, assuming (correctly) the worst.

The more abstract quantitative analyses of reputation's role in conflict cannot match the specificity of this causal connection in the historical illustration of Napoleon and Alexander. But these analyses do provide an opportunity to test

---

[1] Bacevich, 2010; Wood, 2016.

the argument that violence is perceived as incompetence, and thus as aggression. Across time and space, the results show that violence begets violence. Peace through strength turns out to be an elusive result.

This is not a blanket argument against strength, however. The logic and mechanisms of deterrence are still core foreign policy tools for states, and these results should not be interpreted as a call for demilitarization. The reputation model simply shows that the incompetent use of the tools of strength leads to an undermining of the very goal states ultimately seek: namely, security. My approach assumed a basic bargaining process underlying the security interactions between states, and even allows for some conflict to emerge through the standard mechanisms of information and commitment problems. The rare event of militarized violence is one thing, but the emergence of a reputation for war is another. Once that reputation emerges, states are less likely to navigate crises peacefully.

Reputation and Cooperation

Similarly, competence plays an important role in shaping states' reputations in the realm of international cooperation. The focus on alliance behavior provides an analogous rare-events analysis to provide as much comparison with the conflict analysis as possible. Alliance behavior is a blend of institutional compliance and partnership. Contracts emerge between allies, designed to set expectations both between allies and for external observers. In a security alliance, we typically expect those external observers to be potential threats. Yet by focusing on the reputation of states and their willingness to comply with their alliance commitments, we see that potential allies also become external observers. The evidence suggests that states that develop reputations for upholding their commitments are more likely to be sought out as allies in the future, precisely due to the reputational information provided to observer states outside the alliance.

There are, of course, many other dimensions of cooperation that can provide information to states about the reputations of their peers. Other high-profile commitments such as trade agreements could also provide interesting grounds for study. Given that many such agreements are now multilateral in nature, observing defection from the agreed-upon standards could be easier in some circumstances. Tomz, in a landmark 2007 book, demonstrates how reputation can have a fundamental influence on bond markets. It is quite plausible to envision studies of reputation where states or firms use reputational information as a proxy for assessing the quality of an investment. As such, reputation becomes a way for actors to perceive risk—indeed, at times it may be the only source of information pertaining to risk. As more direct information emerges, the reputational information becomes less salient and thus less influential.

Research need not only focus on the ocurrence or absence of cooperation. As Mattes (2012) argues, such reputational information can affect the conditions of future contracts as well as the contracts themselves. Mattes shows that a state with a reputation for failing to live up to its agreements may not be excluded entirely from future agreements. Instead, it may be forced to accept more stringent or disadvantageous contracts in order to be a part of an agreement. Thus, contracts may become more binding, or include more punitive clauses that are enforced upon defection. As such, we can see that reputation affects not only the likelihood of cooperation, but also the qualities and efficiencies associated with cooperation.

Building from Here: Extensions and Implications

Beyond this immediate extension of examining additional dimensions of cooperation among states, there are several directions for improving and extending this basic work. Here I consider just a few such options, focusing on the changing role of reputation depending on the type of actor in world politics, as well as the potentially differential dynamics of building versus losing reputations.

Reputation and Non-State Actors

The bulk of research in this book has been about states and their leaders, working from the assumption in the quantitative analyses that the function of learning is certainly heterogeneous across states, but leads to consistent findings about competence that can be aggregated to the state level. But how do reputations matter for actors in world politics that are not states? The reputation model is ultimately about information provision, and as such it is relevant for non-state actors at multiple levels of analysis in international relations. Scholars need to identify, however, the informational needs of the protagonists in order to properly specify the role of reputation.

For example, in some recent coauthored work,[2] we examined the role of reputation in determining the viability and success of non-governmental orga-

---

[2] Gent et al., 2015.

nizations (NGOs). In this context, we were interested in understanding how an NGO develops and maintains a reputation for competence with respect to the funds it receives from donors. NGOs rarely supply their own funds, and almost always rely on donors for survival. And, NGOs have been frequently vilified in public, ridiculed as incompetent organizations with lofty goals that never seem to be realized. But what if these organizations face unseen constraints that hobble their ability to achieve their goals? One such unseen constraint is the need to maintain a good reputation in the eyes of the organization's donors. For the donors, the information needed is the competence of the NGO in terms of using the donor's investment properly (where "properly" is defined by the owner of wealth, that is, the donor). We can think of the donors as the protagonists, searching for information about whether their investments will succeed. The NGOs are antagonists in this study, purposefully conveying information through their behavior over time that donors use to assess competence. Applying the insight that NGOs are viewed by their donors as rapidly changing, fragile organizations, we in effect demonstrate that NGOs become their own proxies. Specifically, past behavior by the NGO serves as a proxy for competence in the next round of funding.

Indeed, we found that because NGOs are dynamic, perishable organizations, they constantly face the need to convey their competence to donors. This constant informational need can in turn trap NGOs, forcing them to allocate too many resources to maintaining their reputations as good investments. Our findings explain why NGOs sometimes seem to spend too much time on seemingly trivial or minor policy products. These products may or may not contribute to the more ambitious policy goals that both the NGOs and their donors seek, but because they are attributable to NGOs and can be used to show competence, they dominate daily activities. Most importantly, this research demonstrates that when NGOs have to choose between investing in attributable activities that bolster their reputations and non-attributable activities that serve their policy goals, there will be a strategic incentive to prioritize reputation over policy goals. At the very least, this incentive can produce tension and frustration within the organization. At worst, the organization finds itself trapped by its constant need to prove it is a worthy investment. At a time when accountability is necessarily a top priority for NGOs, the need for attribution is ever-present, and so we observe NGOs allocating their scarce resources toward attributable outcomes in order to satisfy the informational needs of donors.

Reputations may also be important in civil conflicts, both for rebel groups and the state. Rebel groups may use reputations to attract external support from donor states, much in the way that NGOs attract funds from donors. In a logical analogy, donor states considering external support for rebel groups are in the same protagonist role as donors seeking to make worthwhile investments in NGOs. Rebel groups have a similar need to demonstrate their worthiness of an investment, and thus play the role of antagonist here. Because rebel groups are highly perishable and ever-changing, past behavior serves as a proxy for future investments. Rebel groups may need to establish a portfolio of outcomes that demonstrate they are able to achieve their policy objectives without being decimated by their state target. These same rebel groups may face different reputational concerns with respect to popular support, which is critical for many rebels. In such cases, groups must establish a reputation for achieving their objectives without compromising the security of their host populations. In cases where popular support is not required for group survival, this reputational need may not exist.[3]

States experiencing civil conflict may also seek to form reputations with respect to their behavior toward rebel groups. Here the state assumes the role of antagonist, with rebel groups playing the roles of protagonists and proxies. Walter demonstrates, for example, that states sometimes have a reputational incentive to fight separatist groups.[4] The key insight that Walter provides is the fact of the existence or expectation of future challenges from other groups. When states face singular challenges and no expectation of future challenges from other groups, the motivation to form a reputation for denying self-determination movements does not exist. When states have an expectation that accommodating or compromising with one group will lead to future challenges by other groups, however, then there exists a strategic incentive to establish a reputation for denying claims by current groups. This need to provide reputational information to future groups can make states look particularly over-reactive or unsympathetic in the moment, often leading to stark criticism from the international community. Indeed, these reputation concerns can dwarf the immediate concerns of both groups, producing policy behavior that only makes sense when we take into consideration the reputational goals of the state. Walter's analysis "strongly suggests that in the case of self-determination challenges, governments are influenced more by the risks and

---

[3] This complication brings up an interesting challenge for reputation research: how can protagonists (and the scholars that study them) untangle reputational information when more than one context is relevant for the antagonist?

[4] Walter, 2004, 2006, 2009.

costs of future challenges than by the costs of current ones."[5] Her analysis leaves little doubt that reputations are so important to states that they can define policy behavior.

Despite the wide range of actors and interests, the role of reputation remains consistent. As long as there is a need for information in a political environment that contains protagonists, antagonists, and proxies, reputation can matter. As in the case of the NGO and its need to demonstrate its reputation for competence to its donors, the failure to recognize the impact reputation can have on behavior can cause scholars and practitioners to arrive at erroneous conclusions. More applications abound, but these three serve to demonstrate how, across contexts, reputation remains important. In the next section, I discuss some additional extensions concerning reputation dynamics.

Reputation Dynamics: Building versus Losing a Reputation

Thus far I have built the reputation information model such that states' reputations change quickly through shocks, and gradually through the passage of time, and that these processes work similarly across different contexts of actions. Two interesting extensions are worth pondering for future research. First, it is possible that different types of reputations fade faster than others. Trust, for example, is a characteristic that is often difficult to obtain and easy to lose. As Benjamin Franklin once put it, "It takes many good deeds to build a good reputation, and only one bad one to lose it." The model built in Chapter 2 is easily adapted to such a structure, where competence is difficult to demonstrate and easy to lose.

There are many ways to model this loss dynamic, but two particular mechanisms may be the place to start. First, returning to the example of the violation of alliance commitments, one could weigh violation behavior as more salient or impactful than upholding agreements. This raises the question of how: is an agreement violation two times as noticeable as upholding one's commitments? Five times, or ten? In effect, any choice in this matter imposes an assumption on the theoretical predictions of alliance behavior and future alliance formation. A second way to model an easy loss of a positive or competent reputation is to increase the speed with which such reputations diminish over time. If it is the case that some kinds of reputations wear off more quickly than others, this is easy to model in the exponential decay function of the reputation information model.

---

[5] Walter, 2006, p. 319.

Like in the last example, the question of how quickly reputations diminish is both theoretical and empirical. Scholars can customize the reputation information model to suit either need, creating a highly specific version of the model for particular states or contexts as needed. Because I have focused my empirical tests as broad, large-n analyses, I have not imposed additional assumptions on these dynamic structures. Scholars who have more focused empirical frames can tailor these assumptions to generate more accurate measurements of reputation. The trade-offs are classic, falling along the lines of prioritizing internal versus external validity.

A second extension of the standard reputation dynamic in the model developed herein is to examine the ability of actors to build reputations in the first place. Put simply, it is much more difficult to build some types of reputations than others. I have conceptualized reputations as moving along a continuum, with sudden movements coming from new information and gradual movements coming from decay over time. The shape of this continuous function can be tailored to suit the context or frame within which reputation informs the protagonist. Treating this dynamic as a continuous function is the proper baseline starting point, but it would be interesting to see how reputation could be conceived of and measured discontinuously, to imitate the intense challenges of some reputations. For example, if a protagonist is examining an antagonist's reputation for trust, and the protagonist views *any* divergence from trustworthy behavior as evidence that the antagonist is instantly untrustworthy, the reputation dynamics could be adapted accordingly. The dynamics of a reputation for honor may also work this way.[6]

Policy Implications

So what does all this mean for policymakers? It means that reputations can be useful and important foreign policy tools, but one can never forget the need for perspective and context. The key to using reputation to improve foreign policy is to keep the focus on maintaining a reputation for competence within the appropriate context, rather than as a static characteristic. One of the most attractive aspects of the old notion of needing a reputation for toughness and strength at all costs was the simplicity of the policy implications. Moving away

---

[6] See Dafoe, Renshon, and Huth (2014) and Dafoe and Caughey (2016) for an excellent analysis of reputation and honor in world politics.

from a focus on strength to a focus on context-related competence may seem like a daunting task from a policy perspective, but ignoring the protagonist's contextual information needs can lead to ineffective and potentially counter-productive policy outcomes. Consider, for example, a 2016 series of high-level executions by Kim Jong-un's regime in North Korea. The regime typically lists disloyalty and disrespect for Kim as the motivation for the punishments, but leaks suggest that Kim's deeper intent is to reinforce his reputation for punishing defectors.[7] The 2016 defection of a high-level official in North Korea's embassy in London angered the Kim regime, prompting its strategy to signal its willingness to punish. But this signal overlaps considerably with the message of instability and indiscriminating aggression. Using dramatic techniques such as execution by anti-aircraft artillery in lieu of a traditional firing squad may be contributing to the problem. More troubling is executing these officials for what appear to be misdemeanor offenses, such as falling asleep during a meeting chaired by Kim. The hope of the regime is clearly to use fear and violence to encourage obedience, but if the protagonists (the high-level officials, in this example) infer from Kim's erratic behavior that there is a high likelihood of indiscriminate violence in proximity to Kim, they will only be more likely to flee. The result is likely to be counterproductive, pushing more North Korean officials out of the regime, rather than deterring them from leaving.

This example illustrates how reputation concerns in policy decisions can be dangerous to individuals within the North Korean regime. Policies that focus on the wrong reputational information need can also be dangerous to the entire globe. Consider the War Scare of 1983, in which the Soviet Union came close to determining that the United States was about to initiate a nuclear first strike, and the world came closer to nuclear annihilation than any time since the Cuban Missile Crisis.[8] Until recently, few people realized just how close we came to war, and that the Soviets' perception of US intentions was clouded by America's reputation for aggression. As a result, the Soviets became increasingly convinced that America was determined to gain and use a first-strike advantage. Here, as elsewhere throughout history, one state's attempts to project a reputation for strength and toughness was perceived as a reputation for aggression, and a global catastrophe nearly ensued.

---

[7] Kang and Lee, 2016; McCurry, 2016.
[8] Also known as the Able Archer War Scare.

Fearing the Incompetence of Aggression: A Cold War Illustration

Never, perhaps, in the postwar decades has the situation in the world
been as explosive, and hence, more difficult and unfavorable as in the
first half of the 1980s.   Mikhail Gorbachev, February 1986.[9]

Toward the end of the 1970s and throughout the early 1980s, the Cold War
between the United States and the Soviet Union dominated seemingly every
aspect of the global political arena. In this regard, this time period was little
different from the rest of the Cold War. A series of events involving the United
States, however, combined with unexpected fragility in the Soviet elite to create
what we now refer to as the Soviet War Scare at the end of 1983. In November
of 1983, NATO command forces conducted an exercise designed to simulate a
period of conflict escalation that would result in a NATO-coordinated nuclear
attack against the Soviet Union. The simulation triggered a Soviet panic that
Western forces were actually initiating a first-strike nuclear attack, and an internal
debate raged in an attempt to ascertain the extent to which the states in the
Warsaw Pact were in grave danger. Perhaps most disturbing is that American
intelligence agencies failed to realize the gravity of the situation until years later.
As such, this illustration demonstrates how important reputations can be, while
also highlighting how challenging they are to manage.

Three statements summarize the crisis and its importance in illustrating the
use of reputation as a foreign policy tool. First, the Americans were engaged in
what they thought to be classic signaling exercises, projecting nuclear strength
and capability through the use of war exercises such as Able Archer. The foreign
policy goal of these exercises was to demonstrate readiness to the Soviets and
America's allies in the event of a nuclear attack. Second, the Soviets did not fully
believe that these exercises were meant only to signal readiness. Instead, a strong
current of near-panic gripped Soviet leadership, as many became convinced that
the United States was preparing to launch a first-strike nuclear attack. Third,
the notion that the Soviets might have truly thought that the United States
was aggressively planning to attack was not seriously considered by American
intelligence or the Oval Office until the end of the the 1980s. In a report by the
President's Foreign Intelligence Advisory Board in 1990, analysts concluded that
Presidents Carter and Reagan were not properly advised of these Soviet fears.[10]

---

[9] Quoted in Board, 1990.
[10] Board, 1990.

In short, the crisis passed before the Americans understood the gravity of the situation.

A full recounting of the war scare requires its own venue, so here I will only focus on the role of America's reputation in the crisis.[11] Setting the stage for this discussion, in this illustration the Soviets are the protagonist, trying to ascertain the intentions of the United States. There is a key need for information, including the need for enough warning time in the event of a first strike to ensure the Soviets' ability to retaliate. For those uninitiated in the unique logic of mutual assured destruction, maintaining the ability to retaliate in the face of a surprise first strike was considered essential at the time in order to credibly deter the strike. Continuing to set the scene, so to speak, here the Americans are the antagonists, and their foreign policy behavior toward Afghanistan and Iran make these countries proxies for the Soviet Union.

The Soviet Union needed information about whether the United States was defensive or aggressive in its nuclear policy. The status quo expectation was that the United States was defensive, and that its military exercises merely served as signals of its defensive capabilities. But as the Soviets struggled to maintain sufficient warning times to enable them to launch a counterstrike in the event of an American first strike, this expectation started to crumble. American force deployments and technological advancements reduced the Soviets' warning time to roughly eight minutes by 1983, despite extensive attempts to improve their own warning system.[12] These conditions exacerbated the need to know more about the United States' intentions, and here is where reputation enters the story.

Toward the end of the 1970s, the Soviet leadership began to perceive American aggression as a dominant policy characteristic. The United States seemed to be improving ties with communist China, and the Soviets observed large numbers of American troops deployed around Iran. Combined with the (covert) American military intervention into Afghanistan, these policy actions became pieces in an increasingly frightening puzzle. By 1980, the Soviets began to connect these dots, forming a picture of American reputation that suggested aggression rather than deterrence. Looking back, the impact of World War II on Soviet perceptions of the West set a reputation stage for this crisis. Fischer (2006) argued that Operation Barbarossa (Hitler's surprise attack on the Soviet

---

[11] See Board (1990), Andrew and Gordievsky (1991), Pry (1999), Fischer (2006, 2007), Manchanda (2009), and DiCicco (2011) for a more complete discussion. See also Manchanda (2009) for a counter-analysis examining why the war scare did not escalate to an actual nuclear event.

[12] Board, 1990, p. 39.

Party Secretary Suslov and Defense Minister Ustinov, the
senior guardians of Soviet ideology and national security, were
among the first to express these apparent misgivings.   In an
address before the Polish party congress in February 1980, Suslov
asserted that there was a "profound interconnection" to recent US-
inspired actions: the "aggression" by China against Vietnam, the
NATO decisions "aimed at a new arms race," the deployment of
"enormous numbers" of US armed forces around Iran, and the
"training and sending of armed terrorist groups" into Afghanistan.
Several- days later, Ustinov condemned alleged US and Chinese
interference in Afghanistan, US delay in ratification of the SALT
II treaty, the NATO theater nuclear force decision, and the
buildup of US naval forces in the Persian Gulf as "interconnected
elements of an aggressive US policy."

Figure 6.1 Page from "The Soviet 'War Scare'".

Union in 1941) continued to haunt Soviet leadership into the 1980s. In that case,
just as with the example of Treaty of Tilsit and Napoleon, a secret agreement
turned into a Western attack on Mother Russia. Thus, in the winter of 1983, many
Soviet leaders were reluctant to once again trust the West in its proclamations of
peace, while it seemed to be preparing for war.

Some in the Soviet leadership were even making explicit comparisons between
Reagan and Hitler. Marshal Ogarkov, then chief of the Soviet General Staff, held
public and private beliefs that Reagan was akin to Hitler, and that America's
war exercises were akin to the Nazi preparations that led to Germany's invasion
of the Soviet Union in 1941.[13] Not everyone shared Orgakov's belief regarding
this comparison, but there were others who feared American aggression. Yuri
Andropov, then General Secretary of the Communist Party, had grave concerns
that the NATO exercise could be real. Figure 6.1 reproduces Fischer's assessment
that the Soviets had put together the pieces of American foreign policy behavior
and perceived them in aggregate form as an emerging reputation for aggression.
Fischer details this shift from the status quo of the Cold War to the heightened
fear of attack: "In the past, [Andropov] noted, the United States had counted
on its nuclear weapons 'to deter' and 'to contain' the Soviet Union; now there
was talk of actually fighting and prevailing in a nuclear war. 'It is difficult to
say where the line between extortion and actual preparation to take a fateful

[13] Fischer, 2006, p. 508.

step lies."[14] To the extent that reputation played a role in this crisis, it was not the role of establishing credibility in deterrence. Instead, the Soviets perceived aggression by the West, and all that context fomented an American reputation for aggression that undermined the conclusion that the Able Archer exercise was merely a simulation.

Although the crisis may have peaked during the days of the Able Archer exercise, it would be nearly a year before the Soviets began to step away from the precipice of war. Preparations continued into the spring of 1984, and the Soviets rapidly tried to counter the reduced warning times that accompanied new NATO weapons deployments. To the extent that the Americans did finally perceive themselves through the eyes of the Soviets in the aftermath of the Able Archer exercises in 1983 and the Soviet response, these perceptions had a significant impact on the Cold War. Manchanda writes, "*Able Archer* 1983 was the climax after which Reagan realized the true extent to which the Soviets misinterpreted and misunderstood him."[15] Of course, the initial reaction to this new understanding was that the Americans finally realized the extent of the Soviet Union's paranoia about a possible nuclear war. Regardless of the framing here, Reagan finally understood that he was being perceived as aggressive, rather than capable. This realization contributed to the softening of his stance and rhetoric, and explains (in part) his new focus on reducing tensions moving forward.

This final illustration highlights two important lessons. First, states will eagerly seek out reputation information when they face uncertainty with respect to the intentions of their direct partner or opponent. Proxy information that varies across space and time can still be useful if the need for indirect learning exists. The Soviet need for information about America's *intent* was desperate, and without the ability to observe direct and credible assurances from the United States, the Soviets turned to proxy information to learn what they could. As such, reputation mattered in this crisis. Second, the reputation for aggression that the Soviets observed was not the reputation that the United States sought to project. Reagan's peace through strength approach was designed to look tough. Indeed, the idea was to look too tough and capable, such that the Soviets would not think about more encroachments or a first strike. But Reagan never intended to appear as if he *wanted* to start a nuclear war. It was not until he realized how the Soviets were interpreting American and NATO actions that he understood how his

[14] Fischer, 2006, p. 506.
[15] Manchanda, 2009, p. 128.

intended reputation for toughness was transformed through Soviet perceptions into a reputation for aggression. Thus, reputations matter, but are more difficult to control than we may realize.

Final Thoughts

The study of reputation in world politics has been through cycles of boon and bust. But as political scientists strive to better understand the causes and consequences of world politics, we have steadily improved our understanding of how reputation dynamics operate and how they impact international relations. The revitalization of reputation studies has enabled scholars to make real progress toward understanding when and how reputation matters in international relations. Hopefully, this book also makes a similar contribution. Ultimately, it is clear that there are many ways to think about, model, measure, and evaluate reputation, and as such, this book makes a partial contribution to the overall research need.

One of the clearest conclusions coming out of this research is worth repeating one last time. History is replete with examples of wars that were not supposed to happen, and for many of these examples one of the key triggers of these conflicts has been the distance between the reputation we think we have and the reputation others perceive. Nixon's "madman theory" (perhaps more properly credited to Schelling) provides a recent illustration of a flawed logic with roots that extend as far back as Machiavelli, and are as recently visible as the current regime in North Korea. Leaders of countries have too often sought out inordinate gains through the projection of what they hope will be rabid toughness. But when the opponent feels backed into a corner, or unable to walk away from the situation or even resolve the crisis through compromise, they begin to plan for the inevitable violence they perceive to be coming from their aggressively incompetent opponent. When that occurs, non-violent conflict resolution becomes more difficult, and the risk of war increases. Reputation does not always impact global politics, but there are times when it has indelibly shaped the world. In many of those times, such as when Napoleon's reputation for aggression served as Alexander's warning to prepare for invasion, the result bore little resemblance to the best-laid plans.

All of this is not to say that violence is never necessary or unavoidable. Such a conclusion would be trivial, and we need not deal in absolutes in order to glean lessons from the analyses above. Based on the research in this book, leaders of states who seek to use violence with the intention or hope that their actions will create a reputation for toughness will be routinely disappointed. Outside of the clear frame of immediate deterrence, the pursuit of a reputation for toughness is more likely to result in a reputation for incompetent aggression and an increased propensity for violence. In such cases, the reputation earned diverges from the reputation desired, and the result is a decrease in security.

BIBLIOGRAPHY

Achen, Christopher H., and Duncan Snidal (1989). "Rational Deterrence Theory and Comparative Case Studies." *World Politics* 41.2, pp. 143–169.

Adams, John Quincy (1914). "Memoirs of John Quincy Adams, Comprising Portions of His Diary from 1795 to 1848". *Memoirs of John Quincy Adams: comprising portions of his diary from 1795 to 1848* (Vol. 12). JB Lippincott & Company. ed. by Charles Francis Adams. Vol. 3. J.B. Lippincott and Co.

Allen, Franklin (1984). "Reputation and Product Quality." *The RAND Journal of Economics* 15.3, pp. 311–327.

Alt, James E., Randall L. Calvert, and Brian D. Humes (1988). "Reputation and Hegemonic Stability: A Game-Theoretic Analysis." *American Political Science Review* 82.2, pp. 445–466.

Altfeld, Michael A. (1984). "The Decision to Ally." *The Western Political Quarterly* 37, pp. 523–544.

Andrew, Christopher M., and Oleg Gordievsky (1991). *Comrade Kryuchkov's Instructions: Top Secret Files on KGB Foreign Operations, 1975–1985.* Stanford University Press.

Axelrod, Robert (1984). *The Evolution of Cooperation.* Basic Books.

Axelrod, Robert and Robert O. Keohane (1985a). "Achieving Cooperation under Anarchy: Strategies and Institutions." *World Politics: A Quarterly Journal of International Relations* 38.1, pp. 226–254.

— (1985b). "Achieving Cooperation under Anarchy: Strategies and Institutions." *World Politics* 38.1, pp. 226–254.

Bacevich, Andrew J. (2010). *Washington Rules: America's Path to Permanent War.* Macmillan.

Barney, J. and M. H. Hansen (1994). "Trustworthiness as a Source of Competitive Advantage." *Strategic Management Journal* 15.1, pp. 175–216.

Beck, Nathaniel and Jonathan N. Katz (1995). "What to Do (and Not to Do) with Time-Series Cross-Section Data." *American Political Science Review* 89.3, pp. 634–647.

Beck, Nathaniel, Jonathan N. Katz, and Richard Tucker (1998). "Taking Time Seriously: Time-Series-Cross-Section Analysis with a Binary Dependent Variable." *American Journal of Political Science* 42.4, pp. 1260–88.

Bertie, Francis (1927). "Memorandum by Mr. Bertie." *British Documents on the Origins of War 1898–1914.* Eds. G. P. Gooch and Harold Temperley. Vol.2. London: His Majesty's Stationary Office.

Beschloss, Michael and Hugh Sidey (2009). *Ronald Reagan—The White House.* Online. URL: https://www.whitehousehistory.org/bios/ronald-reagan.

Board, President's Foreign Intelligence Advisory (1990). "The Soviet 'War Scare.'" George H.W. Bush Presidential Library.

Boehmke, Fred, Daniel Morey, and Megan Shannon (2004). "Selection Bias and Continuous-Time Duration Models: Consequences and a Proposed Solution." *American Journal of Political Science* 50.1: 192–207.

Boot, Arnoud, Stuart Greenbaum, and Anjan V. Thakor (1993). "Reputation and Discrestion in Financial Contracting." *The American Economic Review* 83.5, pp. 1165–1183.

Box-Steffensmeier, Janet M. and Bradford S. Jones (1997). "Time Is of the Essence: Event History Models in the Political Science." *American Journal of Political Science* 41.4, pp. 1414–1461.

Brands, H. W. (2016). *The General vs. the President: MacArthur and Truman at the Brink of Nuclear War*. Doubleday.

Bremer, Stuart A. (1992). "Dangerous Dyads: Conditions Affecting the Likelihood of Interstate War, 1816–1965." *Journal of Conflict Resolution* 36, pp. 309–341.

Brody, Richard (1984). "International Crises: A Rallying Point for the President?" *Public Opinion* 6, pp. 41–60.

Bueno de Mesquita, Bruce (1981). *The War Trap*. 1st ed.: Yale University Press.

Bueno de Mesquita, Bruce and David Lalman (1992). *War and Reason: Domestic and International Imperatives*. Yale University Press.

Bueno de Mesquita, Bruce and Randolph Siverson (1995). "War and the Survival of Political Leaders: A Comparative Study of Regime Types and Political Accountability." *American Political Science Review* 89.4, pp. 841–855.

Bueno de Mesquita, Bruce, Randolph Siverson, and Gary Woller (1992). "War and the Fate of Regimes: A Comparative Analysis." *American Political Science Review* 86.3, pp. 638–646.

Burnham, Robert (2000). "Documents upon the Overthrow of the Spanish Monarchy." http://www.napoleon-series.org/research/government/diplomatic/c_spain.html.

Bush, George W. (2003). "President Bush Announces Major Combat Operations in Iraq Have Ended". United States White House Archives. http://georgewbush-whitehouse.archives.gov/news/releases/2003/05/20030501-15.html.

Cate, Curtis (1985). *The War of the Two Emperors*. Random House.

Chang, Chung-Fu (1931). *The Anglo-Japanese Alliance.*: Johns Hopkins University Press.

Chauvin, Keith W. and James P. Guthrie (1994). "Labor Market Reputation and the Value of the Firm." *Managerial and Decision Economics* 15.6, pp. 543–552.

Chiozza, Giacomo and Ajin Choi (2003). "Guess Who Did What." *Journal of Conflict Resolution* 47.3, pp. 251–278.

Chu, Wujin and Woosik Chu (1994). "Signaling Quality by Selling through a Reputable Retailer: An Example of Renting the Reputation of Another Agent." *Marketing Science* 13.2, pp. 177–189.

Clare, Joe and Vesna Danilovic (2010). "Multiple Audiences and Reputation Building in International Conflicts." *Journal of Conflict Resolution* 54.6, pp. 860–882.

Clare, Joe and Vesna Danilovic (2012). "Reputation for Resolve, Interests, and Conflict." *Conflict Management and Peace Science* 29.1, pp. 3–27.

Cleves, Mario A., William W. Gould, and Roberto G. Gutierrez (2002). *An Introduction to Survival Analysis Using STATA*. STATA Press.

Conybeare, John A. C. (1994). "The Portfolio Benefits of Free Riding in Military Alliances." *International Studies Quarterly* 38.3, pp. 405–419.

Copeland, Dale C. (1997). "Do Reputations Matter?" *Security Studies* 7.1, pp. 33–71.

Coser, L. A. (1956). *The Functions of Social Conflict*. Free Press.

Craik, Kenneth H. (2009). *Reputation: A Network Interpretation*. Oxford University Press.

Crescenzi, Mark J. C. (2007). "Reputation and Interstate Conflict." *American Journal of Political Science* 51.2, pp. 382–396.

Crescenzi, Mark J. C., Rebecca H. Best, and Bo Ram Kwon (2010). "Reciprocity in International Studies." *The International Studies Encyclopedia*. Ed. by Robert A. Denemark. Blackwell Publishing.

Crescenzi, Mark J. C. and Andrew J. Enterline (1999). "Ripples from the Waves? A Systemic, Time-Series Analysis of Democracy, Democratization, and Interstate War." *Journal of Peace Research* 36.1, pp. 75–94.

— (2001). "Time Remembered: A Dynamic Model of Interstate Interaction." *International Studies Quarterly* 45.4, pp. 409–431.

Crescenzi, Mark J. C., Andrew J. Enterline, and Stephen B. Long (2008). "Bringing Cooperation Back In: A Fully Informed Dynamic Model of Interstate Interaction." *Conflict Management and Peace Science* 25.3, pp. 264–280.

Crescenzi, Mark J. C., Jacob D. Kathman, and Stephen B. Long (2007). "Reputation, History, and War." *Journal of Peace Research* 44.6, pp. 651–667.

Dafoe, Allan and Devin Caughey (2016). "Honor and War." *World Politics* 68.2, pp. 341–381.

Dafoe, Allan, Jonathan Renshon, and Paul Huth (2014). "Reputation and Status as Motives for War." *Annual Review of Political Science* 17, pp. 371–393.

Danilovic, Vesna (2002). *When the Stakes are High: Deterrence and Conflict among Major Powers*. University of Michigan Press.

Das, T. K. and Bing-Sheng Teng (1998). "Between Trust and Control: Developing Confidence in Partner Cooperation in Alliances." *The Academy of Management Review* 23.3, pp. 491–512.

— (2002). "The Dynamics of Alliance Conditions in the Alliance Development Process." *Journal of Management Studies* 29.5, pp. 725–745.

Deutsch, Karl W. (1954). *Political Community at the International Level: Probelms of Definition and Measurement*. Doubleday.

Diamond, Douglas W. (1989). "Reputation Acquisition in Debt Markets." *Journal of Political Economy* 97.4, pp. 828–862.

DiCicco, Jonathan M. (2011). "Fear, Loathing, and Cracks in Reagan's Mirror Images: Able Archer 83 and an American First Step toward Rapprochement in the Cold War." *Foreign Policy Analysis* 7.3, pp. 253–274.

Diehl, Paul F. and Gary Goertz (2001). *War and Peace in International Rivalry*. University of Michigan Press.

Dixon, William J. (1983). "Measuring Interstate Affect." *American Journal of Political Science* 27.4, pp. 828–851.

Dollinger, Mark J., Peggy A. Golden, and Todd Saxton (1997). "The Effect of Reputation on the Decision to Joint Venture." *Strategic Management Journal* 18.2, pp. 127–140.

Downs, George W. and Michael J. Jones (2002). "Reputation, Compliance, and International Law." *Journal of Legal Studies* 31.1, pp. 95–114.

Downs, George W., David M. Rocke, and Peter N. Barsoom (1996). "Is the Good News about Compliance Good about Cooperation." *International Organization* 50.3, pp. 379–406.

Dwyer, Philip G. (2001). *Napoleon and Europe*. Longman.

Farkas, Andrew (1998). *State Learning and International Relations*. University of Michigan.

Fearon, James D. (1994). "Domestic Political Audiences and the Escalation of International Disputes." *American Political Science Review* 88.3, pp. 577–592.

— (1995). "Rationalist Explanations for War." *International Organization* 49.3, pp. 379–414.

Fischer, Benjamin B. (2006). "The Soviet-American War Scare of the 1980s." *International Journal of Intelligence and CounterIntelligence* 19.3, pp. 480–518.

— (2007). *A Cold War Conundrum: The 1983 Soviet War Scare*. URL: https://www.cia.gov/library/center-for-the-study-of-intelligence/csi-publications/books-and-monographs/a-cold-war-conundrum/source.htm#top.

Fyffe, Charles Alan (1896). *A History of Modern Europe, 1792–1878*. H. Holt and Company.

Gartner, Scott Sigmund and Randolph M. Siverson (1996). "War Expansion and War Outcome." *Journal of Conflict Resolution* 40.1, pp. 4–15.

Gartzke, Erik and Kristian Skrede Gleditsch (2004). "Why Democracies May Actually Be Less Reliable Allies." *American Journal of Political Science* 48.4, pp. 775–795.

Gayscone-Cecil, Robert (1927). "Memorandum by the Marquess of Salisbury." In *British Documents on the Origins of War 1898–1914*. Eds. G. P. Gooch and Harold Temperley. Vol.2. London: His Majesty's Stationary Office.

Gent, Stephen E et al. (2015). "The Reputation Trap of NGO Accountability." *International Theory* 7.3, pp. 426–463.

Gibbon, Edward (1819). *Memoirs of the Public Character and Life of Alexander the First, Emperor of all the Russias*. Second American Edition. D & E Fenton.

Gibler, Douglas M. (2008). "The Costs of Reneging: Reputation and Alliance Formation." *Journal of Conflict Resolution* 52.3, pp. 426–454.

Gibler, Douglas M. and Meredith Sarkees (2004). "Measuring Alliances: The Correlates of War Formal Interstate Alliance Dataset, 1916–2000." *Journal of Peace Research* 41.2, pp. 211–222.

Gibler, Douglas M. and Scott Wolford (2006). "Alliances, Then Democracy: An Examination of the Relationship between Regime Type and Alliance Formation." *Journal of Conflict Resolution* 50.1, pp. 129–153.

Goldstein, Joshua S. and John R. Freeman (1990). *Three-Way Street: Strategic Reciprocity in World Politics*. University of Chicago Press.

Gooch, G, and Harold William Temperley, eds. (1926). *British Documents on the Origins of the War, 1898–1914*. London: H. M. Stationary Office.

Greenwood, Sean (1990). "Frank Roberts and the 'Other' Long Telegram: The View from the British Embassy in Moscow, March 1946." *Journal of Contemporary History* 25, pp. 103–122.

— (2000). *Britain and the Cold War 1945–91*. St. Martin's Press, Inc.

Haas, Ernst B. and Allen S. Whiting (1956). *Dynamics of International Relations*. McGraw-Hill.

Harary, Frank (1959). "On the Measurement of Structural Balance." *Behavioral Science* 2.4, pp. 316–323.

Harary, Frank, Robert Norman, and Dorwin Cartwright (1965). *Structural Models: An Introduction to the Theory of Directed Graphs*. Wiley.

Heagerty, Patrick, Michael D. Ward, and Kristian Skrede Gleditsch (2002). "Windows of Opportunity: Window Subseries Empirical Variance Estimators in International Relations." *Political Analysis* 10.3, pp. 304–317.

Heider, F. (1946). "Attidudes and Cognitive Organizations." *Journal of Psychology* 21, pp. 107–112.

Hoff, Peter D. and Michael D. Ward (2004). "Modeling Dependencies in International Relations Networks." *Political Analysis* 12.2, p. 160.

Holsti, Kalevi J. (1970). "National Role Conceptions in the Study of Foreign Policy." *International Studies Quarterly* 14.3, pp. 233–309.

Houweling, Henk and Jan Siccama (1985). "The Epidemiology of War, 1816–1980." *Journal of Conflict Resolution* 10.4, pp. 641–663.

Hummon, Norman P. and Patrick Doreian (2003). "Some Dynamics of Social Balance Processes: Bringing Heider Back into Balance Theory." *Social Networks* 25.1, pp. 17–49.

Huth, Paul (1988). *Extended Deterrence and the Prevention of War*. Yale University Press.

— (1997). "Reputation and Deterrence." *Security Studies* 7.1, pp. 72–99.

Huth, Paul and Bruce Russett (1984). "What Makes Deterrence Work? Cases from 1900 to 1980." *World Politics* 36.4, pp. 496–526.

— (1993). "General Deterrence Between Enduring Rivalries: Testing Three Competing Models." *American Political Science Review* 87, pp. 61–73.

Ion, Hamish (2004). "Toward a Naval Allianace: Some Naval Antecedents to the Anglo-Japanese Alliance, 1854–1902." *The Anglo-Japanese alliance, 1902–1922* ed. by Phillips Payson O'Brien. Routledge-Curzon.

Jaggers, Keith and Ted Robert Gurr (1995). "Tracking Democracy's Third Wave with the Polity III Data." *Journal of Peace Research* 32.4, pp. 469–482.

Jensen, Kenneth Martin (1993). *Origins of the Cold War: The Novikov, Kennan, and Roberts "Long Telegrams" of 1946: with Three New Commentaries.* U.S. Institute of Peace Press.

Jervis, Robert (1976). *Perception and Misperception in International Politics.* Princeton University Press.

Jones, Daniel M., Stuart A. Bremer, and J. David Singer (1996). "Militarized Interstate Disputes, 1816–1992: Rationale, Coding Rules, and Empirical Patterns." *Conflict Management and Peace Science* 15.2, pp. 163–216.

Kadera, Kelly (1998). "Transmission, Barriers, and Constraints: a Dynamic Model of the Spread of War." *Journal of Conflict Resolution* 42.3, pp. 367–388.

— (2001). *The Power–Conflict Story: A Dynamic Model of Interstate Rivalry.* University of Michigan Press.

"North executes two top officials." (2016). URL: http://koreajoongangdaily.joins.com/news/article/article.aspx?aid=3023234.

Kennan, George F. (1993). "The Kennan 'Long Telegram' Moscow, February 22, 1946." *Origins of the Cold War: The Novikov, Kennan, and Roberts "Long Telegrams" of 1946: with Three New Commentaries.* Ed. by Kenneth Martin Jensen. U.S. Institute of Peace Press, pp. 17–32.

Kennedy, Paul (1980). *The Rise of Anglo-German Antagonism, 1860–1914.* George Allen and Unwin.

Kernell, Samuel (1978). "Explaining Presidential Popularity." *American Political Science Review* 72.2, pp. 506–522.

Kertzer, Joshua (2016). *Resolve in International Politics.* Princeton University Press.

Kim, Joeng-Yoo (1996). "Cheap Talk and Reputation in Repeated Pretrial Negotiation." *The RAND Journal of Economics* 27.4, pp. 787–802.

Kinsella, David and Bruce Russett (2002). "Conflict Emergence and Escalation in Interactive International Dyads." *Journal of Politics* 64.4, pp. 1045–1068.

Klein, Benjamin and Keith B. Leffler (1981). "The Role of Market Forces in Assuring Contractual Performance." *Journal of Political Economy* 89.4, pp. 615–639.

Koremenos, Barbara, Charles Lipson, and Duncan Snidal (2001). "The Rational Design of International Institutions." *International Organization* 55.4, pp. 761–800.

Kydd, Andrew H. (2005). *Trust and Mistrust in International Relations.* Princeton University Press.

Lai, Brian and Dan Reiter (2000). "Democracy, Political Similarity, and International Alliances, 1816–1992." *Journal of Conflict Resolution* 44.2, pp. 203–227.

Langer, William L. (1935). *The Diplomacy of Imperialism, 1890–1902.* Vol. 2. Alfred A. Knopf.

Lebow, Richard Ned and Janice Gross Stein (1989). "Rational Deterrence Theory: I Think, Therefore I Deter." *World Politics* 41.2, pp. 208–224.

Lee, Sung Chull, Robert G. Muncaster, and Dina A. Zinnes (1994). "'The Friend of My Enemy is My Enemy': Modeling Triadic Internation Relationships." *Synthese* 100, pp. 333–358.

Leeds, Brett Ashley (1999). "Domestic Political Institutions, Credible Commitments, and International Cooperation." *American Journal of Political Science* 43.4, pp. 972–1002.

— (2000). "Credible Commitments and International Cooperation: Guaranteeing Contracts without External Enforcement." *Conflict Management and Peace Science* 18.1, pp. 49–71.

— (2003). "Alliance Reliability in Times of War: Explaining State Decisions to Violate Treaties." *International Organization* 57, pp. 801–827.

Leeds, Brett Ashley and Burcu Savun (2007). "Terminating Alliances: Why Do States Abrogate Agreements?" *Journal of Politics* 69.4, pp. 1118–1132.

Leeds, Brett et al. (2002). "Alliance Treaty Obligations and Provisions, 1815–1944." *International Interactions* 28, pp. 261–284.

Lenczowski, George (1990). *American Presidents and the Middle East.* Duke University Press.

Leng, Russell J. (1983). "When Will They Ever Learn? Coercive Bargaining in Recurrent Crises." *Journal of Conflict Resolution* 27.3, pp. 379–419.

— (1988). "Crisis Learning Games." *American Political Science Review* 82.1, pp. 179–194.

— (1993). *Interstate Crisis Behavior, 1816–1980: Realism Versus Reciprocity*. Cambridge University Press.

— (2000). *Bargaining and Learning in Recurring Crises: The Soviet-American, Egyptian-Israeli, and Indo-Pakistani Rivalries*. University of Michigan.

Levy, Jack (1982). "The Contagion of Great Power War Behavior: An Analysis of the Great Powers, 1495–1975." *American Journal of Political Science* 26.3, pp. 562–584.

— (1994). "Learning and Foreign Policy: Sweeping a Conceptual Minefield." *International Organization* 48.2, pp. 279–312.

Long, Andrew, Timothy Nordstrom, and Kyeonghi Baek (2007). "Allying for Peace: Treaty Obligations and Conflict between Allies." *Journal of Politics* 69.4, pp. 1103–1117.

MacArthur, Douglas (1951). "Farewell Address to Congress." http://www.americanrhetoric.com/speeches/douglasmacarthurfarewelladdress.htm.

Manchanda, Arnav (2009). "When Truth is Stranger than Fiction: The Able Archer incident." *Cold War History* 9.1, pp. 111–133.

Maoz, Zeev (1990). *National Choices and International Processes*. Cambridge University Press.

— (1996). *Domestic Sources of Global Change*. University of Michigan Press.

— (1999). "Dyadic Militarized Interstate Disputes (DYMID1. 1) Dataset, version 1.1." Computer File. Tel-Aviv University.

Maoz, Zeev and Bruce Russett (1993). "Normative and Structural Causes of the Democratic Peace." *American Political Science Review* 87.3, pp. 624–638.

Marshall, Monty G. and Keith Jaggers (2000). *Polity IV dataset*. http://www.systemicpeace.org/inscr/p4manualv2016.pdf.

Mattes, Michaela (2012). "Reputation, Symmetry, and Alliance Design." *International Organization* 66.4, pp. 679–707.

McCullough, David G. (1992). *Truman*. Simon & Schuster.

"North Korea executes officials with anti-aircraft gun in new purge–report.: (2016). August 30.

Mercer, Jonathan (1996). *Reputation and International Politics*. Cornell University Press.

— (1997). "Reputation and Rational Deterrence Theory." *Security Studies* 7.1, pp. 100–113.

Milgrom, Paul R., Douglass C. North, and Barry R. Weingast (1990). "The Role of Institutions in the Revival of Trade." *Economics and Politics* 2.1, pp. 1–23.

Miller, Gregory (2004). "The Shadow of the Past: The Influence of Reputation on Alliance Choices." Dissertation. The Ohio State University.

Miller, Gregory D. (2003). "Hypotheses on Reputation: Alliance Choices and the Shadow of the Past." *Security Studies* 12.3, pp. 40–78.

Modelski, George (1964). "Kautilya: Foreign Policy and International System in the Ancient Hindu World." *The American Political Science Review* 58.3, pp. 549–560.

Monger, George (1963). *The End of Isolation: British Foreign Policy, 1900–1917*. Thomas Nelson.

Morgenthau, Hans J. (1967). *Politics Among Nations*. 4th ed. Knopf.

Morrow, James D. (1987). "On the Theoretical Basis of a Measure of National Risk Attitudes." *International Studies Quarterly* 31.4, pp. 423–438.

— (1989). "Capabilities, Uncertainty, and Resolve: A Limited Information Model of Crisis Bargaining." *American Journal of Political Science* 33.4, pp. 941–972.

— (1991). "Alliances and Asymmetry: An Alternative to the Capability Aggregation Model of Alliances." *American Journal of Political Science* 35, pp. 904–933.

— (1993). "Arms Versus Allies: Tradeoffs in the Search for Security." *International Organization* 47.2, pp. 207–233.

— (1994). "Alliances, Credibility, and Peacetime Costs." *Journal of Conflict Resolution* 38.2, pp. 270–297.

— (2000). "Alliances: Why Write Them Down?" *Annual Review of Political Science* 3, pp. 63–83.

Most, Benjamin and Harvey Starr (1989). *Inquiry, Logic and International Politics*. University of South Carolina Press.

Mueller, John (1970). "Presidential Popularity from Truman to Johnson." *American Political Science Review* 64.1, pp. 18–34.

Nalebuff, Barry (1991). "Rational Deterrence in an Imperfect World." *World Politics* 43.3, pp. 313–315.

Newcomb, Theodore M. (1953). "An Approach to the Study of Communicative Acts." *Psychological Review* 60.6, pp. 393–404.

— (1961). *The Acquaintance Process*. Holt, Rinehart and Winston.

Nish, Ian (1985). *The Anglo-Japanese Alliance: The Diplomacy of Two Island Empires*. Athlone.

— (2004). "Origins of the Anglo-Japanese Alliance." *The Anglo-Japanese Alliance, 1902–1922*. Ed. by Phillips Payson O'Brien. Routledge, pp. 8–25.

Nowak, Martin A. and Roger Highfield (2011). *SuperCooperators: Altruism, Evolution, and Why We Need Each Other to Succeed*. Free Press.

Nowak, Martin A. and Karl Sigmund (1998). "Evolution of Indirect Reciprocity by Image Scoring." *Nature* 393.6685, pp. 573–577.

— (2005). "Evolution of Indirect Reciprocity." *Nature* 437.7063, pp. 1291–1298.

Olson, Mancur (1965). *The Logic of Collective Action: Public Goods and the Theory of Groups*. Harvard University Press.

Oneal, John, Bruce Russett, and Michael L. Berbaum (2003). "Causes of Peace: Democracy, Interdependence, and International Organizations, 1885–1992." *International Studies Quarterly* 47.3, pp. 371–393.

Petty-Fitzmaurice, Henry (1927). "Memorandum by the Marquess of Lansdowne." *British Documents on the Origins of War 1898–1914*. Eds. G. P. Gooch and Harold Temperley. Vol.2. London: His Majesty's Stationary Office.

Pevehouse, Jon, Timothy Nordstrom, and Kevin Warnke (2004). "The Correlates of War 2 international governmental organizations data version 2.0." *Conflict Management and Peace Science* 21.2: 101–119.

Powell, Robert (1999). *In the Shadow of Power*. Princeton University Press.

— (2002). "Bargaining Theory and International Conflict." *Annual Review of Political Science* 5, pp. 1–30.

— (2004a). "Bargaining and Learning While Fighting." *American Journal of Political Science* 48.2, pp. 344–361.

— (2004b). "The Inefficient Use of Power: Costly Conflict with Complete Information." *American Political Science Review* 98.2, pp. 231–241.

Press, Daryl G. (2005). *Calculating Credibility: How Leaders Assess Military Threats*. Cornell University Press.

Pry, Peter Vincent (1999). *War Scare: Russia and America on the Nuclear Brink*. Greenwood Publishing Group.

Raknerud, Arvid and Håvard Hegre (1997). "The Hazard of War: Reassessing the Evidence for the Democratic Peace." *Journal of Peace Research* 34.4, pp. 385–404.

Reed, William (2000). "A Unified Statistical Model of Conflict Onset and Escalation." *American Journal of Political Science* 44.1, pp. 84–93.

Reiter, Dan (1996). *Crucible of Beliefs: Learning, Alliances, and World Wars*. Cornell University Press.

Richardson, Lewis Fry (1960). *Arms and Insecurity*. Quadrangle.

Roberts, Frank K. (1993). "The Roberts Cables Moscow, March 1946." *Origins of the Cold War: The Novikov, Kennan, and Roberts "Long Telegrams" of 1946: with Three New Commentaries*. U.S. Institute of Peace Press, pp. 33–68.

Russett, Bruce and John Oneal (2001). *Triangulating Peace: Democracy, Interdependence, and International Organizations*. Norton.

Sartori, Anne E. (2002). "The Might of the Pen: A Reputational Theory of Communication in International Disputes." *International Organization* 56.1, pp. 121–149.

— (2005). *Deterrence by Diplomacy*. Princeton University Press.

Schelling, Thomas (1966). *Arms and Influence*. Yale University Press.

Schiller, Wendy J. (2000). *Partners and Rivals: Representation in U.S. Senate Delegations*. Princeton University Press.

Schrodt, Philip A. (1978). "The Richardson N-Nation Model and the Balance of Power." *American Journal of Political Science* 22.2, pp. 364–390.

Schrodt, Philip A. and Alex Mintz (1988). "The Conditional Probability Analysis of International Events Data." *American Journal of Political Science* 32.1, pp. 217–230.

Schultz, Kenneth (1998). "Domestic Opposition and Signaling in International Crises." *American Political Science Review* 92.4, pp. 829–844.

Sechser, Todd S. (2010). "Goliath's Curse: Coercive Threats and Asymmetric Power." *International Organization* 64.4, pp. 627–660.

Senese, Paul D. and John A. Vasquez (2003). "A Unified Explanation of Territorial Conflict: Testing the Impact of Sampling Bias, 1919–1992." *International Studies Quarterly* 47.2, pp. 275–298.

— (2008). *The Steps to War: An Empirical Study*. Princeton University Press.

Shanker, Thom (2002). "Aftereffects: Korea Strategy; Lessons From Iraq Include How to Scare Korean Leader." *New York Times* May 12, A17.

Shapiro, Carl (1983). "Premiums for High Quality Products as Returns to Reputations." *Quarterly Journal of Economics* 98.4, pp. 659–680.

Signorino, Curtis S. and Jeffrey M. Ritter (1999). "Tau-b or Not Tau-b: Measuring the Similarity of Foreign Policy Positions." *International Studies Quarterly* 4.1, pp. 115–144.

Simmons, Beth (2000). "International Law and State Behavior: Commitment and Compliance in International Monetary Affairs." *American Political Science Review* 94.4, pp. 819–835.

Simmons, Beth and Zachary Elkins (2004). "The Globalization of Liberalization: Policy Diffusion in the International Political Economy." *American Political Science Review* 98.1, pp. 171–189.

Simon, Michael W. and Erik Gartzke (1996). "Political System Similarity and the Choice of Allies: Do Democracies Flock Together or Do Opposites Attract?" *Journal of Conflict Resolution* 40.4, pp. 617–635.

Singer, J. David and Melvin Small (1972). *The Wages of War, 1816–1965*. John Wiley.

Siverson, Randolph M. and Juliann Emmons (1991). "Birds of a Feather: Democratic Political Systems and Alliance Choices in the Twentieth Century." *Journal of Conflict Resolution* 35.2, pp. 285–306.

Siverson, Randolph and Harvey Starr (1991). *The Diffusion of War: A Study of Opportunity and Willingness*. University of Michigan Press.

Small, Melvin and J. David Singer (1991). "Formal Alliances, 1816–1965: An Extension of the Basic Data." *Measuring the Correlates of War*. Ed. by J. David Singer and Paul F. Diehl. University of Michigan Press, pp. 159–190.

Smith, Alastair (1995). "Alliance Formation and War." *International Studies Quarterly* 39.4, pp. 405–425.

— (1996). "To Intervene or not to Intervene: A Biased Decision." *Journal of Conflict Resolution* 40.1, pp. 16–40.

Snyder, Jack (1991). *Myths of Empire: Domestic Politics and International Ambition*. Cornell University Press.

Sorokin, Gerald L. (1994). "Alliance Formation and General Deterrence: A Game-Theoretic Model and the Case of Israel." *Journal of Conflict Resolution* 38.2, pp. 298–325.

Steinbeck, John (1937). *Of Mice and Men*. Cannery Row.

Strassler, Robert B. (1996). *The Landmark Thucydides: A Comprehensive Guide to the Peloponnesian War*. Tran. Richard Crawley. New York: Free Press.

Thies, Cameron G. (2001). "A Social Psychological Approach to Enduring Rivalries." *Political Psychology* 22.4, pp. 693–725.

Thies, Cameron G. and Marijke Breuning (2012). "Integrating Foreign Policy Analysis and International Relations through Role Theory." *Foreign Policy Analysis* 8.1, pp. 1–4.

Tomz, Michael (2007). *Reputation and International Cooperation*. Princeton University Press.

Tomz, Michael, Jason Wittenberg, and Gary King (2001). *CLARIFY: Software for Interpreting and Presenting Statistical Results*. Version 2.0. http://gking.harvard.edu.

Vasquez, John A. (1993). *The War Puzzle*. Cambridge Studies in International Relations: 27. Cambridge University Press.

Wagner, R. Harrison (2000). "Bargaining and War." *American Journal of Political Science* 44.3, pp. 469–485.

Walt, Stephen (1987). *The Origins of Alliances*. Cornell University Press.

Walter, Barbara (2004). "Does Conflict Beget Conflict? Explaining Recurring Civil War." *Journal of Peace Research* 41.3, pp. 371–388.

Walter, Barbara F. (2006). "Building Reputation: Why Governments Fight Some Separatists but Not Others." *American Journal of Political Science* 50.2, pp. 313–330.

Walter, Barbara F. (2009). *Reputation and Civil War: Why Separatist Conflicts are So Violent*. Cambridge University Press.

Waltz, Kenneth (1979). *Theory of International Politics*. Random House.

Ward, Michael D. and Kristian Skrede Gleditsch (2002). "Location, Location, Location: An MCMC Approach to Modeling the Spatial Context of War and Peace." *Political Analysis* 10.3, pp. 244–260.

Weigelt, Keith and Colin Camerer (1988). "Reputation and Corporate Strategy: A Review of Recent Theory and Applications." *Strategic Management Journal* 9.5, pp. 443–454.

Weisiger, Alex and Keren Yarhi-Milo (2015). "Revisiting Reputation: How Past Actions Matter in International Politics." *International Organization* 69.2, pp. 473–495.

Weitsman, Patricia A. (2004). *Dangerous Alliances: Proponents of Peace, Weapons of War*. Stanford University Press.

Werner, Suzanne (1999). "Choosing Demands Strategically: The Distribution Power, the Distribution of Benefits, and the Risk of Conflict." *Journal of Conflict Resolution* 43.6, pp. 705–726.

Wickman, Forrest (2013). "Fact-Checking Spock: Was the "Enemy of My Enemy" Guy Really Killed by His "Friend"?" http://www.slate.com/blogs/browbeat/2013/05/16/star_trek_into_darkness_fact_checked_was_the_enemy_of_my_enemy_guy_really.html.

Wilson, Robert (1985). "Reputation in Games and Markets." *Game–Theoretic Models of Bargaining*. Ed. by A. E. Roth. Cambridge University Press.

Wood, Houston (2016). *Invitation to Peace Studies*. Oxford University Press.

Zametica, John, ed. (1990a). *British Officials and British Foreign Policy 1945–50*. Leicester University Press.

— (1990b). "Three Letters to Bevin: Frank Roberts at the Moscow Embassy, 1945–6." *British Officials and British Foreign Policy 1945–50*. Ed. by John Zametica. Leicester University Press, pp. 39–97.

Zinnes, Dina A. and Robert G. Muncaster (1997). "Prospect Theory versus Expected Utility Theory: A Dispute Sequence Appraisal." *Decision Making on War and Peace: The Cognitive Rational Debate*. Ed. by Nehemia Geva and Alex Mintz. Lynne Rienner Publishers, Inc., pp. 183–211.

INDEX

Able Archer war exercises (1983), 170, 173. *See also* War Scare of 1983

Adams, John Quincy, 64–66

Afghanistan, 127, 171

Agadir Crisis (1911), 74

aggression
  Cold War and perceptions of, 55, 171–74
  deterrence and, 78
  incompetence and, 11–12, 59, 78–80, 90, 163, 170, 175
  Korean War and perceptions of, 87–88
  Napoleon's reputation for, 13, 65–66, 162, 174
  North Korea's contemporary reputation for, 169
  selectorates' preferences for, 94
  US policy in Iraq perceived as, 7

Alexander I (tsar of Russia)
  Adams's conversation (1812) with, 64–65
  Continental Blockade and, 14, 62, 65
  Russo-French War (1812) and, 12–14, 65–67, 174
  Tilsit Treaty with Napoleon and, 12–15, 59–65, 67, 162

Allen, Franklin, 71

alliances. *See also* specific alliances
  autocracies and, 132, 136
  autonomy of individual states and, 125, 127–28
  bargaining power and, 127
  bilateral *versus* multilateral types of, 145–46, 148
  bipolar systems and, 157
  capability aggregation and, 125, 130, 147
  Cold War era and, 157
  collective action problems and, 130, 158

  commitment and, 6, 65, 71
  compliance with, 124, 143–44, 153–54, 159, 163
  costs of, 128
  defections and, 70, 143–44, 167
  definition of, 125
  democracies and, 130, 132, 146, 149–50
  deterrent effect of, 129
  economies of scale and, 125–27
  foreign policy similarity as factor in, 145, 147, 149–50, 152–54
  geographic distance between states as factor in, 147, 149–50, 152, 154
  incomplete information and, 121
  Interstate Interaction Score (IIS) and, 147, 149–51
  joint enemies as factor in, 146, 149–52, 158
  leadership turnover and, 131–32
  multipolar systems and, 157
  Napoleonic Wars and, 13, 61, 63, 65
  post-Cold War era and, 157–58
  Potsdam Conference (1945) and, 53
  power similarities *versus* power differences in, 147, 149–51, 154
  predicted probabilities of, 153
  proxy information and, 137–41, 147
  regime similarities *versus* regime differences in, 146, 149–51
  reliability and, 10, 24–25, 71, 120, 124–36, 141, 148, 152
  reputational learning and, 22, 25, 133–41
  reputation and, 34, 74, 82, 125, 131–59, 163
  shared interests and, 147
  threat approximation and, 147, 157